D0765745

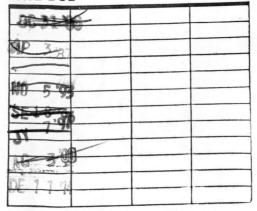
RIVERSIDE CITY COLLEGE
LIBRARY
Riverside, California

MY   '86   DEMCO

THE MALE PREDICAMENT

The Male Predicament

ON BEING A MAN TODAY

James E. Dittes

1817

Harper & Row, Publishers, San Francisco

Cambridge, Hagerstown, New York, Philadelphia
London, Mexico City, São Paulo, Sydney

THE MALE PREDICAMENT: *On Being A Man Today*. Copyright © 1985 by James E. Dittes. All rights reserved. Printed in the United States of America. No part of this book may be used or reproduced in any manner whatsoever without written permission except in the case of brief quotations embodied in critical articles and reviews. For information address Harper & Row, Publishers, Inc., 10 East 53rd Street, New York, NY 10022. Published simultaneously in Canada by Fitzhenry & Whiteside, Limited, Toronto.

FIRST EDITION

Library of Congress Cataloging in Publication Data

Dittes, James E.

    THE MALE PREDICAMENT.

    1. Men—Psychology. 2. Men (Christian theology) 3. Sex role. I. Title.
HQ1090.D58   1985   305.3'1   84-47719
ISBN 0-06-061924-4

85 86 87 88 89 10 9 8 7 6 5 4 3 2 1

For Mercein and for Larry,
my father and my son:

We never had the chance to
say these things to each other

Contents

Preface   *ix*

1. Joseph: Frozen Power   *1*
2. Driven Dreamer: Mystic, Idolmaker, Addict   *30*
3. Confessions of the Golden Bull   *75*
4. Yes-Men: The Empty Yes and the Masked Yes   *92*
5. Crippled Cripplers   *111*
6. Up-manship   *139*
7. Paths of Liberation: Women and Men in
   Tandem and in Conflict   *166*
8. Joseph: Father Nevertheless   *201*

Preface

A real man wouldn't read this book, or write it.

If you are "manly," you don't think the things in this book. You don't admit to yearnings. You don't claim a birthright for more in life, more than the steady, measured march of a manly life. You don't admit to throbs throttled, promises hijacked, dreams dimmed, energies sidelined by that stern, relentless demand: Be a man!

You don't feel a restless tug between "Be a man!" and "Be yourself." It's all the same to you.

You don't admit that you have been programmed, automated, scripted. You insist that you are supremely in control, in charge of your life (and of many other lives, too). You don't admit that you are playing out other people's plans for your life, puppet to their strings, even—maybe especially—when you most act "in charge."

You don't think of "manliness" as constricting, as making life puny and sidetracked. You think of "manliness" as huge, powerful, tough, in the center of the action.

You don't admit to unquenchable longings for tender succor, warm embrace, safe haven, nor do you admit how much of the urgent scrambling is an attempt to earn and guarantee that haven, how much of the tough swagger is a bluff, a poor substitute for the comfort you crave.

You don't admit to manipulating people, especially those closest to you. You insist that you are helping them, or just explaining things, doing it all for their Own Good; you are only the patient, slightly suffering, Good Scout.

You don't admit to lifelong dreams, dreams so urgent that you fashion others into the props and machinery to enact and ensure them, to make the dreams come true.

You don't admit that "Be a man!" demands from you more than you can possibly deliver, that it forbids you from asking for more than you are getting. You don't admit that you have shriveled the wanting to the size of the getting.

So this book is for those men for whom the shell of manliness is cracking or never did fit comfortably, for those men who are discovering that manhood is far richer than the charade of manliness. I try to give voice to the restlessness of yearnings long buried and muted, to the stress and weariness of bearing the heavy armor of manliness and of pretending to wear it nonchalantly and unimpeded.

If I were "manly," I wouldn't have written this book the way I have. I would present sustained, logical arguments, stating the theories clearly and mustering the evidence. I wouldn't mostly tell stories, stories that open more than they settle, stories that try to reach from my experience to yours, stories that sometimes bypass the mind just because resort to conceptual apparatus—one of the ways of being "manly"—can so readily bypass experience. I wouldn't trust you with some of the tenderest parts of myself, in the hope that you will reciprocate and find yourself vulnerable in the reading of this book. If I were "manly," I wouldn't make so much out of Bible stories, the soft stuff women teach in Sunday school, just because I think these legends and parables display the seemingly ageless male predicament in a particularly earnest and revealing way. The key figures of this book are the biblical Josephs—Jacob's favorite son sold into slavery in Egypt, and Mary's spouse, the father who was not the father. Both were promised power and place, both scripted and frozen by those promises into mutely obedient chore boys, scurrying about in the night. Yet both also found in this very sidelining, the very drudgery of the chores, in the fitful sleep of the night, new dreams and new place. Their story is my story, made manifest and made hopeful. Your story, too, I think.

If I were "manly," I wouldn't tell so many stories drawn from the experiences of ministers—a wimpy, powerless profession in the eyes of many, each year sinking lower in the charts of social status—just because that is the profession I happen to know best and because what I think I see in the predicament of ministers trying to be manly and trying to be human is what I think I see in the haunts of any profession. Change the words a bit and see if their story is not your story.

The stories I tell are all true stories, each in its own way. The stories about myself are literally true, told as accurately as I can remember them, except for changing the names and in other ways disguising the other people. (I thank "Judith" for letting me discuss in detail in the chapter entitled "Up-man-ship" the conversation that she and I shared.) Some stories, essentially, are composites of the Bryans and Jennys, the Marilyns and Rogers that I have known, and been. Other stories are obviously inventions of fantasy and fable. If I were more "manly," perhaps I would be more scrupulous about the line between what is literally true and what is true to life. The stories are here because they make, for me, one true story, my story, the story, I dare to suppose, of the male predicament of our time, and therefore your story. Is it?

This then is a book about men's liberation, the freeing of the human being from the stultifying burden of being manly. But it differs—profoundly, I think—from other recent books about the male experience because of three assumptions I make about the relation of men to women. These are: (1) Women are not the enemy. I do not regard women as the oppressors, as either the manufacturers or principal enforcers of the manly role. Women are often, however, the conveyors, the sometimes supremely effective teachers of the male role. But the male role that women sometimes convey is a common creation of our culture, in which we all participate.

(2) Nor are women the present problem. This book does not regard women's changes in their role as a problem for men.

Many authors do think that learning to live with liberated women, learning to live in a world of liberated women, is the major male predicament these days; perhaps you assumed that when you picked up a book called *The Male Predicament*. Living with women who refuse to fit a traditional role *is* a large adventure. But that is not what this book is about. We men have even more urgent business in dealing with our own obstacles and stereotypes. We can learn from women, perhaps, something about the process of liberation, about becoming conscious of the stereotypes into which we fit too comfortably and about finding the power to break out. But even here we will be distracted if we try to imitate women too closely. For their methods have had to be the methods of people commonly denied power, of those for whom the stereotypes are more obviously disabling. We must devise methods necessary for those encumbered with power, for those for whom the stereotypes are less obviously disabling, all too comfortable, pay off all too well. Hence, for example, the absolute necessity of encouraging vulnerability among men, mirroring in importance the strategy of empowerment among women. The final chapter proposes a distinctive male mode of liberation.

(3) So if women are not the enemy, nor the present problem, neither are they the solution, the third difference from many men's books these days. There is much talk these days of the new, liberated man being a "feminized" man; men are told to aspire to greater openness of feelings and tenderness, so that they will become "more like women"—somehow reciprocating, apparently, women's efforts to be stronger, "more like men." But I think that living up to the new specifications is at least as deadly as living up to the traditional specifications. This book is instead about surrendering the comfort of all specifications and roles for the zest of authentic living.

*   *   *

This book is dedicated to the two important males in my life, my father and my son, with whom I have had to carry on these conversations in the silence of a still grieving heart. It is also dedicated to those important men in my life with whom I have learned many of these things in vigorous discovery— including Alan Lovins, Ted Mills, Jim Nelson, Barry Seltser; John Higgins-Biddle, Dwayne Huebner, David H. Kelsey, Gene Outka, Leon Watts; Peter Benson, John Hay, Michael Jackson, Al Simons, Tom Stiers, Lewis Rambo, David Ruhe; Richard Newcombe; David Knisley and Jim Ralston; Jeff Edwards and John Wagner; Leonard Hill and John Young; Jim Ashbrook; and Tim Lull (who identified the "Joseph deal")—and to the women who have shared with me the throes and joys of a now and then liberation.

1. Joseph: Frozen Power

It was said about him that he was "a man who always did what was right." A model citizen, a man whose retirement tribute or Chamber of Commerce award or obituary could have written itself, as though the life had been lived just for the tribute—the tribute scripting the life, not vice versa. A model citizen, the kind the neighbors gasp to the reporters about after a violent outburst or an elopement to South America, "He was the last man we expected to do something like *that!*" He was a man who always did what was right.

In every Christmas manger scene, every Christmas pageant, one figure stands tall, central and unnoticed—Joseph, the father who is not the father. Just as in your household and mine, baby and mother, animals and visitors all get more attention than the sturdy, quiet figure in the center of the action. Joseph is an apt symbol for modern men: prominent, dutiful, robust, yet shadowy and marginal, never quite looked at directly. "What exactly is his part in the story?" That's how it is every Christmas in the manger scene. That's how it is all year round for most of us. That's how it was for the first Joseph in the first Christmas story, absolutely dutiful, crucially dutiful, yet kept in the shadows.

The story starts out with Joseph at the center; he has the leading role in the first chapter of the New Testament, in the first chapter of Matthew, the writer whom the ancient church symbolized with a man. Joseph is at the center, but look how the story goes.

"This is how the birth of Jesus Christ took place. His mother Mary was engaged to Joseph, but before they were married, she found out that she was going to have a baby by the

Holy Spirit. Joseph was a man who always did what was right, but he did not want to disgrace Mary publicly; so he made plans to break the engagement privately. While he was thinking about this, an angel of the Lord appeared to him in a dream and said, 'Joseph, descendant of David, do not be afraid to take Mary to be your wife. For it is by the Holy Spirit that she has conceived. She will have a son, and you will name him Jesus—because he will save his people from their sins.' . . . So when Joseph woke up, he married Mary, as the angel of the Lord had told him to. But he had no sexual relations with her before she gave birth to her son. And Joseph named him Jesus." (Matthew 1:18–21, 24, 25)

No matter what happened, Joseph stayed tough. When his fiancée turned up pregnant, he may have been dismayed and humiliated, but no one knew it. He always did what was right. If he was hurt or angry, no one knew it; he stayed in control—in control of himself, in control of the situation. Denied his bride, shunted aside from fatherhood, if he felt wronged, he covered that pain with his own righteousness. Good Scout ever, he would make no trouble, just put her away privately, the decent thing, you know.

Of course, when he was told to do otherwise, he changed his plan and did as he was told, still tough, still righteous. When he discovered that the higher right, the still more self-sacrificing right, was to give Mary a home and to give the baby a name, then, of course, that is what he did—and no sex! If he felt used, abused, or cheated about having a marriage in name only; about being a father who was not a father, no one knew it. Doing the right thing was more important than finding personal satisfaction. He provided for the baby, scrupulously, relentlessly—the second chapter makes clear just how much out of his way he went on behalf of the baby—just as he was told to do.

That is all we know about him: he always did what was right.

No wonder that the Catholic church made Joseph the patron

saint for the modern working man. Although the church invented a Joseph who is a model of the skilled and committed craftsman, we know nothing from the Bible, only from our own fantasies, about his work as a carpenter. What we do know about Joseph from the Bible and what does make him a close model for modern men's lives is his mute obedience; his steadfast acquiescence; his "Yes, sir!" when a promise made to him was broken; his "Yes, sir!" when a new assignment was given; his impulsive, take-charge activism on behalf of that project. In short, we know about his eagerness to play out energetically and unhesitatingly the script assigned to him, without pausing to question its suitability, the male predicament.

I learned to play Joseph, quite literally, the year I became a teenager. Miss Gardener and Miss Swearer, who produced the Christmas pageant that year, cast me in the lead role, they said, and they taught me how to do it just right. Though their script was only one of many in a boy's life, not even the first, not even the most rigid, it was a clean and spare script, pure manliness, as taught by women—which is how most of us have learned it.

First, they enticed me with promises: a big part, an important role, top billing, right next to Mary. I said I would do it. Joseph had exchanged promises, too; Mary would become his wife and bear his children. Then, like his, my expectations were shattered. The script turned out quite different from the billing and the built up expectations, different in the same way. Once recruited and on stage, my instructions were simple and absolute: don't move!

Eyes down, one hand benignly on Mary's shoulder, the other hand out in open receptive gesture, welcoming all pilgrims, I was to freeze, stock-still, the only person in the pageant unmoving and unmoved, the lead role become part of the scenery. I was the centerpiece, even the altarpiece of all the action, yet totally removed from the action, denied action, a figurehead. Presiding, in charge but uncharged, steadfastly going through the motions without moving a muscle. I stuck it out as man-fully as Joseph did, the father who was not the father.

Going through the motions while standing still. Going through the motions of standing still. Going through the motions by standing still: Miss Gardener's and Miss Swearer's script for me was Matthew's script, Scripture's script, for Joseph and the most common script for men. Learning to be Joseph for Miss Gardener and Miss Swearer, I was learning to be a man for them, and for all for whom they spoke, and shaped. For is this not every man's assignment in our culture, that we run in place? We must strike a decisive posture without moving, without effecting anything or affecting anyone, thoroughly do-mesticated, leashed, mute.

When men believe the promise of top billing, the invitation to be the center of the action, but don't understand that the script requires them to freeze—when they misperceive the promises as the script—then they spend many heartbreaking and ulcer-plagued years trying to make a difference, trying to have impact and effect, trying to leave the world different from the way they found it. Spent, burned, and burnt out, at last they discover what the Miss Gardeners and Miss Swearers knew all along, that the script only requires them to freeze, to simulate action, to be prop and scenery for others to act out their pageantry.

When a man looks up in twinges of pain and anger from his fruitless efforts, the Miss Gardeners and Miss Swearers are watching him blankly, truly dumbfounded and perplexed, appalled not at their own unresponsiveness but at the man's feverishness. "We thought you understood the script. All you're supposed to do is stand still and be the centerpiece."

Suppose I had taken Miss Gardener and Miss Swearer lit-erally when they said "Be the hero." Suppose I had been busy playing Joseph as I conceived him: concerned husband, tender father, generous host, thoughtful sage. I might have fussed about the manger, urged Mary to take a nap while I kept the vigil, graciously received visitors and their gifts with flourishes and with speeches. Suppose I had moved into the role and about the stage with such vigor? Suppose I had played Joseph as I thought I had been invited to? Suppose I had played Joseph as I most wanted to? Suppose I had played Joseph in the way that felt most authentic?

If I had tried to be a vigorous, genuine Joseph, then I would have encountered what any man encounters whenever he ventures authenticity.

Wise men, shepherds, and Mary would have been confused and balky. Instead of matching my spontaneity with their own, all action would have come to a chaotic standstill. My own version of Joseph as God's man would have been an obstacle to their playing out their own scripts, instead of an invitation to leave their scripts and to become authentic wise men, shepherds, and mother. The audience would have been offended and dismayed; a real living Joseph is not what is expected. Miss Gardener and Miss Swearer would have dissolved in fury (expressed in typical code of course: one would simply have said, "Well...!" with the other standing close behind, hands on hips). An unscripted, spontaneous, expressive Joseph, especially an emotional Joseph, was not wanted, is not wanted. I was not wanted, at least not unscripted.

"Freeze!" the police say to the robber caught in the act.

Any man who has ever followed the script, or even accepted casting—that is, every man—has discovered that the casters and the scriptwriters don't mean it, at least not in the way he thought they did, at least not consistently, at least not as something to live your life by, at least not with you having the power to carry through. Seducers never do mean it as earnestly as the seduced supposed.

For me, as 13-year old Joseph, the abrupt discovery, the unveiling of the script, came promptly and therefore almost painlessly: "Leading man?" they said, "Forget the busy hosting and benign fathering. Just freeze!" I didn't have time to take the role of leading man seriously and bustle about the stage acting out this role to which I had been recruited and was committed, before being chagrined and stranded with the countermand "Freeze!" I have seldom been as lucky since. Few men are. Far more often, we have been energetically preoccupied in midstage greeting shepherds, rocking the baby, performing whatever other chores we have been assigned, content to be doing "what was right," secretly savoring the admiration and merit we believe we are earning, when suddenly the houselights go up and a voice booms out, "Cut! What are you doing! You were just supposed to freeze!"

The abrupt discovery came late and painfully for my grandfather, one who most decidedly and most admirably "always did what was right," as a faithful and imaginative minister/husband/father. He endured a seven-year engagement while his bride-to-be cared for an aging mother. He laboriously gardened huge plots every summer so as to reduce his claim on church budgets, frequently no more than $1,000 per year. Already successful as minister to a large city church in his thirties, he relinquished that when his denomination asked him to move West at the turn of the century to start a new church. Once he had moved, the denomination abandoned its support, leaving him stranded and a failure. Now off the career ladder, stigmatized, shunted aside by church officials guilty over their own miscalculation, he was unable for years to find another church, and then never one able to fully require or appreciate his talents. He never complained, persisting faithfully and creatively at whatever he was assigned. Never complained, that is, until late in his life, when the houselights suddenly came up on the Psalms he had been reading for most of his life, and he noticed that they were true, that the wicked had prospered and that he hadn't. Aging and semi-invalid, he showed me the newspaper accounts of American Legionnaires cavorting at conventions, thriving while flouting every line of the script he had bound himself to and which still bound him. Bitterness escaped from him in the form of his warning to me:

"Take a good look down the road before you make any big decisions."

Why can't fathers pass on this hard-won wisdom to their sons—or at least wink when they pass on the role assignments—this wisdom that the roles of manhood are isolated roles, not part of a genuinely working ecology, that the people supposed to play those complementary roles that are needed to justify the scripts of manhood aren't doing so. Fathers can't warn or wink because the rules of manhood forbid such confession. Real men don't confess to feeling duped or angry, because that is to confess loss of control.

Cinderella is a woman's story, the dream of escape from the chores, maybe for a grand fling, maybe even for a lifetime of bliss once the hero comes along and makes the slipper fit. Women can dream of escape from the chores, because they know that life is more than the chores. For men, the chores faithfully performed *are* life. Women, hardly to their advantage, can imagine and sometimes wait for the rescuer, the prince to awaken them with a kiss, the fairy godmother to brandish a wand, the hunter to slay the wolf, the wonderful wizard of Oz to take them home. Indeed, women assign these roles to their men, to no one's advantage. But men cannot depend on such a savior (any more than be one, for the women), only on their own efforts—fully as futile as waiting for Prince Charming. It is not from their chores that men seek a saving. Men may seek rescue from loneliness and meaninglessness (and cast women as rescuers), but not from their chores. For men, chores are the solution, not the problem. Chores are to be pursued, pursued even to the breaking point.

The biblical Aaron is known now mostly for how he ended up, faithless manufacturer of an idol, the infamous gold bull, that so angered his scriptwriters, God and Moses, that they destroyed him. But read the whole story (Exodus 4–7, 32) as we shall in the next chapter, to see how Aaron was seduced into this fateful deed by venturing to do a good deed. He was only doing his best to follow the very script they had set for him. They had commissioned him into a ministry of assuaging his people's plight, and they had taught him to use props at hand for miraculous effect (for example, "Tell Aaron to take his walking stick and throw it down in front of the king, and it will turn into a snake" Exod. 17:8b). So (in Exodus 32) when the people were desperate and leaderless, when they felt abandoned by both God and Moses, when they needed drastic help, Aaron undertook an honest ministerial chore, a good deed, the best he knew. He took gold jewelry at hand and fashioned a gold bull—it looked strong and saving! And God and Moses said: you should have known better; even with all that responsibility you were just supposed to freeze.

Oedipus is now known, thanks to Sophocles and Freud, as the villainous murderer of his father and seducer of his mother. But he was lured into such disaster precisely by playing the hero flawlessly, just as everyone wanted and for which they applauded. Volunteering exile from what he thought was his native land, in order to avoid causing disaster there, he went to Thebes and played hero as all scripts taught: he killed a threatening marauder, answered the riddles, saved the city, and married the queen. This impeccable record of noble intentions and heroic deeds was turned on its head by fate and Freud to make Oedipus—and the Oedipus in each of us—the villain and victim, a just man faithful to his duty and lured by it into disaster, when it turns out that the call to duty is a seducing lie.

Doug Abbott, a man well known to me, has performed his life's chores with a vigor and a skill and an effectiveness that deserve praise (and get a lot from some people) but earn only fearful disapproval from his wife, who wants a faithful chore boy, a "good boy." Doug brings a single-minded zest to the male script.

Provide for, give of yourself to your family, your church, your community. These are the rules Doug has obeyed, precisely and unswervingly. Providing for the family has meant working hard, and taking risks. It has meant starting his own business, building his own factory on the edge of town, trying new products. Every move has resulted in more comfort and more security for his family; the changes have also meant, in this case, more time with his family and a happier disposition. But every move he has made has been resolutely opposed by his wife as a threat to the family security. She has attacked him as reckless and uncaring, as deliberately risking his family's welfare for crazy new ideas. His wife, fearful and unhappy, has mobilized neighborhood support, and Doug now lives with the reputation of being foolhardy and selfish—a reputation he has earned precisely by being careful and selfless.

When his church sponsored Cambodian refugees, he quietly offered some jobs in his factory and just as quietly refurbished one of the buildings on the property in back of his factory for housing. Deserving praise, he got more accusations: you're taking a chance hiring so many of them—suppose it turns into charity? Why can't you let the others in the church carry their share?

Doug is Don Quixote, spurned for taking the impossible dream seriously. He is Oedipus, made the villain and the scapegoat for the ills of his city, for undertaking no more and no less than his city wanted. On the whole, Doug is warmly liked. It is only his overcommitment—as people see it—his unabashed seriousness and energy in pursuing the role he was taught—that is what offends the community. Somewhere, Doug has missed or has ignored the fundamental message: freeze. But they will have their way with him and subdue his spirit. Lacking appreciation and instead villainized, in late middle age, he is gradually subsiding. "Let them do it their way. Let them make their own mistakes." He is gradually surrendering. They will have their way with him, and their way is: freeze. It's another word for "burn-out."

Employ a man as leader, whether as President or as a school principal, whether as new Kiwanis president or Boy Scout leader, and there is much rhetoric from others about high

expectations for new accomplishments. But the real expectation is: don't rock the boat. Most men get the message well
and play out this dream effectively, meeting both expectations
at once, appearing to move while standing still: the appearance
of being a leader while frozen. Quick promotions, new job
offers abound for the man who plays well enough to make
others feel energized and led while no one has to move. Everybody knows that except the intrepid good Scout Joseph, taking
expectations and promises more seriously than they were meant,
building castles doomed to crumble.

 The other Joseph of the Bible acts out the same male script,
the better-known Joseph actually, the one with the colored coat
and the jealous brothers, the one who spurned a military
captain's wife and interpreted dreams for Pharaoh and then
took over agricultural management for all of Egypt. (You can
read the whole story in Genesis 37–45 or in Thomas Mann's
multivolume reconstruction, or go see your high school kids
perform Webber and Rice's musical update of the church pageant, *Joseph and the Amazing Technicolor Dreamcoat*.) Joseph starts
out as his father's favorite son, and through his whole career
he plays favorite son, teacher's pet, obedient Scout, dutiful
choreboy. He always did what was right, a script that regularly
left him stranded.

 At seventeen: Jacob's favorite of twelve sons, Joseph spies
on his brothers' delinquencies for his father and is paid off
with a special robe (either "many colored" or "long-sleeved,"
depending on the translation you read). He dreams of grandeur and trustingly shares his dream with the brothers, who
shove him into a pit. Later they drag him out and sell him as
a slave to a caravan heading for Egypt.

 In Egypt: dutiful and reliable, "Potiphar was pleased with
him and made him his personal servant so he put him in
charge of his house and everything he owned." (Genesis 39:4)
Good boy Joseph of course coldly refused a proposition from
Potiphar's wife, in the name of duty, without even a gallant

"No, thank you." Such goodness so angered the woman that she grabbed his robe and used it as evidence to frame him. So, off to a dungeon for being dutiful son.

In prison: a trusty, pleasing the jailer this time, so "he put Joseph in charge of all the other prisoners and made him responsible for everything." (Genesis 39:22)

Before the king: telling him what he wanted to hear about his dreams, getting assigned the role of favorite son again, this time in a big way, governor over all Egypt. "I will put you in charge of my country" (Genesis 41:41) with the assignment to hoard grain against the coming famine.

Now the governorship: locked into playing harsh and scheming bureaucrat incognito, always doing the right thing, when his brothers come to buy grain from his stores, needing to hide his feelings—still the good boy, the real man:

"The sons of Jacob came with others to buy grain, because there was famine in the land of Canaan. . . . When Joseph saw his brothers, he recognized them, but he acted as if he did not know them. He asked them harshly, 'Where do you come from?. . . . You are spies; you have come to find out where our country is weak. . . . This is how you will be tested: I swear by the name of the king that you will never leave unless your youngest brother comes here. One of you must go and get him. The rest of you will be kept under guard. . . .' With that, he put them in prison for three days. . . . Joseph understood what they said, but they did not know it, because they had been speaking to him through an interpreter. Joseph left them and began to cry. When he was able to speak again, he came back, picked out Simeon, and had him tied up in front of them.

"The famine in Canaan got worse . . . so the brothers took gifts and twice as much money and set out for Egypt with Benjamin. . . . They took the gifts into the house to Joseph and bowed down to the ground before him. . . . Then Joseph left suddenly, because his heart was full of tender feelings for his brother. He was about to break down, so he went to his room and cried. After he had washed his face, he came out, and controlling himself, he ordered the meal to be served. . . . Joseph commanded the servant in charge of his house, 'Fill the men's sacks with as much food as they can carry, and put each man's money in the top of his sack. Put my silver cup in the top of the youngest brother's sack, together with the money for his grain.' . . . When they had gone only a short distance from the city, Joseph said to the servant in charge of his house, 'Hurry after those men. When you catch up with them, ask them, "Why have you paid back evil for good? Why did you steal my master's silver cup?" . . .

"When the brothers came to Joseph's house . . . they bowed down before him. . . . Joseph was no longer able to control his feeling in front of his servants, so he ordered them all to leave the room. No one else was with him when Joseph told his brothers who he was." (Genesis 42–45)

Joseph, the perpetual boy wonder, set apart and aloof for his pageant by garments draped on him by his father and by Pharaoh, garments as strange as those draped on me by Miss Swearer. Joseph, locked into positions as frozen as mine on my teen-age Christmas stage. Joseph's obedience, virtue, and competence earns the favor of the fathers—Jacob, Potiphar, jailer, Pharaoh, God—and earn him his own role of authority, a kind of father who is not a father. But it cuts him off—as surely as I was cut off from authentic talk with the wise men, shepherds, or Mary—from companionship and intimacy with brothers, fellow prisoners, women. Manhood means being a dutiful prisoner, obeyer of authority, dispenser of authority—all the same thing, really.

The Joseph deal—being the man who always does what is right—is to exchange action and authenticity and access to others for the posture of special place and privilege, a kind of power, as we shall see more clearly at the end of this chapter, but a frozen power. A good man, if not a real man. Joseph gives up being his own man, with its promises of grandeur and risks of humiliation, in order to be a scripted man, a hero.

Joseph accepts a posed, less than life-size role in order to be solidly part of a larger than life-size script. You are our leading man, Miss Gardener and Miss Swearer had promised, and indeed I was.

COMPULSORY LIMPNESS

Renouncing intimacy for obedience to authority. More devastatingly: renouncing sexuality for obedience to authority; renouncing natural fatherhood, with all its vulnerability, for the role of father, with all its rigidities. Now it's time to say what is at the chilling heart of the Joseph story: Joseph is required to renounce his sexuality. The story is relentless in its harsh and unambiguous assault on a man's jauntiness—on his self-image—because it is an assualt on his sexual self-image. For however much it may be exaggerated by *Playboy*, and scorned by puritans, a man's potency and his capacity to father are the most basic, distinctive, and pleasurable aspects of his manhood—and precisely what is dismissed by the Joseph script, Matthew's Joseph script, other Joseph scripts.

"Abraham fathered Isaac, and Isaac fathered Jacob, and Jacob fathered Judah and his brothers, and Judah fathered . . . and Matthan fathered Jacob, and Jacob fathered Joseph. . . ." These opening verses of Matthew (1:1–17)—the opening verses of the New Testament—beat out the litany of paternity. Joseph is in the patrilineal line from Father Abraham. Because of all his fathers, 40 generations of them, Joseph's fatherhood is important, his son credible. And as his fatherhood is celebrated, sexuality is promised: the next verse announces his engagement to a woman named Mary. Joseph is to become someone important, through his sexuality and through his paternity. The Joseph promise is every man's promise. For any man whose God-given exultancy in his own sexuality has not been scoffed into limpness, deep and primitive pulsations of joy and destiny are aroused inside him by the promises Matthew registers, sheer unabashed delight in his own tumescence, utter awe at his own prospects of paternity.

But it is a buildup for a letdown. For the Joseph experience, the Joseph script, is the devastation of legitimate and appropriate pride in male sexuality. Matthew's genealogy promises and celebrates paternity, but Joseph's sexual role in fathering is dismissed, rendered totally irrelevant. He's the standby, the eunuch in attendance, his seed precisely what is not wanted. Thirty-nine times, in Matthew's drumroll of paternity, a man fathers a son ("begat" in the King James translation's mounting staccato). And the next verse should read, in a climactic drumbeat, "and Joseph fathered Jesus." But it's not there. Betrothal promised sexuality, but sexual relations are explicitly banned. Marriage but no sex. That's how Matthew's first chapter, Joseph's big chapter, ends. Down, boy. This is too important to let you toy with. No admittance. Authorized personnel only—and mortal sexual males clearly are not authorized. Virgin father.

Freeze. Hold still. Don't make a move, Miss Gardener and Miss Swearer told me. This pageant is too important for that. Just follow our directions, our script. Be Joseph. The last thing we want is a turned-on Joseph.

When Dr. Freyda Zell became pregnant, the man she had picked (without consulting him) to father her child, asked if the child were his. Her answer: "Look, I don't feel it's really your business." ("When Motherhood Doesn't Mean Marriage," by Georgia Dullea. New York Times, November 30, 1981, page B16.) She is one of those who want children while denying as much as they can the man's role in the process. Perhaps the men can form the Joseph Club, fathers who are not fathers. "Sometimes I think this may have been the way women lived long ago in tribal times," another says, conjuring a golden age to suit her preferences. "A woman would have a baby and raise it on her own with the help of other women." (Ibid.)

"To the Editors: For a book on a single mother's wanted child, I am interested in obtaining biographical or autobiographical information concerning unmarried women who planned their pregnancies and head-of-household status." So Deborah Michelle Saunders cooly queries (*New York Review of Books*, volume 29, number 12, July 15, 1982, page 45). Mary, at least, was startled and perplexed by male-less pregnancy. "How can this be?" (Luke 1:34). Ms. Saunders "planned," with male sexuality frozen out, sometimes literally, in a sperm bank.

Consider another group of fathers who are not fathers—the clergy. "Father" we often call them, especially the celibates! But even when they are not officially declared "Father" and celibate, we still treat clergy that way. "No marital delights on Saturday nights," a veteran Baptist minister warned when his assistant got married. When God's men set out to do God's work, they must leave behind what it is that makes them men. The churches, or, more accurately, the culture for which the churches speak, prefers its clergy to be eunuchs; or prepubescent boys; or slaves on God's plantation, living in housing provided by their masters and permitted little private home life; if Protestants, married to desexualized women, if Roman Catholics, more explicitly rendered sexless; and if women, often denied the role of minister altogether because they are perceived more sexually and are less willing to repress their sexuality. (It is probable that one of the basic resistances women experience when they try to enter the ministry is precisely the conflict church and culture experience between their own perceived sexuality and the desexualized role imposed upon the ministry and on the men who have, on the whole, comfortably occupied that role.)

"Cut the dirty jokes, hide the *Playboy* magazines, here comes the minister!" "I didn't expect to see *you* here in a movie like this!" Ministers are expected to be no less than our ideal good men, close, even intimate, but frozen sexless. Any studs the culture offers as models to stir adolescent fantasies are, the message is clear, out-of-bounds and not to be copied.

"How *do* you become pregnant if you are married to a minister?" A minister's wife told me she was asked by an earnestly perplexed teenager.

"How nice that you could find an older man to marry," the church people told another minister I know, making clear their perceptions that neither "older men" nor "women ministers" are sexually active.

All these fathers who are not fathers, the fathers of the church, the fathers of the babies of the Ms. Zells and the Ms. Saunderses are reflecting in extreme form what all of us Josephs experience, the epitome of frozen power: compulsory limpness. Have it but don't use it, or use it but don't enjoy it. The stages of life from early boyhood on can be measured by the way they say it: "No, don't touch there while you're in the bathtub . . . Remember to keep your hands outside the covers . . . You guys that hang around the drugstore all have dirty minds . . . Wait until we're more ready . . . There's so much more to a real relationship than sex . . . Try to be more tender . . . Can't you be more patient when I'm not in the mood . . . Let's just cuddle . . . We're getting too old for that anymore . . ." Sometimes they mean just what they say, and what they say is fair. Mostly they mean more than they say; they mean the Joseph message: "Freeze. Down boy. If you want a place in my life, hold back, don't feel as sexual as you are." We want that place, so we shape up, strike the Joseph pose, and become "manly"—their way.

THE FREEZING POWER OF FROZEN POWER

For the place they offer does have power. Joseph does have center stage. Being "manly" their way may be stereotyped, bound, rigid, frozen, but it does have a power, and we can easily get into that stereotype, into exercising that power. I got a charge out of presiding over the manger scene. The difference between bringing my own energy to the role and getting my energy *from* the role is the tragic male predicament. (Reversing that energy flow may be a classic male liberation, as we shall consider in the last chapter of this book.) But once Joseph lets his own power be turned off, frozen, he does feel a new power surging; unfortunately, it too, since it derives from the freezing of the role, is frozen in its own way and freezes others. The frozen Joseph has a kind of Midas touch: everything he touches must turn solid, too, to match his frozenness, an agent of Miss Gardener's and Miss Swearer's freezing touch.

"You were commanding," they said afterwards. "You looked in charge, running things." At the cast party "Mary" stood off by herself giving me long wide-eyed looks, preteen adoration. And for weeks afterwards, kids who had played kings and shepherds would pass me in hallways with eyes averted, a vestige of the deference they had shown me in the pageant. For, as dutifully, even abjectly, as I may have complied with the script, the script called for me to be magisterial. Though I gave up playing Joseph my way, their Joseph played me. Their Joseph dominated me, but in such a way that others perceived me as dominating them. I may have been frozen, impotent, but I was frozen in a pose of power. I may have felt a puppet, I may have been a puppet, but I was a puppet who pulled the strings of others. They didn't say, "You froze well," though I did and though it was important to them and to me that I did. They said, "You were commanding." The role became real. Overruled, I became ruler. The epitome of manhood, the epitome of father: Frozen power, overruled and become ruler.

To become Joseph is to change the axis of orientation from horizontal to vertical. Give up the outward reach (to peers, to frontiers) for a more secure upward grasp. Give up action onstage for approval backstage. Lest abandon bring abandonment, give up abandon for a bonding with the powers, opting for the risks of bondage over the risks of abandonment. Give up being a "real boy" for being a "good boy." The Joseph deal, the Pinocchio deal.

For that is what we all do as men. We comply with the script for the payoff. To avoid all the ignominy and scorn that it would have cost to be my own Joseph, I complied with being Miss Gardener's and Miss Swearer's Joseph. Led man rather than leading man. But it still felt like being on top, on high. I had an in on high. My status was now derived, not self-defined, but it was still status. I was making the deals all teacher's pets make: give up spontaneity, its delights and its risks, and get the security of sponsorship, the comfort of patronage. Give up the risks of excess for the privilege of access. To authorities. And the power that brings.

Joseph, Jacob's son: enslaved and imprisoned, deprived of his place in one household after another (Jacob's, Potiphar's), he narrowed his fantasies down to hierarchical dreams of grandeur and acted them out, escalating the teacher's pet role into a princely and commanding rule. Joseph: denied open brotherly relations with his brothers, he resorted to trickery and manipulation to regain their attention and respect. Joseph: ejected from his family, he contrived, not without cruelty and cunning, to reassemble the family—around himself. Joseph: so "full of tender feelings" (Genesis 43:30) that he required strenuous measures to "control himself." (Genesis 43:31) Joseph: discovered that the only way he could relate to his brothers—not so much by his choice as by theirs—was hierarchically, either cast down by them into a pit in the wilderness, or lording over them, compelling them to bow down before him.

Jacob, Joseph's father, knew about these things, too. Jacob, who had been maneuvered by Rebecca into manipulating and deceiving his own father and his brother; Jacob, who had been tricked out of the bride of his choice and compelled to contend for her; Jacob, whose sex life and fathering was managed by Leah and Rachel. "Give me children, or I will die" . . . "Here is my slave girl Bilhah; sleep with her so that she can have a child for me." . . . "You are going to sleep with me tonight, because I have paid for you." (Genesis 30:1, 3, 16) Joseph was the son of the Jacob who was compelled to play superstud.

Joseph, Matthew's Joseph: frozen out of the decisive promised action, he found a decisive commanding pose. Joseph,
also a Jacob's son, also a dreamer who claimed unique and
self-enhancing messages from on high. Joseph, who craftily
outsmarted two kings (Herod and his son, Archelaus), in a
high stakes drama. Joseph, who staged a daring nightime
escape, undertaking commanding, decisive action in his brief
moment of glory and opportunity.

Joseph, Matthew's other Joseph: the one who was so cool
and generous at the end of the story. "When it was evening, a
rich man from Arimathea arrived; his name was Joseph, and
he also was a disciple of Jesus. He went into the presence of
Pilate and asked for the body of Jesus. Pilate gave orders for
the body to be given to Joseph. So Joseph took it, wrapped it
in a new linen sheet, and placed it in his own tomb, which he
had just recently dug out of solid rock. Then he rolled a large
stone across the entrance to the tomb and went away."
(Matthew 27:57–61) A man of power, boldness, comfortable
with authority, a man who digs a tomb from solid rock and
who moves large stones, a man prepared, a man committed
to disposing of a body traditionally and humanely, a prominent citizen and generous benefactor, the factory owner who
sits on all the nonprofit boards of directors, buys full-page
ads in benefit programs, and opens his parking lot gates to
the Scouts for weekend baseball; a very good man. A man
who did all things necessary and good for the dead Jesus,
privately, without a tear, and then went away, maybe never to
know that his doings, the wrapping in linen and the rolling of
a large stone, good doings all, decisive and final doings, did
not end the story.

Joseph: frozen power, controlled and controlling. Man: frozen power, controlled and controlling.

Frozen is not relaxed, but just the opposite; not open, not
receptive, not responsive, frozen is fixed, intense, determined,
addicted, addictive. Frozen is hard at the task. Frozen is not

waiting for something to happen, but making something happen, a something that is narrow, so as to be manageable, something restricted, constricted. Frozen is intense pursuit, controlled energy, determination—in all senses of the term—to do right, to do well, the mission impossible. Frozen is not inert, waiting to follow others' leads, not even ready to accommodate, adapt to, relate to others, but the opposite; frozen is fixed, laden with gravity, leaden with gravity, the center of gravity, able to relate to others only as they are pulled into close orbit. Frozen is the coldness of the dying star, collapsing densely on itself, and pulling others into it, like so much debris. That dying star is Joseph. That star is American manhood.

Macho manipulation of others is not the expansion of power but contraction; not centrifugal but centripetal, not the imposition of strength but the armoring of weakness. Others are frozen in place because the frozen man has no choice. He is determined. The constriction is imposed on others because it is imposed on him.

The manipulator must manipulate because he is manipulated. The stereotyped must stereotype. The idolized must make idols of others and of programs and of agendas and of institutions, because that is the nature of idols; they must breed support of their own kind or they perish. The frozen man must freeze others because he fears that if he doesn't surround himself with frozenness, he will melt—into nothing. Once fixed (whether that feels like what happens in the veterinarian's office or in the darkroom or at the back door of the police station), the man needs to equip his world with fixtures, whether these are persons or groups or organizations or schemes or creeds or uniforms or rituals. The drugged becomes pusher to hook others, pushing others into their proper places in his scheme of things and pinning them there. The man cast in a role requires a supporting cast, all in roles, to prop up his own.

VICTIM AND VICTIMIZER ARE ONE

Men are often and readily portrayed as victims of sterotyping and role typing. The principal purpose of this chapter so far has been to draw that very portrait. Men are just as often and just as readily portrayed as perpetrators of stereotyping and role typing, forcing people into postures and roles to fit their own schemes. Other chapters in this book draw that portrait. The remaining pages of this chapter propose to show that these two portraits, stereotyped and stereotyper, pushed and pusher, are one portrait. These pages will try to make it clear and plausible that the man, frozen in place, fixed, stereotyped, role typed, once he comes to fill the role, to play the script as his, must support that role by enlisting others in the same script.

The key is in the artificial, manufactured nature of the role; the role is not necessarily fragile or precarious, but it is artificial. The role imposed upon the man has not evolved; it has been constructed. It is not part of an ecological balance—or perhaps it is an archaic survivor from the balance of another era—so that it is not in a natural give-and-take relationship with the environment around it. It is constructed and imposed on, inserted into, the environment—more like rape than embrace—so that the man is forced to construct an environment to match the role.

If he, the man, is puppeteer, shoving his fist inside of other people's lives to manage their doings, then he is also a puppet, compelled to just such doings, such managing, by fists shoved inside his life. Sometimes, in a fine, if constricted, symbiotic balance, the hand maneuvering him, the puppet, is the hand of the puppet he is maneuvering—the self-sustaining, self-defeating arrangement of many a married couple, many a professional and client, many a parent and child, many a politician and voter—mutually paired idols all, mutually dependent (not interdependent), mutually freezing.

When I was Joseph, a thirteen-year-old Joseph learning to be a lifetime Joseph, Miss Gardener's and Miss Swearer's Joseph, I was definitely not employing method acting. I was not told to get into the spirit of being Joseph, then let my inner promptings, my inner prompter, take over. That may have been what I wanted, what I had first thought I had been promised; but I was not allowed that. I was told what to do, and all attention was on my doings, Miss Gardener's and Miss Swearer's attention and energy, therefore my attention and energy, and therefore the attention of my fellow players and of the audience. This was not less true because my doings were so constricted, but more true. If what I had to do was to freeze, to stay fixed in place, then my doings were all the more important to everyone. "Be sure to keep your eyes on the manger and not look around!" they said. "Keep your eyes there, don't move!" I recited to myself all during the performance. "How still you stood!" everybody said admiringly, quite different from a remark such as "You were really Joseph," which I might have aspired to and earned had Miss Gardener and Miss Swearer—and hence, I—been part of a different Christmas message. To be Joseph was to be defined by these assigned doings, no more and no less.

Later, people would say to me and other Josephs: "How tidy you keep your lawn," and "Your voice sounds so good from the pulpit," and "You have such a nice smile and broad shoulders," and "You tell jokes well," and—a more insidiously freezing role casting—"You are so sensitive." Narrow doings all. Me. Feeding such comments and fed by them, Joseph redoubles his energy on lawn care, voice projection, body building, joke telling, and sensitivity—if this is who Joseph is, then this is how he must try harder to be somebody—in a way that inevitably enlists others in this project. Children must dig up weeds—they need the discipline and the exercise; it's good for them. "Keep Off" signs go up. "Do Not Interrupt" signs are strictly enforced when he is working at voice practice. People must be smiled at and they must smile back at jokes or people must expose their vulnerabilities so Joseph can "do sensitivity."

A frozen Joseph, limited to a narrow task, limits and shapes how other people can relate to him. People in the pageant had to adjust their roles to mine: I wasn't going to adjust to them. They had to come to where I was, and kneel reverently, because my posture demanded it. They had to let their eyes go where mine did, not meet mine. They had to handle their gifts themselves; I stayed aloof, above such transactions. My doings shaped theirs. My fixedness limited them, shaped them.

If I was learning to be Matthew's Joseph, as well as Miss Gardener's and Miss Swearer's Joseph, then I was learning how relentlessly and insistently Joseph would play his role and sweep others into the action. Take Mary as my wife? Certainly! So Matthew 1:24 seems to say. Abstain from sex? Firmly! Escape to Egypt? Immediately! "Joseph got up, took the child and his mother, and left during the night for Egypt." (Matthew 2:14). Joseph will play his part in Mary's script and Jesus' script when he has to, and he will do it determinedly. But when his time comes to take the lead, then they will play their parts in his script, their supporting roles, and they *will* do it. "Right away, Mary. I have the travel orders. No time for breakfast or laundry or saying goodbye. We're going now."

Cast and garbed by his father as favorite son, Jacob's Joseph played his role vigorously and tried, equally vigorously, to impose the appropriate supporting roles on his brothers: they should bow down. Cast by Potiphar as chief steward, that role then became the boundaries and the boundedness of his personality; others could relate to him only as chief steward. (In the only human encounter we know of while he was in that role, he rejected and rebuked Potiphar's wife, with no personal acknowledgment of her except as a potential compromiser. This was a unilateral and stereotypical dehumanizing of her—however "wrong" her proposition and however admirable his refusal—which understandably angered her to the point of revenge.) Cast by Pharaoh as governor of all Egypt, he found no way to relate with his brothers—much as he genuinely seemed to want to—except by imposing upon them the machinations and deceits of his bureaucratic office. Brothers became pawns in a characteristically devious Middle East power game because Joseph had become a Middle East power. But unnaturally and artificially so, a bureaucrat not grown into that role but shoved into it in a manufactured way that required manufactured props, props frequently made of other people.

Suppose in my eighth-grade pageant, on the crowded stage, one of the shepherds trips on his unfamiliarly long robe and falls toward me. My natural impulse is to put out a hand to catch him and to ward him off, so he doesn't bump me or Mary. But Miss Gardener's and Miss Swearer's Joseph is frozen—"Don't move"—and in obedience to that lofty posture I must withhold my hand, let the shepherd fall. But when he does bang against me, knock me out of my pose, Miss Gardener and Miss Swearer or not, I reflexively throw up a hand, which is now too late to help but strikes him alongside his head. The hand that would help while protecting is frozen into a hand that can only defend and hurt. To be Joseph is to be trapped into this defensive belligerence, so that it seems to become inevitable even when it doesn't come naturally. Joseph, Jacob's son who became govenor of Egypt, was somehow forbidden, as govenor, the natural emotions he felt for his brothers at their reunion. (See pages 11f.) He hid his spontaneous reactions, until his feelings burst forth in bizarre and hurtful ways: planting money and silver in their grain sacks in a way that thoroughly frightened them, commanding them (backed with threats) to bring their youngest brother and father to him.

TO BE JOSEPH OR NOT TO BE

To be Joseph is to want to wear to school a brightly striped sweater, your sister's, because you feel good and look good in it, but then to think of the jeers it would get on the bus, then to put on the usual jean jacket and mix with the crowd at the bus stop, ready to be the first to jeer at any striped sweater.

To be Joseph is to impulsively compliment a woman in your workplace on her new hairdo, just because you like it, only to have her pull back haughtily as though you had made a pass, then to resolve to henceforth withhold any such friendly gestures and to remain strictly businesslike. Or else—really only another version of frozen power, another constricted and safely emotion-free pattern—to accept the assignment in her response and to fall into the habit of making flirtatious wisecracks, suggestive remarks, and innuendos: "Long lunch hour today?" "I can see why your blouse popped a button, and I am glad." It's easier, really, a more smoothly predictable pattern, to treat each other just as sex objects, a familiar script you can both follow, no unnerving surprises.

To be Joseph is to say to a lover or a daughter or a wife, "You seem tense and upset today," offering sympathy and support and caring, only to have her shoot back, "You can be so critical sometimes," so—especially after a succession of such episodes wears down your warmth—you pull back into a properly masculine stony silence or else begin to return the fire, gradually growing into the judgmental role in which she has cast you, casting her as victim of the constant critic she has cast you as. Instead of risking warmth, risking rejection, it turns out, somehow, to be easier to play along with this script; at least you know where you are, and at least you have some place in her life. As judge, you are somebody she knows how to deal with. As object of scrutiny and correction, she is somebody you know how to deal with.

To be Joseph is to be prowling with a couple of other five-year-olds through the big field at the end of the street and to come to some thick bushes and to have the others, both girls, pull back. "You go in first. You're the daddy." So you swallow your fears, hard, stand tall as if you were brave, and plunge in, letting the fear and loneliness, the wish that you were with the girls instead of leading them, give way to pride that they wanted you in the lead, and to exaggeration of the new difference: "Come on in, sissies, it's all right. What's wrong with you?"

To be Joseph is to be a five-year-old walking with your mother in a strange part of town looking for a toy store that had advertised special bargains in the paper and, after she says, "I wonder where it is," you impulsively run over to some men to ask where the toy store is, and she is embarrassed and scolds you, "Don't bother them like that. You're a big boy." And, chagrined, compliant, and proud, you grow up to be a man who is self-reliant, a man who will study the road map by flashlight, drive around blocks and blocks, never pull into a gas station to ask directions, curse the incompetence of the highway engineers, and snap at the passenger who makes a suggestion.

To be Joseph is to pull alongside the woman standing beside the stalled car and offer to help, meaning to give a push or to give a ride or to find a police car or a tow truck. But she wiggles and coos, "Oh I'm so glad you stopped. I just know you can fix this." So you are hooked, helper on her terms, not yours, her savior, and you dive under the hood, resenting her fawning even while fearing to fail, needing and savoring success—meanwhile establishing interim success by establishing her helplessness: "You're taking chances being out here on the road by yourself."

To be Joseph is to rush to hug your son after he falls while climbing up on a wobbly chair, only to have the hug interrupted by a voice—over your shoulder or in your head?—"Warn, teach, don't coddle, be firm, don't pamper, be strict, be a father," so you pull away and scold, "That's what happens when you climb up places you're not supposed to be." That somehow feels right. The voice is stilled, and you've done what you should have done, in spite of the wistful tug for the aborted hug, a father who is not a father.

To be Joseph, frozen and outwardly unmoved, is to be the

50-year-old man, immaculately dressed, dominating a class reunion dinner. He has just been dismissed from a significant, publicly visible position. Not visibly bitter, not defensive, not recriminatory, he is analyzing, in detail and adroitly, the sociological and political and institutional processes that has made this decision inevitable. He is holding a kind of seminar on institutional decision making—it all might have happened to somebody he had heard of once a century ago and a thousand miles away. Only his insistence in imposing this seminar on the dinner party suggests that something personal is at stake, but not a tremor shows in his voice, not a hint of pain or anger. He is a Joseph who "always did what was right." He stayed in control, in control of himself by keeping control of the situation: he dominates the conversation (lest someone offer sympathy?) and he is master of the institutional processes (lest the whole thing seem too personal?).

To be Joseph is to go to the beach at the age of six, no longer afraid of the water and eager, after a week of constant anticipation, to splash and dig and run and skip stones and collect shells and play catch and jump waves, only to have your mother say as she lies on the blanket, "David, you be responsible for your own toys, okay?" You know she really means. it—no whining "Where's my . . ." when it's time to go, and no chance for her to say as you head to the car, "Where's your . . ." So the day changes abruptly; it's unpleasant at first, but then you get into it. You build a castle to safeguard the toys. You discover how to jump the waves so you can see over the top and keep an eye on the toys. You build a police station by the water and then discover how fast you can rush up to the toy fort and rescue the toys from robbers. You get your sister to be a robber and shoot her dead, and yell at her when she starts to take a shovel and pail from the fort, "Those are mine. Mom said so, and they've gotta stay right there."

To be Joseph is to go to the beach 25 years later with David, Jr., now just 4 and ready to enjoy the water and you want to romp with him. Your wife is nervous and says, "Hold on to

Daddy's hand all the time you're in the water," and he does hang on tight and approaches the water timidly. Soon you find yourself not playmate, but lifeguard and swimming coach, and really getting into that. "See, nobody goes beyond those yellow ropes. We'll get you one of those life vests like that little boy has and you can buckle it on real tight. Here I'll show you how you can float on the water, just lie flat on my arms. Sure you can do it, go ahead, I won't let you go. Now try sticking your face in the water and blowing bubbles so you get used to it and know it can't hurt you. See, just like me. Now go ahead. Go ahead." To match your coaching, he becomes trainee, but he likes it a little less well than you like your coaching—and a little less well than either of you would have liked the romping.

To be Joseph is to be outraged over a piece of political skullduggery in your office and to prepare a memo that says so, only to remember that your outrage will offend many, so you mute the outrage with a more "balanced" analysis and a retreat into abstract principles. You eventually discover after several such episodes that you enjoy the feeling of an undivided community and that you savor compliments such as "He certainly keeps people together"; you savor them so well that you begin to inflict "peacemaking" on others and to rebuke "troublemakers," those who get agitated about injustice at work.

To be Joseph is to be a teacher recognizing with awe the growth of a class—as steady and as lovely as watching a flower bloom in time-lapse photography—thrilled at the mounting discoveries, the deepening risks the students take, the questions and theories they venture, the building of trust and bonds, the increasingly muscular skills they display in analyzing problems, and their increasingly loftier imagination in dealing with them; and to be equally awestruck and thrilled and grateful at your own capacity for intervening at just the right point to keep it rolling—to permit yourself a brief glow of satisfaction—"This is what you are called to do and what you do well"—only to have one frustrated student whine,

"We've wasted an hour going around in circles instead of asking the teacher to get us straightened out." Momentarily intimidated and easily regressing to a more familiar pattern, they fall silent and you become talkative, begin to play the new/traditional role assigned by this student. You make a lucid analysis of the problem they have been discussing, the alternative solutions, and the reasons for choosing one solution over the others. To your simultaneous delight and consternation, the rest of the day and even in bed that night, what you remember with relish and a tingle is your vigorous analysis, your decisiveness, and the enthusiasm the class showed afterward. So, despite yourself, you open the next session with a speech. "Let me help you get started by laying out the questions today."

To be Joseph is to yearn all day, and longer, for a relaxed, loving fusing with your wife at the end of the day, just that blend of relaxed nurturing and high excitement that marriage is all about, but then to get so busy playing husband, managing household chores, managing your wife's upset, managing to stay awake, that all romantic yearnings, once again, vanish, her own tentative tenderness now misfitting your mood as you say, "But we've got to decide by tomorrow whether to roll over this certificate of deposit."

To be Joseph is (1) to yearn for the richness and color and depth of life which you know is your natural birthright and a God-given promise; (2) to be assigned, instead, a task, a fixed role; (3) to adopt that task as yours, that role as you, and to devise ways of sustaining it, to the point of (a) enlisting others into the script implied by your role and assigning them their corresponding tasks and fixed roles, and (b) bringing vigor and energy and imagination into protecting those roles, theirs and yours, from the erosions and ravages of that rich birthright of life, once—and still?—your treasured promise.

2. Driven Dreamer: Mystic, Idolmaker, Addict

A man is daydreaming—as he does every day of his lifelong adolescence, his lifelong religious quest, his lifelong thirsting for the waters that will at last leave him unthirsty. I am the man. You are the man. This day, as many days, he daydreams about his homecoming. *She* will be *there*, "there" as crucial as "she". She will be fully present and fully present to him. She will be there for him in ways that complete the unfinished, fill the emptiness, enlarge the smallness, satisfy the craving, quench the thirst. It is not simple stroking he daydreams of, verbal fondling, sexual caress. These are not male-chauvinist daydreams, and it is not doting servant or plaything that he craves. Such a charade would only increase the hunger. The attentiveness and responsiveness will issue from her strength, from her will, from her choice, not from grudging or tamed duty. It is a larger than life-size Woman he daydreams into life (and therefore expects), not smaller. These are religious, mystical daydreams, not chauvinistic. She will be—she *will* be—bubbling and warm and witty and knowing and generous and wise and alert, not *because* he needs her that way, that is the cheapening, gutting catch-22 of one's own hand in the puppet, or even because she thinks that he needs her this way. She will be full, she will be fully there, she will be fully there for him, because she is that way. She will be the larger than life-size person who welcomes him home and makes *him* feel life-size at last. A pretty face, luscious figure, attractive dress, witty greeting, culinary prowess, sexual finesse, artistic taste, cultural sophistication: her fulfilling largesse may be expressed in any of these ways or none. But she will have a fulfilling largesse, and it will be for him, this Woman whom he daydreams into life, daily and lifelong.

Another man, another day, probably another culture, another century: the daydream, the mystical craving, is more explicitly religious. Rather than a Woman who awaits his homecoming with fulfilling largesse, it is God. "Our hearts are restless until they find their rest in Thee," Augustine wrote in his *Confessions*. For this man of another time, God is as real in his daydreams as is the Woman in yours and mine. For this God of the homecoming comes to him out of the same primordial blend as that out of which the Woman comes to you and to me: out of yearnings admitted; out of those moments memoried and memorialized, when God gave taste or promise of presence; out of the stories of others' encounters, stories shaped and believed by the important people in his life and therefore true stories, someday to be his. This is how some men have known that God is waiting to make them real and true and whole and full. That is how most men, these days, know that the Woman is waiting.

But on some days, in some daydreams, for some men, it is not God, not even the Woman who waits to save, but the confirming embrace of a boss or a coach or a therapist, or those at the convention or the class reunion who will wrap you and your accomplishments in admiration and unguarded congeniality. Maybe it is the readers of the book or the hearers of your lecture whose daydreamed embrace sustains, or maybe— in a lifelong pathetic daydream—the readers of your obituary and mourners at your funeral. Maybe it is the next job or the next year on this job "after a few things get straightened out," or maybe it is the next marriage or the next year of this marriage "after a few things get straightened out." Then all will be well, all *will* be well, *all* will be well. Maybe it is the professor who lit a spark and to whom you plan to carry back the flaming torch or the board members who wait to admire your clever presentation. Maybe it is the smooth feel of the wood you will turn in the lathe, or the feel of the car purring to your touch, or the unblemished sweep of the green lawn next July, even while the neighbors' lawns are spotty with weeds and rot. Maybe it's just the next house, or your present house in a couple of years, which will finally surround you with comfort and security and not demand constant repair and endless dollars. Maybe it's the array of tools on the wall, complete and neat, and the workbench in place, solid and yours. Maybe it's just the money in the bank, at last growing and not depleting. Maybe it's the perfect game, the perfect vacation, the perfectly grilled steak, the perfectly behaved child, the mountain climbed, the sailing trophy brought home, the new computer, the new staff organization, the new secretary, or new boss. Something awaits, already palpable in the daydreams. You can already smell it and feel it and touch it and hear it and taste its goodness. It will save you.

Men are, stereotypically, known for our doings, for our achievements, for our performance. But our doings are just a means to the end, the end that is so urgent it has to be hidden by buzz and ado. The doings are a giving to earn a getting. The doings are to make the daydreams come true, daydreams in which the man is at last at rest from all doings and embraced, getting more than giving, daydreams in which you know yourself because you are known.

Women, of course, daydream, too, with yearnings no different and no less urgent and no less concretely lodged in particular people and places and things: no less religiously ultimate, no less idolatrously doomed to disappointment. But it may be that women are more often led in their daydreams, as elsewhere, to wait patiently and passively for the dreams to come true. The Sleeping Beauty, the homebound Cinderella, awaiting prince's kiss or godmother's wand—these may be the more typical daydreams of women. Men's daydreams are more imperative, more imperious. Men endow their daydreaming with the power of doing, confusing dreaming and doing, dreaming and drudgery. For men, led to make things happen, to shape with their bare hands, suppose that the daydreaming is making something happen, that they can shape with their bare wish. Pygmalion and Pinocchio are the stories of men's daydreams making themselves come true.

So the man's daydreams take form. Imperiously and automatically, wish becomes expectation. Because he dreams her there, she will be there, primary process, to be sure, his dreaming sovereign because it is his. What she feels as demand (to be defied) he feels as promise (to be disappointed). Because he thinks, she is. His dreams recruit and conscript her, without her consent, without her knowledge. His own construction becomes covenant and contract. He goes home confident: she is in covenant. Her largesse is his. He has done it.

Daydream is confirmed and enacted by courting. The momentum of the daydream is sustained and doubts quieted by dreaming come alive in a one-sided but confident contract.

You get out of a daydream, like any other idolatry or any other addiction, only what you put into it. Since these are religious daydreams, dreams of getting all, they require a religious-like faithful, dutiful giving of all.

He courts confidently. To the creation of daydreaming, he adds the confirmation of his courting. He brings a gift and walks in the door with breezy wit, as his part of the covenant. The courting escalates his investment, and hence his sureness in the outcome. The courting is his part of the bargain, so there must be a bargain. His daydreams take form. The saving Woman is there. He has made it happen.

But, of course, she is not there.

The idol falters, is propped up, then crumbles. Seduction ends in betrayal and abandonment, as the promise of fulfillment turns into bitter emptiness, gnawingly deeper than before. It is self-seduction. Or is all seduction self-seduction, the victim reading private daydreams into the face and words of the seducer? Is the setup by the victim's own desperate wishes? Seduction: the desperate pursuit of ultimate fulfillment into the despairing pit of nothingness. The savior he constructs is but idol, as constructed saviors always are, and the idol crumbles, as idols must.

There are just two differences between an idol and a god: (1) The idol is created and sustained by the worshipper, and (2) The idol cannot deliver what it promises. God saves; the idol must be saved. The idol is but a puppet in the hand of the worshipper, so its promises are as great as the worshipper can manage—and so are its powers to deliver on those promises—that is, huge promises and meager powers.

What is the connection between these two facts: (1) The man must save the idol; and (2) The idol cannot save the man. The usual lesson is that the first leads to the second: because it is only human construction, it cannot deliver you from your human plight. True enough. But here we emphasize the more poignant lesson: the second leads to the first. Not getting his saving, the man redoubles his efforts to make a better savior.

The idol cannot save because it is only the construct of the man: that is the conventional wisdom of prophets who, quite properly, warn us away from idols. As we are cautioned about the modern idol called a computer, you can't get out more than you put in, and you would destroy yourself if you were to try. But just as true and even more important here is the opposite wisdom: it is just because the idols do not save us that we persist in trying to save them. The idol cannot save, so we construct it all the more feverishly. Every faltering of the idol, every doubt about its saving power, every discovery that the ideal moment is not just around the corner—every time the idol fails or falls—we must rush to save it. We have so much invested already, we count so much on its saving power, that we need to prop and patch and weld and gild, all to enhance and guarantee its power. We accord it reverence so that it will deserve the reverence. We recruit new converts to reassure ourselves. We prop our commitment with flying buttresses of elaborate theory and creed and rationale and fuel it with our most frantic energy. My woman not as warm, responsive, and orgasmic as I need? I will coach, insist, engineer, manufacture the warmth and responsiveness and orgasm. What I fail to see is that the responsibility for success or failure is hers; it's not my doing.

When Aaron constructed the most famous and futile idol of the Bible, the golden bull, he buttressed it with the usual religious devices. He built an altar, and he announced a religious festival; the worship would enhance the powers of the idol. All the while, of course, he had to deny his own hand in its making. When questioned about the bull he had sculpted, he shrugged his shoulders and said simply, "I threw the ornaments into the fire and out came this bull!" (Exodus 32:24).

When the war is failing, then you escalate its global significance by escalating your commitment to it and by minimizing your responsibility for it; it is happening *to* you. Throwing good money after bad makes the bad good. So with the commitment to a woman or a new car or a church or a presidential candidate or a word processor or a long-planned trip to Europe or whatever you count on to make a huge, redeeming difference in your life. When it falters, as it must, for it is but an idol, then it needs reinforcement and gets it: new embellishments, new recruits, new veneration, new courting, new explanations; new ways of treating it like an exalted saving moment or figure in your life, so it will be that.

So lawmakers and regulators invent ever more intricate laws to cover loopholes created by the last laws, physicians prescribe more pills to correct the side effects of the last pills, clergy hold out new visions as solace for the hungers and guilts induced by the last visions promised and withheld, militarists demand new missiles to protect from the instability created by the last round of missiles. A stiff drink is the only cure for the morning after, once you are hooked on the stuff.

The persistence and sovereignty of the daydreams, and then the insistent courting—the unacknowledged hand in the puppet: this is what separates men's daydreaming from women's. Women, too, daydream and paint their daydreams on the blank faces of their partners. But they seem better able to separate reality from hope. They know that they are "only" hoping, though desperately. Women seem less ready to reach a hand inside the puppet as though they could make it become what they want. Or if they do, they know they are doing that. They have a clearer sense of the otherness of their partner, and of the gulf between. They have been well trained in their own limits. Men are afflicted still with a small-boy sense of impatient omnipotence: what they want is, or can be made to be. There is always something to be *done* to make things right. And that something should be done *now*.

When the daydreams confront reality, the daydreams stay in control, the daydreams and the expectations and the courting that expresses the expectations. Champagne signals "be bubbling," candy, "be sweet," theater tickets, "be alert," a joke, "be witty," and—a condition that idols share with gods—it is all or none. No human partialness is tolerated. The first signs of reality—she is not the ideal total woman he daydreamed—are met with continued courting, escalating the expectations. Then, as some hints of panic begin to erode the daydreams, remedies ("Why don't you take a shower and freshen up while I have a cocktail?" or "Why don't you have a cocktail and relax while I have a shower?"), then diagnostic questions ("What is wrong with you?"). (It is the male way for remedies to precede diagnostic questions, indicating that the questions are more attacks than inquiries). The callously alleged "wrong" measures the intensity of the pain now felt. It also measures the intensity of the yearning that started it all, the yearning that generated the reckless daydreaming that generated the unblinking expectations that generated an empty panic. By the time he begins to coach and diagnose and scold and call on the other strategies in his male bag of tricks to make things become what he wants, by the time we see him playing up, we may forget that he started down, looking up, yearning.

The idol cannot save. The idol must be saved. We cannot speak of the building of the idol without speaking at once of its failure. We cannot speak of daydreams without speaking of rude awakenings. We cannot speak of hopes—no, much stronger than "hope": expectation, certainty, conviction, contract, covenant—without speaking of disappointment—no, much stronger than "disappointment": shattering, wounding, catastrophe, grief. But neither is it possible to speak of the shattering of the daydreams without speaking of their rebuilding. For a man cannot live without his daydreams. He lives by them. He must have them. And he is accustomed to conceiving the musts as blueprints for him to build by. What must be he must make to be. If the sales curve or the production speed is down, it is up to the man to get it up. If the computer is down, it is up to the man to get it up. If the idol has fallen off its pedestal—even of its own weight—it is up to the man to get it up. It is up to the man to get it up. Whatever it is that the man counts on getting *him* up, it is up to the man to get *it* up.

So goes, perpetually, the constructing and reconstructing of the idols, in dreams and in deed, courting them, according them a power and caring and covenant they cannot and do not possess except in his according it to them, counting them accountable. We can talk about it in sequence: first the construction of the idol, then the hints of its mortality or even its shattering, then its reconstruction and saving. But the rhythms are more blended than that, more counterpoint and fugue. Even in his most naive, romantic, and hopeful daydreaming, the man fears and therefore scrambles to buttress, patching, certifying, guaranteeing as best he can, wooing his own mannequin. The anticipatory grief and the grief work become one.

The man's daydreaming is the urgent religious searching of the mystic wanting to be one—wholly one—with the fount of life. It is honorable, honest, and healthy yearning, and our daydreamer is neither the first nor the last to suppose that the fount comes in the form of a woman, a nurturing, responsive woman. There is nothing peculiarly or distortedly male or macho in the search or in the riskily idolatrous targeting of the search on another mortal. And there is nothing peculiar to men in the crushing disappointment of discovering the yearning unrequited. The male imprint is in the impatience, in the do-it-yourself, barehanded, unilateral, unspoken shaping of the other to fit the daydreams, in the transformation of daydreams into insistent expectations, in the change from "I hope," to "you will," in the supposition that courting guarantees covenant, in the equation of ideas in one's own head with a covenant between two people, in the relentless addiction. Anyone can make idols, and most of us do. It is usually men who make them as puppets. In the absence of guarantee and in the need of guarantee, manipulation serves.

But frozen founts do not flow freely.

LEARNING TO DAYDREAM

A boy—a four-year old boy—daydreams a homecoming, shaping and scripting, as best he can in his head, the sure nurturing presence he so craves and finds so unsure. It is a late spring afternoon. He is playing lazily on his front lawn. He moves his yellow plastic tricycle around in a slow, fixed circle, while he leans far backward, mouth wide open and eyes staring straight up at the sky. Then he dismounts to study the patterns of ants crawling in and out of the sidewalk cracks. Then over to lie limply across a large beach ball, it the turtle and he the shell wrapping it up. But laid back and limp as he may look, he is finely tuned. He will hear and see his father's car when it first turns the corner, though he will not betray his notice with the slightest twinge. He will stay limp turtle shell protecting the beach ball. For he is most finely tuned of all to his mother who waits on the porch, and it is her welcome of his father, not his, that is important. Whether he is looking up at the sky or down at the ants, he is scanning and recording her every move, straining with inner body English to shape her moves to match his needs.

He may be a beginner, a clumsy and bored novice, in reading books, but he has long ago mastered reading his mother. He has learned to read her face and her gestures with highly nuanced precision. As an Indian boy might learn to read tracks silently and swiftly or to tell the slight difference between good berries and poisonous as though his survival depended upon it—both his physical survival and his survival as an acceptable member of his clan—so this boy learns to read his mother's signs, as though his survival depends on it.

This moment at the end of the afternoon becomes an all-or-none, almost life-or-death, moment of decision. Her eyes down on her sewing, or out on him mean one verdict: thumbs up. Life will continue, the life he has had with her during the day. But if her head is cocked down the street or back toward the kitchen door, it is thumbs down. She is focused on his father, not on him, and she is listening for the bell that means the early supper—his early supper—is ready. He will eat alone, and he will go to bed early, and alone, with a perfunctory kiss and no cuddling. If she goes into the kitchen, he can tell clearly whether the sounds are his special dishes and mean a lonely supper for him or whether the sounds mean a family meal. He has learned to detect the different tunes in her voice, as he overhears her on the phone in the late afternoon. It matters not to whom she is talking or what she is saying. It matters whether her voice has that slight harshness and shrillness that speaks distance and that seems to shut him out, or at least to hide her from him, or whether it has that warmth and lilt that promises embrace.

The homecoming verdict is decisive. One verdict leaves him feeling calm and warm and full—"fuzzy" his mother sometimes calls it—limp like taking a nap on her lap on a warm summer afternoon. The other verdict leaves him feeling tight and tense and empty, limp like after having run very hard to catch his father's car one day and missing it, like gasping for breath instead of feeling gently inflated. Will he be with his mother? Will she be with him? Will she look right at him and hear him out and speak with him in that sweet, full, patient way with the voice that seems to be hugging him and patting him? Will she make him feel like running and chattering and teasing and being the "delightful cherub" as he heard her once describe him on the phone, "full of the dickens," as she says to him? Or will he feel lost and lonely and wobbly on his feet and oh-so-stiff and brave, "the good soldier" (as he hates to hear her call him)? The verdict has this life-and-death, all-or-none effect on him. Life either continues or he droops, like a balloon pricked. It all seems to depend on her. Maybe it shouldn't; after all, he is four years old now. But it always has, and that seems to be the way it is. There isn't much he can do about the verdict, except watch astutely for it.

He knows it's important to accept the verdict, whatever it is, to be the good soldier, because protesting never works, only makes matters worse. It makes the next day's verdict colder. He knows that when he does protest and gets her to be with him, she isn't really with him. The emptiness persists. And when she applauds his unfeeling bravery, that feels, sort of, "with" him. So he won't appeal the verdict.

But maybe he can try to sway it.

He has spent the afternoon in the shadow of the coming verdict and has shaped his behavior, hoping he has been shaping hers. He knows that clean clothes at the end of the afternoon count, and not having begged for a Good Humor when the truck came by, and keeping the ball and the tricycle away from the curb but carefully in sight. And he has day-dreamed. He has heard, in his head, her warm voice, saying, "You look so nice. I'm going to have supper with my two favorite men." And he has seen, in his head, her warmest smile. And he has felt her rubbing his back, while he has lain on the beach ball. All those responses that matched and completed his own behavior. He has done everything he can. He has completed his part of the bargain and some of hers. He is learning to be a man.

As he grows he will find other ways of shaping and seeming to guarantee her response, whoever "her" happens to be at the time, even if the shaping has to go on entirely in his head.

CAREER MAN AS MYSTIC

A man becomes enamored of the sunshine and courts it. He loves to lie, secluded, draped open, exposed to the sun, bathed by it. He comes to adjust his schedule, his daily schedule, his annual schedule, to maximize his time with the sun, to be flexibly available for a sudden sunny hour or a sunny day. He learns to read the fine print of the weather reports and to scan the clouds and wind patterns—as surely as the four-year old scans his mother's face—to chart the coming of the sun, to assure the coming of sun. So when he adjusts the reclining chair and plants himself in his favorite and proper alcove, having invested heavily in the sun by adjusting his schedule and meteorological plotting, he naturally assumes a reciprocal commitment on the part of the sun. He naturally assumes that the total enveloping warmth for which he has turned to the sun in the first place, and for which he has made heavy commitments, and which he has shaped to the best of his not-slender ability, will be there. He lies back relaxed, expecting the best—not merely wanting, not merely hoping, but expecting—feeling it assured as his earned desert. So when the clouds come, when the sun deserts, when the idol fails, there is humiliation and resentment and panic. "How dare those clouds!" And he lies there strenuously commanding the clouds to follow the course of his choosing and orders the patch of blue sky off in the northeast to come to him.

Another man is enamored of stereo music and courts it. He selects only records with advanced digital processing and with exactly suitable microphone placement. He chooses his equipment with scrupulous attention to the subtleties of concert hall fidelity. He arranges his furniture and his way of life and his schedule to maximize and to assure the warm bath of splendidly flowing sounds. Wearing his puffy earphones, he leans back in the recliner—"this has to be it"—expectation and investment have fed each other to a spiraled peak. But courting cannot guarantee. There is a flaw in the record. So courting is escalated, to guarantee what cannot be guaranteed and yet must be guaranteed. Intense, paranoid, and fervid, as in any other idol-making, idol-worshipping ritual, he writes an angry letter to the record company, an angry notice that he tapes to the stereo prescribing the sacred rituals of record handling and cleaning, an angry warning that declares the stereo off limits to any nonordained. Sinking back into the recliner, exhausted from the impassioned orgy of furious importuning, he is reassured that *now* all is at last well, for he has poured out the spurts of energy that will make it so.

Yet another man is enamored of the rhythms and rituals of TV football and courts the experience of being absorbed, enveloped by it. He masters the esoterica of the plays and players, learns the liturgies of the announcers and how to talk back to them. He fine-tunes the television, chills the beer, and commands the family to keep their places. But the substitute announcer introduces a strange patter, or one cameraman loses the ball, or the instant replays—those mystical moments of intimacy that transcend time—are slow in coming or fuzzy in detail, and that heady experience of oneness, heavily courted and fully expected, does not materialize. So the shaper shapes anew and as fiercely as he can, commanding, as though magically, others into the postures of fulfillment for which he has turned to his electronic ark of the covenant.

For other men, or the same men at another time, the mystical moment is a day of fishing, an early morning on the jogging track, a lunch hour of sex, an afternoon in the bleachers, an evening at the bar, a period of marriage.

But for most men, mystical craving is lodged in career, work, profession. The high is in an intense morning in the office, or in the courtroom, or in the operating room, or in the pulpit.

These experiences are ultimate in the urgency with which men insist on them, the addiction, the intoxication, the mustness to which all else must finally defer, and toward which, finally, all energies must be deployed.

Mystics want it all; they want ultimacy, the promise of a totality of experience that somehow registers the fullness, the wholeness of life, the feeling that "this is the way it is," "this is it." These are moments of mysticism. These are moments of intoxication. These are moments in which one finds oneself losing oneself. Even while letting go normal self-consciousness and vigilance, one feels absorbed and filled and lifted up and enveloped and bathed and nurtured, rooted again, home.

Mystics also want it immediately: not mediated, nothing in between, no masks, no fears, no role playing, no political maneuvering, just me and it, all there, totally, face-to-face. Another of the mystic's words is "union": oneness, together, blended, belonging, wedded. All of me, not lttle pieces of me, nothing held back, all of me engaged and supported and nurtured and present because somehow all of me is acknowledged and made part of, absorbed, by something that is larger than me, yet all for me, nothing held back. No defensiveness, no need to posture, to analyze, to maneuver, to manage. Just let go and let be. Mind and senses all a delicious blend.

These are the mystical cravings of all of us. These are the mystical cravings that propel men into daydreaming into life a woman at home, and more often and more steadily into daydreaming into life an absorption with work, a buoying engagement with the energy that makes the world move. Men are looking—and why not?—to the primitive powerful energies and alliances that make the daytime world spin for this mystical sense of immediacy, of wholeness and oneness, wholeness and oneness of self, and wholeness and oneness with others and with God. Men want—expect—this self-confirming, self-abandoning, absorbing experience as they handle the throbbing holy stuff of industry, commerce, science, travel, harvest, mining. The workplace is the sun, the stereo music, the TV football game, the nurturing mother, the totally present lover. Why not? These mystical longings are honest and honorable, inevitable and insistent, and the idols of the workplace are no more or less life-giving than any other idols, no more or less life-draining than any other idols.

These are the mystical cravings for wholeness—for "being wholed"—which everyone invests in one target or another, and which men, especially, invest in busy doings, especially their own doings designed to sustain others' doings. These are the cravings that are part of what it means to be a full, healthy, and religious human being. These are the cravings that inevitably become lodged in particular targets, idols if you will, which seem, and for a time do, fulfill. We are not to be faulted for our idol making. It, too, is part of what it means to be a healthy and religious person. It is a legitimate and a mandated part of the human religious quest (even though some want to reserve the words *mystic* or *religion* for removal from the world that God has created and is redeeming and has placed us in) to find those signs and sacraments within history and within experience that give reasonable surety of conveying the affirming, confirming graciousness of God for which we ultimately crave. We are consigned, most of us, not to see God face-to-face in this world, and so we are consigned, most of us, to find something in this world that mediates the immediate. It is impossible. It is inevitable. Most of us do so find, for a time, then search and construct and find again, and again, as sacraments become idols, and idols failing become puppets to be forced back into life.

"What do you want to be when you grow up?" they asked you as a boy. "What do you want to be when you grow up?" you ask yourself the searching question all your life, as growing up always seems to be just ahead.

"Fireman, astronaut, baseball player, truck driver . . ." They asked about "be," but the standard answers they waited to hear, were of *doings*, and later on, as television teaches other

sorts of heroics as well, "doctor, lawyer, private detective . . ."
Then, still later, maybe "accountant, architect, banker, engineer, minister, foreman, professor . . ."

But though the language is of heroic doings, the question
was about "be," and the most urgent, the most poignant, even
the most desperate cravings of the young man are not these
dreams of doings. They are the cravings to belong, to be a part
of, to find oneself by finding oneself part of a team or a club
or even a crowd. Like most things in a man's life, these cravings come to rest on his career, on his job. There is a prior
and private wistfulness which is part of the small boy's longing—the small boy of any age—as he turns to career for the
salving of his longing. He does want to be someone, and the
brave doings, like the brave answers, are important finally as
promising means to that end. As surely as he found himself
in his mother's embrace before he looked for himself as heir to
his father's heroic daydreams, he wants to perform in order to
be recognized, acclaimed, welcomed, wanted. He craves to be
part of something, part of a team, to share an arm across the
shoulder, a wink across the room. He looks to be greeted by
openings made for him, the cocktail party group opening its
circle as he approaches, a job opening, eyes opened wide, a
pair of arms opened for him.

A young woman waits for fulfillment, stereotypically, by
becoming engaged, by being in a relationship. But so, too,
does a young man wait and crave to be engaged, to be in a
relationship. Engaged in a career, that is, in a relationship
with work. Engaged: like a gear meshing smoothly, a productive and essential and well-cared-for part of the larger machine. It is in your work that you most often look to be recognized, embraced, wanted, identified, made to feel useful and
productive, made to feel someone. The things a woman wants
from you, at least in the early years, you want from your job
(even though in midlife you may both change, you looking at
last in the marriage for what she turns to a career for).

You carefully select your career. You court it, you shape it as best you can, and you shape yourself to fit it, even as you suppose or daydream you are shaping it to fit you. You treasure those moments of recognition, those signs of welcome and embrace, and you redouble your efforts to increase them, in more finely tuned and more closely meshed engagement. You give it your all because it promises to give you back your all. And when it reneges on those promises, you redouble your courting, all those gifts of yourself that should win the blessing: the extra hours, the extra energy, the extra imagination, the more finely honed shaping of yourself to fit the gears you want to mesh with you. When the gears grind, even when they grind you, at first you confess to the fault—just as women have learned to take the blame when gears grind in relationships and marriage—and you refine your courting. What you once gave to a promised abundance of nurturing you now give to its withholding. Escalating the stakes because you are hooked on the game. Lyndon Johnson pouring more and more into the Vietnam War for the fulfillment it promised him, and denied. Richard Nixon pouring more and more into the Watergate coverup for the security it promised him, and denied.

Until finally the idol crumbles and disappoints, beyond even the powers of your hopes to sustain it as a sustainer for you. The machine lumbers on, mindless and uncaring. The machine chews up the people, it doesn't nurture them, *and it never promised otherwise*. The promise was only in your own wanting and waiting.

But who dares say "only." There is nothing more urgent, more compelling, more honest, more honorable than that craving to be engaged, to become someone by becoming an essential part of something. This craving, this vision, is the essential religious throb of the human spirit, that which sustains and beckons life from womb to beyond the grave. Our hearts are restless until . . . a yearning that is misplaced, of course, when affixed to a career, or even to a woman, but a yearning that is perhaps doomed to always be so misplaced and disappointed, and a yearning that is more sustaining when fully ventured and acknowledged (even when misplaced and disappointed) than when reined in and denied in vain virginal hopes of avoiding trafficking with idols.

FOUR FABLES OF SEASONED FAITH

One bright October afternoon a small boy scuffed through the leaves, feeling good. The sky was bright blue, the sun beamed warm on his face, he was in no trouble with his teachers or his parents or his sisters. The leaves made him feel like the meat of a sandwich, a Big Mac, between the puffy golden top, branches of leaves arching all around him, cocooning him, and the leaves into which his feet dripped like hamburger juice—and that felt cozy and good. He jumped into a pile of leaves and said "eat me" and giggled—and that felt good. He reached for a pretty leaf with red spots, just as a gust of wind blew it away, and he felt a moment of panic and lunged and missed. Then he noticed it was getting dark, the day was almost over; he remembered somebody at home talking about a rainstorm coming, and he didn't want this crisp, bright, warm, golden, meaty day to end. He wouldn't feel this good if it did. So he thought to himself: I will find the brightest and biggest leaf there is in the whole world and I will take it home with me so that it will not get wet and won't blow away and the day will never end and I will feel good forever and ever and ever. And that is what he did. He found the biggest and most golden leaf and held it in front of his face and said "You are this beautiful day and you are mine and I will feel good forever and ever and ever." The day was so beautiful and he so much wanted it for himself forever and for sure that he took the leaf in both his hands tight and put it in his pocket and he held his hand tight against his pocket all the way home feeling the leaf and feeling sure and feeling good.

At home his sister frowned at him and said, "It's about time you got home. It's the end of the day." But he said, "It's not the end of the day. I have this whole day in my pocket, and it's mine. Do you want to see it?" And he reached in his pocket and held out his arm triumphantly stiff right in front of her face and said, "See!" And she said, "All you have is a dumb crumpled leaf," and walked away. And his mother said, "You got your pocket all dirty with that thing. Come wash your hands for supper." A noisy bus churned past the house. When he looked out to watch it, he saw blue smoke pouring out behind the bus, and, through the smoke, the sun going down behind the garage across the street.

On a cold January morning the same boy looked out the window as best he could, for the window was veiled with a cold frost. He was lonely. Now he was in trouble with his mother and his sisters, and his best friend was sick. He scraped a hole in the frost and looked out at the wide lawn; not even a dog had yet made tracks in the fresh snow. The bleak crust stayed unbroken, but in his mind he saw his friend run across the lawn, stand under his window, and call up to him. And he rushed outside and built a snowman just where he had seen his friend standing. He pounded the snow hard so it would stay forever. And he took a stick and jammed it into the icy shoulder and aimed the arm, in friendly greeting, at his window. Then he ran back inside and peered out through the hole in the frost and waved at his friend, and the friend waved back. This was his, all his, and nothing could ever take it away, ever. That afternoon the weather changed to a warm rain, and he watched his snowman dissolve into a sad slush.

On a windy April day, the boy saw butterflies flying and birds flying and blossom petals fluttering and said, "I want to fly." So his father said, "You will fly. You will fly a kite." So they went to a store and carefully picked out just the right kite and they came home and worked very carefully and followed all the directions exactly. They tied just the right length of rags on the tail in just the right colors, and then they tied string to the kite. When the kite was ready and the boy was ready to fly, the father gave him one end of the string. Then the father yelled at him, "Now run, now pull, now let up, no, not that way, here, let me!" And the father grabbed the string just as the kite dived into a tree.

One lazy July afternoon, the boy lay in a hammock by a lake and felt very good. His father felt good because he had just caught a big fish, and his mother felt good because she had been sleeping in the sun all afternoon, and one sister felt good because she had a new bathing suit and liked the way she looked in it, and another sister felt good because a boy had just called, and the boy in the hammock felt good because they all felt good. It didn't happen often. The boy remembered his new birthday camera and he called everyone and he said, "Let me take a picture so we can keep this good feeling," and he made everyone come and stand by the lake, and he did everything to make the picture good because the feeling was so good. So he had them move away from the tree, then kneel on the grass, then turn their faces more toward the sun, then he stepped back, then he turned the camera sideways, then he told them to all move closer, then he got mad because they wouldn't all smile together, the way he needed so the good feeling would be in the picture. But finally the picture was taken and he had captured the good feeling. He took more pictures of the lake that day, then pestered his father to take the film to the drugstore that very evening.

In the following days the family never had that good feeling all at once again, but the boy didn't care, because he had the good feeling in a picture and that was enough to make him feel good, and them, too. Then came the day when his father put the package in his hands. He went back to his hammock and pulled out the picture and had it right there and he was bursting with good feeling. He and his picture would make everyone feel good again. He waited until just the right time, when the family was grumpy and sitting down to supper, ready for the miracle of the picture. No priest ever had a flourish more spellbinding than his when he pulled the picture from underneath his napkin and held it aloft, ready for its power to transform them all. His sister reached for the bread and said, "Oh that's the day you made us squat so long in the sun when I wanted to go swimming with Bobby."

It has to be a child's life we fashion into such fables, a child's expectancy, a child's open pain at the empty places in life, a child's trust that they can be bridged and filled, a child's energy to make a commitment—too much of a commitment, we now know to our sadness—to the fashioning of bridges for the gaps and plugs for the empty places: a child's persistent trust in the promises of life, a child's trust that there are deliverers on those promises, and a child's readiness to give himself or herself to those deliverers in exchange for the saving they promise. The rest of us know too much about crushed leaves and crashed kites, about melted snowmen and other dissolved companionships, about how our frantic efforts to preserve the promises prove filmy in deed, about how our efforts destroy the promises they would save. So we wince at the boy's vulnerable reliance on the products of his own expectancy because we have shared that vulnerability and the painful grief. Now our energies are spent in making sure that we don't do that again, in barricading ourselves against such vulnerability, in mounting vigilance lest we trust again such a deliverer who cannot deliver. For, as wholeheartedly as the boy in the fable, we have covenanted with gods, or so they surely seemed at the time, and with the messengers of the gods, for they seemed sure to deliver; and we have been stranded. Every time we have put a sure messenger or message in our pocket or on a string, pounded or posed one into sure place, we have found ourselves holding debris and tatters and shreds and cinders. So we wince at the boy and at our own temptations to imitate him and we put all that energy at the service of ensuring that we do not.

But we cannot turn our back on the boy in the fable, for we are still him. We have shared his expectancy and vulnerability—and still do—even if we have also found that hope over and over dissolving into grief and that grief armored in cynicism. We are still him, and we still have a childlike hope. If we were not, if we did not, we would not need the armor. If we could shed the expectancy, with all of the yearnings and trust that have fashioned it, we would not need the armor, for there would not be the expectancy to lead us into vulnerability, the vulnerability that opens us to grief. One can peek through the armor to find the hope it points to: if there is armor and barricade and stockade—resolute mistrust and refusal to yearn—then there is fear of grief, risk of vulnerability. And if we are feeling vulnerable, fearing loss, it means we still have hopes we need to protect from disappointment. It is one of the paradoxes of the spirit that the more mistrust we wear as a facade, the more trust (latent, to be sure) we are testifying to. Our scoffing at the boy of the fable proves we are him, as much as do the tugs and tears.

Probably it is a boy who best fits this fable, not a girl. Not because of the intense hopes and hungers and yearnings, for those are shared by all of us. Not because of the intense shattering and disappointment and grief, for that is shared by all of us. But it is a boy, or the manhood that is stuffed into a boy, that is more likely to make idols. If I am wrong, if women recognize this experience as their own, they can tell me. For now, I know that part of learning to be male is learning to build idols.

I know that part of the experience of being male is lodging much yearning and much promise in concrete objects, this leaf, this photograph, this kite, this snowman, this job, this woman, this night with this woman, this book, this book review. Women are perhaps more likely to expect fulfillment in some larger form, some less concrete form, some more collective form, some form that lasts over the long haul, some slow growing form that can be patiently awaited. It is the man who focuses sexuality on genitals and on orgasms. It is the man who pushes urgently from problem to solution. It is the man who wants to comb through questions, piece by piece, with fine logic; who needs to fine-tune his car, his television, his children, all his machinery; who needs to reduce all problems, from getting telephone messages to deploying nuclear weapons, to a push of the right button. It is more likely a man who picks a single target, a small target, a savior, a sacrament small enough to be held in the hand (and hence easily controlled, though, also easily crushed) to count on something countable, to fashion something fashionable.

It is more likely a boy who will actively fashion, control, capture, manufacture his savior, his sacrament. Just as a woman is more likely to know that life and saving are larger than any single object, so she knows that life and saving are larger than herself. She can wait. She can receive. A male learns to limit his trust to what he can construct.

So it is more likely a boy who relies so ferociously for saving and guarantee on his own doing and his own products, on capturing something capturable, on managing something manageable, on fashioning and clutching in his own bare hands something to banish the bareness of his soul. A boy is more likely to deflect longing for embrace and nurture to mechanisms and techniques, to replace the urge for soaring mystical union with sacramental surrogates, to shift so quickly from lofty ends to meaner means.

It is the professions created by men that undertake to abridge the mysteries, to replace uncertainty with structure, foreboding with precision. So men have begotten medicine and its cults out of illness and death, law and its cults out of disorder and injustice, religion and its cults, science and its cults, out of sin and alienation and helplessness, the academy and its cults out of ignorance. Arcane and esoteric vocabulary, formal hierarchical titles, priestly robes, distinctive and elaborate temples—sometimes called hospitals, sometimes called courthouses, sometimes called houses of worship, sometimes called universities, in which to practice and amaze—these are the devices by which the professionals have long reassured themselves and persuaded others that they were in control and all was well. And if these same devices turn out to confuse and frighten, to enhance the mystery rather than allay it, well, that only creates more need for the profession and the professional. The needs generate the idolatry of the profession and cult, but the idol's need to be protected and enhanced generates more need.

TIGHTFISTING THE TREASURE

"There once was a man of high rank who was going to a country far away to be made king, after which he planned to come back home. Before he left, he called his ten servants and gave them each a gold coin and told them, 'See what you can earn with this while I am gone.' . . . The man was made king and came back. At once he ordered his servants to appear before him, in order to find out how much they had earned. The first one came and said, 'Sir, I have earned ten gold coins with the one you gave me.' 'Well done,' he said, 'you are a good servant! Since you were faithful in small matters, I will put you in charge of ten cities.' The second servant came and said, 'Sir, I have earned five gold coins with the one you gave me.' To this one he said, 'You will be in charge of five cities.' Another servant came and said, 'Sir, here is your gold coin; I kept it hidden in a handkerchief. I was afraid of you, because you are a hard man'" (Luke 19:12, 13, 15–21).

It's like a six-year-old boy trudging warily to the drugstore to choose his own *Star Wars* comic book, his quarter clutched tightly in his fist. The stakes are high—it's his first trip to the store on his own, with his own quarter, in determined pursuit of the long coveted comic book. But the perils are even higher: there are dogs to give chase and maybe jar the quarter loose; there are bigger boys who are ready to assert that he is too small to have his own quarter; in the drugstore there are candy bars luring the quarter out of his hand. Most dangerous, perhaps, are the boys with enough quarters to spare, so they don't have to be tightfisted—enough talents to risk investing—they are matching quarters on the street corner and want him to join them. So the stakes are high and the risks are high and he is only a small boy and it is his only quarter, so he clutches it very tightly—maybe even so tightly that his sweaty hands make it slippery, so the clutching only increases the peril, but he clutches nevertheless.

No, it's even more tense than that: it's like the six-year old boy *sent* to the store. It is *their* mission and their money; *they* expect him to make good on the mission. The judgment waiting if he fails—scoffing, rebuke, anger, belittlement, whatever—makes him feel all the smaller, all the more inadequate to the mission. So the stakes are higher and the perils are higher and he clutches the quarter all the more tightly and fixedly—increasing its slipperiness and increasing his chances of tripping over an obstacle he doesn't see while he fixes on the quarter.

Our idols are the inevitable products of our hope—or others' hope—and our hope is the product of the tantalizing circumstances in which we find ourselves: we are given glimpses of a saving (and sometimes of the gods who will deliver it), yet the saving is ever withheld or held precariously. We are exiles from Eden, wanderers on the verge of reaching the promised land, fugitives from our homeland, aliens seeking citizenship, pilgrims to a shrine ever just beyond the horizon, frontiersmen seeking homestead out beyond the reach of the corrupting civilization, perpetually adolescent lovers sure of the next romance, the ill crying out "one more doctor," the condemned awaiting the promised reprieve, the standby passenger with eyes riveted on the dwindling red stickers on the seating chart, the standin, well rehearsed and eager, watching every show from the wings, perpetual honeymooners, perpetual rising executives, perpetual students, perpetual movement people, perpetual rainbow trackers, intent on that saving that is just around the corner, just over the hill, just as soon as . . ., perpetually reaching out of our mire for the fruit just overhead, perpetually expectant.

Our hope is based on a glimpse and on a withholding.

Our glimpses of saving come from dreams, from deliberate utopian fantasizing, from stories told to us, from reconstruction of what other people's lives must be like, from assembling fragments of saving moments, from embellished memories— all hints and foretastes of a state of sublime well-being, with energies mobilized and flowing and responded to and effective and recognized, with knowledge whole and effective, with affects full and met, with will channeled and right, a state of oneness within and a state of oneness with others, nurturing and being nurtured, serving and being served. There is a life for which we are created—a sustaining ecological niche, our very own—that is hinted at, but only hinted at tantalizingly, by the life we now live. It is hinted at by the small boy's exhilarating flying leap into a pile of crisp leaves, by his placid bond with his own snowman on a bleak and lonely day, by his fantasy of flying, by his contentment in a hammock in the bosom of a momentarily contented family.

But the glimpse is only a glimpse and is threatened or withheld or fragmented as soon as it is given. This may be part of the Fall, but it is not our fault. Our expectant yearning and craving is our persistent demand of a scheme that says a simultaneous *yes* and *no* about what is most important to us, the promise that is only a promise. That yearning, which is both the vision and the grief, both the glimpse and the withholding, is all one move of aspiration: we reach, unable to grasp, just as what we grasp is not what we reach for. Saving must come from a distance. The promised land and the promised life are beyond, must be beyond. It is the wilderness we are in that defines the promised land, just as the promises beyond define the wilderness as wilderness. What is not fragmented and partial and withheld and threatened and unavailable is not worth yearning for, cannot become part of an important expectancy, is not fit candidate as a savior. If it is true that a god must visit us to save us, it is no less true that a god must be elusive to be saving. A savior for whose visit we yearn must visit from afar.

So it is the very intensity of our hope that fates us to make idols and to be vulnerable to their crumbling. Oh, we do not set out to make idols. We set out to reach for the saving that we know is there and that we know we need and that we find so elusive. But because our faith is in a savior beyond our reach and because the urgency is too great to be long teased, we grasp in our reaching for what we can. We grasp, like the boy clutching the leaf or the kite string or the photograph or pounding the snowman into fixed place, for those surrogates and sacraments, those symbols and signs, those messengers and mediators, which promise to enact the saving on behalf of the savior ever near, never here.

Our reaching is shrewd, sharply directed by our need and our intuition, acutely honed into a vigilant wariness by the elusiveness of the saving; we reach with skill and knowing. Our reaching is helped, too, by the wisdom of our culture, which has placed effective mediators and sacraments within our reach, and—we sometimes dare to believe—by the graciousness of the saviors who have moved themselves and their surrogates closer to us. The mediators we trust and the surrogates we hold—unlike the small boy's first futile lonely experiments—do deliver their pledges of saving. They *are* sacraments and mediators, even though they are *only* sacraments and mediators, and therefore destined to become idols and to crumble. They are as close to the absolute as we can get—and so is our need and hope—so we make them absolute. We dare not let ourselves see through them to see them only as mediators and therefore look beyond them for the immediate, to see them only as sacraments of the savior and therefore look beyond them for the savior. For that is to put us back into the same perplexed, unfulfilled hope that made us reach out and grasp. Our commitment is inevitably overcommitment, for to do less is to withhold ourselves from the covenant and to achieve only the bereftness of undercommitment—a grayness of the spirit (which we do eventually and defensively achieve, a costly immunization). If the small boy let himself be aware of the limited promise and power of leaf and snowman, kite and photograph, they would have no power for him.

But the surrogates and mediators are only surrogates and mediators, and thus limited in their efficacy and range and relevance. They cannot respond to the overcommitment we invest in them. They cannot keep up their part of the covenant we unilaterally impose upon them. They are not the saviors we must take them to be. So they must fail. We are doomed to rely for a saving on the unreliable savior we have forced the mediator to become.

It is our expectancy of a saving, that authentic, gracious, inevitable hope informed by yearning, which impels us to rely on surrogates more than we should dare, to transform sacraments into idols. It is the weight that we put onto the idols that makes them crumble. It is our own hope that sets us up for our own grief.

People who talk to us about our idols usually scold us for making them. They are quick to scold us for relying on what is ultimately unreliable, for making absolute what is not absolute, for treating as ultimately true what is not ultimately true, and therefore false. But that judgment is so easy to make as to be glib. That our idols are futile and crumbling, that we are not finally saved by them, that we are trapped in bondage to them—all this is well known by any of us much beyond the age of trusting in leaves and snowmen and kites. The most shrill scolding doesn't tell us as much as the grief we already know. Instead, let us rescue our hopes from the scolding and the grief, and let us celebrate idol making, for our idols testify to our persistent hope, our long-range trust and our capacities for urgent commitments.

Since the idols are the products of our hope, the only way to avoid making idols is to dull the hope. That, alas, is precisely what we learn to do to protect ourselves (sometimes to please the idol scolders, to make one more idol—this one out of abstaining-from-idols). We learn to shuffle through leaves on a golden day without wonder, or to stare at a bleak landscape or at birds in flight without longing. We learn to mute the joy we feel at special moments of rapture. We learn to disengage from life, at the gain of lessening grief, and at the cost of lessening life. To satisfy the idol scolders and to spare ourselves the idol suffering, we smog our vision, flatten our path, drug our sensibilities, and siphon off our energies in dull routines such as jogging and cocktail parties and cable TV.

To the extent that we find ourselves still afflicted with idols and with grief over their crumbling, to that extent we can treasure the animated, risking spirit that has impelled and permitted the idols.

AT THE FOOT OF SINAI

So it is the most honest and most human of yearnings and the most sublime of trusts in the promise of fulfillment that leads us to make idols—yearning and trust in the face of the fragility and failure of the promisers. We want and expect, we promise and perform, and then don't get, so we want all the more and expect all the more and promise all the more and perform all the more, in an escalation of idol making and idol saving and idol serving. We clench our fists and stuff our pockets with golden leaves, crushed.

That is exactly the story of the most famous idol maker of all time. It was Aaron who fashioned a golden bull to be god for the Hebrew people, an act of insolent idolatry that so angered Moses that he smashed to the ground his brand-new tablets of the Ten Commandments.

The Hebrew people were wandering in the hot and dry

wilderness, a long way from Egypt where they had been comfortable, though oppressed, and still a longer way from the Promised Land. Huddled at the foot of Sinai, while their God and their leader Moses conferred so long at the top, they felt abandoned and wanted rescue. Aaron did his best—it really was his best. He made a golden bull, and lest his best seem a little puny, he fashioned worship, an altar and a festival, to court it and enhance its saving powers. The story is told in Chapter 32 of Exodus:

"When the people saw that Moses had not come down from the mountain but was staying there a long time, they gathered around Aaron and said to him, 'We do not know what has happened to this man Moses, who led us out of Egypt; so make us a god to lead us.' Aaron said to them, 'Take off the gold earrings which your wives, your sons, and your daughters are wearing, and bring them to me.' So all the people took off their gold earrings and brought them to Aaron. He took the earrings, melted them, poured the gold into a mold, and made a gold bull.

"The people said, 'Israel this is our god, who led us out of Egypt!'

"Then Aaron built an altar in front of the gold bull and announced, 'Tomorrow there will be a festival to honor the Lord.' Early the next morning they brought some animals to burn as sacrifices and others to eat as fellowship offerings. The people sat down to a feast, which turned into an orgy of drinking and sex. . . .

"When Moses came close enough to the camp to see the bull and to see the people dancing, he became furious. There at the foot of the mountain, he threw down the tablets he was carrying and broke them. He took the bull which they had made, melted it, ground it into fine powder and mixed it with water. Then he made the people of Israel drink it. He said to Aaron, 'What did these people do to you, that you have made them commit such a terrible sin?'

"Aaron answered, 'Don't be angry with me; you know how

determined these people are to do evil. They said to me, "We don't know what has happened to this man Moses, who brought us out of Egypt; so make us a god to lead us." I asked them to bring me their gold ornaments, and those who had any took them off and gave them to me. I threw the ornaments into the fire and out came this bull!' " (Exod. 32:1–6; 19–24)

Moses had been gone a long time, and with him any sense of the presence of God. The people feel forsaken, naturally and desperately so. This story is in the Bible to tell about the faithlessness and futility and wrongness of making idols, in Aaron's self-righteous words "how determined these people are to do evil," and to tell of how angrily—and how mercifully—God responds to such faithlessness. But we need —we really do—to read the story also as a record of the powerful urgency of those cravings that lead, perhaps inevitably and universally, to the making of idols. The people are forsaken and lost, bereft of what they and all people most ultimately need: that which tells them who they are, whom they belong to, which steps shall be their next, where their last steps shall take them. "Make us a god to lead us."

This is not an infantile longing, though we first know it as infants, urgently craving the totally embracing comfort of our mother's warm, strong body, and often separated from it. This is not, in itself, an idolatrous craving, although it does generate the futile scrambling of idolatry. This is the fundamental, insistent religious yearning of the human spirit living after the Fall and before the fulfillment, living in alienation from God and in perpetual hunger of God. Human efforts to bridge that gap with *some*thing and to fill that void with *some*thing cannot be stayed any more than Aaron could stay the clamor of the Hebrew people, "Make us a god." The hunger, the addiction presses too desperately. That is as much the message of this story as the disheartening and warning message that the human efforts to bridge the gap, to fill the void, are futile and only increase the alienation and hunger. Of course idols are wrong, futile obstacles to growth in faith, foreclosure of grace, fruit of impatient and untrusting longing. Aaron knew this, and the Bible wants us to know it, and we need to know it. But knowing this is only the start, not the end of our struggle with idols. This book is meant to track and accompany that struggle for those already in it, not to summon to the struggle or to warn off any who have so far managed to avoid it.

It is important to know, if you are truly relying on an idol to save you, that it cannot. The Bible is right to insist on this, and so, perhaps, are many of the preachers and prophets who scold our idolatry. But most of us, now, know all too well the futility of our idols and don't need to hear any more about this. Our problem is more often the opposite: wounded, grief torn, and scarred as we are from the failure of the idols we have trusted, we are far more likely to stay gun-shy, idol shy, promise shy, to avoid trusting any new promises and—still more tragic—to suppress and deny those yearnings and hungers that have propelled us into past reliances and alliances and into their biting disappointment. Burned by our hot bondage to idols, we freeze, in cold bondage to those same idols and keep the throb of our dreams locked up in our own frozen power.

Here we need to rescue those honest cravings, the naive capacity to trust, and to say a powerful word *for* the idol-making Aaron in each of us, and for the craving, sometimes even the finding (albeit partial), we lodge in each of our golden bulls.

These cravings are not distinctively male. They are the blessing and the curse of all human beings. What is male, I am convinced, is precisely what is Aaron's way of dealing with the cravings. He does three things:

He manufactures the idol.

He organizes a ritual to establish and enhance the idol's status, to sell it, if you will.

He denies that the idol is his creation.

The first move requires the other two: the two ways by which Aaron and most of us (try to) make the idol more than an idol, to disguise its defects and the impossibility of its mission to save. These are the two ways of exalting the idol, of magnifying it, of treating it like the god it is not; as though the treatment will make it so. One way is to worship it. The other way is to endow it with independent power by denying our power in creating it.

These cravings and these idol making ways of meeting them are not distinctive to professional men, but it is in the professions—especially among ministers, as it happens—that I best know them. Professionals are caught both ways, both as the golden bulls that others have manufactured, and as the fervent makers of bulls. But maybe so, too, are hardware store clerks, automobile mechanics, football quarterbacks, bus drivers, butchers, and any other man with a service or art or skill to offer a constituency; in other words, just about any man. Church members, hospital patients, lawyer's clients, butcher's customers try to make a saving idol out of their minister, physician, lawyer, butcher, and he does the same to them. They fashion him, in their minds, and he fashions them, in his mind, into the larger than life-size, better than human, glittering god who will embrace, engage, envelope, and save. He will make good for them, and they will make good for him what past churches or ministers, past patients or physicians, past clients or lawyers, past customers or butchers—not to mention spouses, lovers, parents, children, hobbies, jogging, and other frenziedly pursued saviors—have left sullied and soured. When a church installs a new pastor, when a patient visits a new physician, when a client visits a new attorney, when a customer finds a new butcher, each side is seeing a glistening golden bull, created in the wilderness of their own fantasies and needs and in the searing heat of their own past disappointments. *This* will be *it*. They have manufactured it.

This is a manufacture they not only fail to make explicit but even deny; it is, however, a manufacture they are quite prepared to ratify with orgies of worship.

NOT MY WISHING: IT REALLY IS SO

The record is very clear about what Aaron did. "He took the earrings, melted them, poured the gold into a mold, and made a gold bull." There is no evading what happened. The record is also very clear that Aaron tried to do just that, to evade the truth. He said. "I threw the ornaments into the fire, and out came this bull!" Out came this bull! If only Hebrew permitted the same commentary that American idiom automatically makes about this alibi! Picture the scene that Aaron is picturing as he stands there shrugging his shoulder, palms up in helpless wonder. He is picturing the scene of the bull coming forth from the oven door, full-fashioned, wonderous and surprising gift, with its own authority, its own power, quite beyond his own ken and doing. Indeed, that is precisely the point: the idol must be beyond one's own ken or doing or it has not the power it must have to lift you beyond yourself.

"Out came this bull!" Aaron, of course, is trying to dodge Moses' wrath and God's. But since he knows he can't really fool them, perhaps even more desperately he needs to fool himself, which he can do. Idols are not created to be idols but to be gods. And a god cannot be created, cannot be manufactured, dare not be needy or mortal, dare not itself need to be saved. It must empower and nurture me, not need my energy or fashioning. If the idol/god is a puppet, needing my constant manipulations so it can do and be for me what I need, I must never know this. (Neither must the idol know, so we surround it with courting and worship to mask its feebleness with grandeur. More about that at the end of this chapter.) If the machinist see his new position, after a series of frustrating ones, as an ideal position, it must really be that way. If the physician, or the lawyer, after a week of boring routine work, turns his new case into a really intriguing problem, demanding his best, if not heroic, talents, it must really be that way. If a man rebounding from a painful romance turns the next woman into the long-awaited ideal, she must really be that. If a minister turns his people into the magnificent sustainers of faith and champions of prophetic mission that will fulfill his ministry, they must really be that way. He does not just wish or hope. He expects, takes for granted, presupposes, in a way that establishes the objective existence of all these saving attributes. They really are full of faith and energy, they really are eager and responsive covenant partners in his ministry. They really have initiated and promised all those things he wants and needs. "Out came this bull!" He can count on their promise. So, of course, the stage is set for the crushing disappointment and rage when the idol crumbles, when they renege on those promises on which he has relied, leaving him abandoned and lonely, promises they never knew anything about, or only dimly intuited were being attributed to them.

For the secrecy veiling the manufacture of the idol extends to the idol itself. No one asked the bull or told the bull. The bull made no claims and no promises. It was molded and it was ground to powder again through no initiative or fault of its own. The idols that we mold—and then grind up again because of their failure—don't ask for that and seldom even know what is happening. Spouse or lover, parent or child, career or hobby, minister or congregation, new boss or new partner or new assistant, whomever we mold in our head as the one with the power to save us not only doesn't make those promises, but seldom even understands how we have attributed the promises to them. And when the unmade promises are broken, to our fury, despair, and anger, the idols don't even know what hit them.

This plight of the golden bull gets earnest voice in the "Confessions" of the next chapter.

Here we need to notice how it works both ways for men. Men know what it is to be the unwilling golden bull, to be set up on high, the one from whom so much is blindly expected, sternly expected, fearfully expected; to be the one set up to fail, to offend, to be resented, punished, the one ground up and swallowed up. Men also know what it is to fashion the golden bull, gilded into Godhead unwillingly, to demand a saving from it without negotiation or consultation, so that disappointment is inevitable, dreadful, and—compounding the man's pain—totally baffling to the one doing the disappointing. In the "Confessions" of the next chapter, the golden bull is speaking for men, and to men.

If you are an executive, especially a male executive, you know what it's like to be left holding the bag, on the spot. Other people—maybe above you, maybe below you—want something done, need something done, and so of course you can do it. If it doesn't get done, promptly and well, it must be because you didn't want to do it or try—their urgency imputing power to you. You are set up to be the god who grants or withholds or—the same thing—the omnicompetent servant. As an executive, your power, omnipower, is simply assumed, and you are either on the pedestal or on the carpet. You know how uncomfortable and unfair those positions are and how there is no way to fight back, to challenge or question these attributions because they are done so insidiously and slyly. To say honestly, "I can't do it" sounds like feeble alibi. People's needs for you to have power endow you with power. Their need to disguise their need disguises the endowment.

If you are an executive, and especially if you're a male executive, and if you feel as if you are the golden bull, you can perhaps recognize how you do it to others, and don't know it: how you rankle and fester at others' "unwillingness" to exercise their power—which you, of course, take for granted that they have (since you have accorded it to them) and could use, if they would. They are, naturally, part of a machine, the machine you feel part of, and the machine you feel responsible for running smoothly. Flaws and breakdowns are not tolerated. The uncooperative piece is simply ground up into powder. And all of this goes on without your being aware of it, while you suppose you are treating others quite humanely, and, indeed, are. They are as puzzled and as dismayed by your attributions, of how you need them to fit perfectly into your system, as you are by theirs.

If you are a man, you know what it is to have a woman attribute power to you, power to save or to destroy, power that you do not recognize. You do not know about it until you, the idol, get ground up for failing. When you have withheld this power, when you have been silent or less than reassuring, or less than expressive, then you discover how these things mean you have withdrawn and withheld a saving power she assumes and counts on. Or when you discover that even innocent remarks are taken as attempts to control or dominate, then you discover again what huge power you have over her, which you knew nothing about. When you feel as if she has turned into a fierce enemy or an ice maiden or a helpless little girl—when you least expect it and feel least warned—these are the signals that you have been cast as dazzling and powerful, a golden bull, and never knew it.

But if you are a man and feel scarred and baffled by such frustrating encounters, then you know how she feels. For you have taken for granted, have naturally expected, a warm, emotional, succoring, constant presence. Any deviation, anything less than perfect, any intrusion of the real or human woman tainting this golden goddess, feels like an attack. The denial of what you need and expect and take for granted feels like a deliberate withholding.

If you are a minister, especially a male minister, you can feel what it's like to be the golden bull, how silently it happens. They don't tell you how they are fashioning you into God's superman. It just shows, but only if you have the patience and courage to notice, in the slight but devastating ways in which they set you apart, put you on a pedestal, treat you as more holy, more pure, less human, less manly than you perceive yourself. It may be the traditional "sorry, pastor, for the profanity," or the still persistent request, trivial but freighted, to visit, to pray, to heal rifts, to still anger, to fulfill the traditional pastoral roles in ways that distort you. It may be they dismiss your earnest political or theological views as only the expected and therefore discountable rantings of one who is somehow different, "set apart," somehow non-human, non-citizen, somehow above and beyond all that. Other times it is non-sexual, non-masculine you must be. You know yourself to be the golden bull when others start to grind you up because they are angry that you have disappointed their expectations that you will play out the myths of their needs in ways you never asked for, certainly never pledged to, and barely even discerned.

If you are a minister, especially a male minister, this experience as the golden bull may help you understand the experience of your congregation. They frequently feel just as baffled or disoriented or knocked off balance or twisted or distanced by the ways in which you unthinkingly take it for granted that they are committed partners in faith, mobilized to complement (as well as compliment) and thereby sustain and fulfill your ministry. And they are just as dismayed when you grind them into pieces for failing these expectations and failing you.

If you are any other man, you too know what it is like to be placed, misplaced, in the lives of others who need you to act out their saving by knowing what you don't know; by believing what you don't believe; by accomplishing what you cannot achieve and don't aspire to; by compartmentalizing your life into boxes that perfectly exalt their lives and stifle your own. For them—boss, children, spouse, clients, lovers, employees, customers—you are to be the hero/expert/lover/nurturer/gladiator/sage/scout/conqueror/martyr/prince/god/bull—and you manfully struggle to comply—but seldom the partner/mortal/pilgrim/explorer/companion/bum/nurtured/hungerer you know yourself to be and want to be known as. You want to be close, and you are distanced, made object.

But then, if you are any other man, you know too what it is like to build those boxes and stuff other people into them as part of the furniture of your life—the same bosses and children and everyone else—who are cast into those supporting roles you so earnestly need to act out your own role. You make the other nurturer/goddess/bum/cripple/lover/mother/father/child. However close they want to be, they are distanced, up on that stage, enrolled, coached into acting out those roles that derive from your own and support it.

It is so crucial to the saving powers of the idol, whether it be the partner in love or the partner in work, that the savior freely and fully wants to give succor and embrace and is not coerced or wished into it. Thus the power of a true God's love, freely and unconditionally bestowed, unearned and unmerited and untrammeled and uncoerced. That crucial, devastating question: "Does he really mean it?" Does the lover really love? Is my partner my partner?

We are talking about the arts of seduction and self-seduction. Seduction is very different from rape. Rape is sheer attack and never comes close to yielding satisfaction. Seduction must be done in such a manner that the seducer—never mind the seduced—doesn't notice it. The molding of the god must be invisible, so the god's response is genuine self-generated and not induced or shaped.

But we are also talking about the subtle arts of creation—"making" in a more exalted sense. We are talking ultimately about the dilemma God must face. God intends, we believe, for creatures to be responsive and responsible partners in creation. God opts to endow freedom and opts to exercise not the power to mold, but the power to withhold the power of molding. We similarly need our creatures, including the god/idol, to have freedom and responsibility; we may *wish* to renounce or deny our determined and determining shaping. But, in fact, we do not appear to have the power to withhold the power of molding, only to pretend that we do. The greater power, God's power, is the power to create in and by genuine vacuum, luring galaxies and souls into frantically expanding growth.

We seem to be in touch here with an insight into men's

ambiguities about the exercise of power and the distortions that accrue from that ambiguity. Men appear to be both excessive and timid, at the same time, about their use of power, closet machos. Men exercise power, as in the shaping of idols. But as they then sense that it may be illicit, trespass, excessive—as indeed it usually is—they hold back, deny, freeze. But the denial creates a false vacuum, a distorted emptiness, and in rushes more power, usually reckless and uncharted. So men end up as victim to their own creatures. Aaron would have been better off admitting to himself just what he did— "I took the earrings, melted them, poured the gold into a mold, and made a golden bull." That's what he did, no less, but no more. If he could have said that to himself, he could have measured his deed and the consequences and not fallen down before it. Aaron might have known that he was the monster, but then would not have had to suffer thinking the bull was the monster.

COURTING THE IDOL TO MAKE IT REAL

Aaron made the bull and immediately courted it. He built an altar and staged a feast. The courting extends the manufacture. Men who court, whether by whistle or champagne, are said, quite accurately, to be "on the make," and at the consumation are said to have "made" the woman. (This is quite different, but not different at all, from the ways in which, as we say, a woman "makes" a man, similarly to her own specifications.) Molding the bull (or as another reliable translation has it, fashioning it with a graven tool) was not enough. The idol had to be taught its place in life, its place in the lives of these people. A true deity doesn't have to be courted: genuine power generates a genuine veneration. Idols have to be courted to become gods. Any hints of ungodliness—such as a cold unresponsiveness or such as recent memories of having fashioned the bull bare-handed—need to be eradicated and undone. Worship of a deity flows naturally, is drawn out of you like love, like a spontaneous erection. But worship of idols is different. It has to be manufactured, as part of manufacturing the god, like forcing an erection. If the woman falters in her beauteous reign, ply her with more gifts, gifts suitable only for reigning beauty: therefore she is a reigning beauty. If the job fails to satisfy, fails to engage and reward your best talents, as the ideal job should, and as this one promised, then give it longer hours and more energy, as an ideal deserves: then it must be the ideal job. If an idol falters in its saving, then bring out the repertory of gifts and courting, gifts and courting suitable only for a true savior: therefore the idol must be a true savior.

But courting is a strange kind of teaching or shaping or molding. The target of the courting, though the courtiers must never acknowledge this, is inert, whether golden bull or golden-haired woman or golden years in one's career or marriage. Courting is a strange, magical, one-sided, self-defeating kind of drama in which one person plays a role that presupposes the other's role, and in that presupposing, pretends to establish. If I treat you like a loving, beautiful woman, committed to me, then you are. No need to check your behavior for confirming or disconfirming evidence, no need to ask you, no need even to tell you. It is my behavior that does the work. I am making you. If I treat you, a minister, like a powerful priest with special access to holy power and the readiness to deliver it to me, and me to it, then you are. If I, the minister, treat you as a biblically informed, radically committed member of my congregation, then you are. If I speak difficult theology to you, you are, thereby and therefore, a ready partner in theological conversation. If I instruct you to testify as the witness or take the medicine as the patient or if I coach you on how to respond as the lover who will complement my expertise, then you are; no need to check your wants, feelings, intentions, or even your willingness.

SWAGGER AND BLUFF

Aaron built an altar and staged a festival of sacrifices and feasting so intense it turned into an orgy. Why so much swagger? He must have been scared. That is the male posture: the scared swagger. The swagger that changes the world, except that it changes nothing, so that finally—the pretense unmasked—it only fuels the fear. Aaron's stakes were high: he had a lot to lose and not much going for him, only the image he had manufactured, and no one knew as well as he did just how impotent and puny that image was. The gold they had put into it—that was real—but the shaping of the image— that was only his doing.

A real deity doesn't need an altar or sacrifices—that's why a real deity objects to such things, being treated as precarious or unsure—a real deity doesn't have to be courted or wooed. And real trust doesn't court and mold, only unsure faith. But Aaron's manufactured bull needed a lot of buttressing, a lot of acting as if it were something it was not, so it would become so. Aaron knew that better than anybody. His own terror needed the swagger of behaving as if he were confident, as though the swagger could make it so. The swagger covers the terror with a thin veneer that just may hold, but it also may be easily punctured and let the terror out with a blast. The swagger builds a structure that may house and protect or that may be the trap.

Aaron is everyman playing the emperor with new clothes, conned and conning by the elaborate rituals of tailoring and getting dressed up. It works just fine as the emperor swaggers down the street—until a small boy (the small boy within the emperor, never fooled about his puny nakedness) calls out the truth and leaves the frightened, foolish, swaggering emperor more devastated and humiliated than ever.

Aaron is the man who, baffled by mechanics and intimidated by salespeople, chooses a car, and feeling his choice challenged in the faces of his friends and in the unsureness within himself, proceeds to exalt his choice with elaborate courting of the car. His behavior will make it securely what he fears it is not: he praises it, he polishes it, he guns it, he protects it, he makes it taboo—he will let no one else touch it or drive it—he scoffs at its rivals. He denies its failings as they occur; they only exaggerate his courting. And when mechanical failure or poor performance finally shatters the swagger and crumbles the image it established, the hurt and anger is keen and widely disbursed at all within range.

Aaron is the Little Leaguer boy at bat and quite unsure about its powers in his hands. So he cocks his hat forward and his hips back, chews gum, and shuffles his feet, bull-like, in the batter's box—all the standard rituals to make his arms and bat perform better than he fears they can. The ritual works, sometimes. It makes him believe, and that may even make his bat perform. But making him believe, and making him believe that he has made others believe, only escalates the stakes—and the eventual devastating chagrin.

Aaron is the friendly family doctor from Kansas, somehow cast as the Wizard of Oz. He can meet the challenge only with an elaborate facade of bluster and swagger, commanding others to venture on impossible missions to slay wicked witches and venturing his own impossible promises to satisfy all requests.

Aaron is on a first date, unsure about his choice—since it is only his choice and since it is with somebody who is willing to go out with him—and unsure about his prowess at these things. He is unsure about the date that he is manufacturing. So his courting, his swagger are more to mold the event he has manufactured and programmed and feels responsible for than to woo the partner, though she must be coached and shaped into her part in the event. So he swaggers through the postures of "having a good time," as he makes clear by hearty jokes and knowing chuckles, by smooth moves with waiter and with car and with date. He guarantees, at least to the

temporary satisfaction of his own gnawing doubts, that everything is going fine and that they are having a great time. He
announces it frequently to her and to his friends afterward.
Any slight signs to the contrary from her only escalate the
courting and the swagger and the assurance it gives that all is
well. So when the message finally gets through, through the
network of friends, and through her own reaction next day—
when the date gets ground into powder that he has to swallow—he is incredulous and furious. Intensely so because it is
an idol he so thoroughly fashioned with his bare hands, refin-
ing the manufacture through stages of courtship—which is to
say that it is an idol he badly needed.

Aaron is a man, scared and therefore swaggering, swaggering and therefore all the more scared.

Aaron is the young ensign assigned his first tour on ship-
board; the new minister suddenly at the bedside of a dying
person or in the pulpit giving the second sermon of what will
now be weekly encounters with these real people; the young
physician having to make a decision with no immediate backup
or consultation; the new executive with a secretary out there
to type his reports today and a board upstairs to read them
tomorrow; the foreman on his own making decisions—the
productivity they affect is being closely monitored but there is
never a chance to explain or justify or discuss those decisions
themselves. Wedding nights may be less traumatic these days,
but never the wedding night of the job. All is as demanding,
as absorbing and as intensely urgent as successful batting or
successful first date or successful sex once was to the beginner
in manhood. And as crucial as priestly power and a potent
god were to Aaron, the stand-in leader of the Hebrew people.
Yet the man is unsure about his role on the job, unsure because he may have manufactured it himself, unsure because
it may not really deserve his sacrifice and others' respect,
unsure that he is not an imposter. So he needs to pose—in
exaggerated stance—the postures of the office, the swaggering

equivalent of the gum chewing for the Little Leaguer and the flourished tipping for the boy on the first date. He postures his job in uniform, in slightly affected speech, in exaggerated hearty cheer. Aaron plays his job.

Aaron is the veteran Shakespearean actor grandly playing the cities on his tour, his proud postures puffed up by his fears of fading, as unsure of his place in history as he is oversure of his lines on the stage. Aaron is the small boy playing grownup, dressing up in father's clothes and imitating father's swagger.

Aaron is the poker player who has anted big. He has all that money, and—more crucially—his reputation, riding on this game. Eyes on him, this is no time to fold, especially when a peek at the cards shows him that the hand he is building is not nearly as strong as he is pretending. This is the time for bluff. This is the time for bravado and swagger to the utmost. There must not be the slightest doubt in anyone's mind, especially his, that his hand is big and strong. That's the only way to make it so. It is the way to make it big—all the way to the final disaster. Posturing makes it so, swagger and bluff, daydreams and golden bulls.

3. Confessions of the Golden Bull

"So all the people took off their gold earrings and brought them to Aaron. He took the earrings, melted them, poured the gold into a mold, and made a gold bull. The people said, 'Israel, this is our god, who led us out of Egypt'. . . .

"When Moses came close enough to the camp to see the bull and to see the people dancing, he became furious. . . . He took the bull which they had made, melted it, ground it into fine powder and mixed it with water. Then he made the people of Israel drink it." Exod. 32:3, 4, 19, 20.

I never wanted to be a golden bull, yours or anybody's. I was content to adorn you as earrings, to jingle when you danced, to glisten with sweat as you labored through the day, to be admired sometimes, and, at those other times when you found other adornment, to be quietly stored away. I was content to be a part of your life, an important part, but only a part. I never wanted to be your golden bull. I never wanted to be the center of your life, the focus of your most intense and most suppressed emotions, the one you danced around, the one you sweated for. I wanted to be close to you, not set apart, not cast and frozen, not pedestaled, not altared, not altered, neutered in pretense of endowing potency. I never wanted to be the one to whom you attributed your saving, your past and your future. Why did you say I had brought you out of captivity? You had brought me.

Why did you expect me to be the answer to your prayers, to show you the way you had lost, to fill your loneliness, to rescue you from the wilderness? How did you expect me to find you, to guide you, to be intimate and potent with you, when you stripped me from yourself, when you molded me into something I am not, gave me face and form that you needed but that are not mine, when you set me apart and lifted me above you?

I never promised any of the things you expected from me. I never threatened any of the things you feared from me.

I didn't want you to believe I was endowed with these grand powers, because the belief was so destructive. How could we live together that way, with you expecting so much from me that I could not deliver, with me wanting to relate to you in an intimate way that was forfeited by your recasting of me.

I never wanted to be the excuse for your frenzy, for your fears, for your fantasies. I never wanted to be the object of those frenzies or fears or fantasies, only to be with you in them.

I never wanted to get caught in the middle of your struggle with the men who still have actual power in your life, the ones who once liberated you, so you thought, and also abandoned you and with whom you remain locked in anguish. I was a standin, cruelly set up by you on center stage even while the drama of your life had yet to unfold with another.

I didn't want to be set up as lording over you. I didn't want to draw fire for making grand promises any more than to draw fire for failing to keep them. Inert as I was in your life, willingly inert, suspended, hanging, even dangling, given motion only by your movement, even as I did nothing to raise myself up, any more than I could raise you up, so I could not bring my own destruction, any more than I could bring on yours. Most decidedly I did not want to be flung into the fire and ground into powdered oblivion, to be swallowed. I only wanted to adorn, to be admired occasionally, to be sometimes joined with you. This final joining now violently imposed upon us is intimate indeed, but so destructive to both of us. If only you had left me dangling as sometime adornment, and had not cast me as your savior. I did not want to be your golden bull.

*   *   *

At supper I ordered champagne because I wanted to share something special with you and to watch your nose wrinkle while you drank and to celebrate our good time that evening. But when I threw my gold into the fire, it became an idol. You were awed. You thought it was a grand gesture and you acted impressed and appreciative—and distant, by just that much. You looked up to me for buying the champagne. And because you were looking up, you were looking at me with fear and defiance, the ambivalence accorded any idol. You thought the champagne was extracting a covenant, that it had a price for you to pay, a demand for you to measure up. You felt you had to converse more gaily and wittily, and so you tried and felt angered by the assignment and inadequate and guilty for your failure to meet it, and I felt the distance of your trying, and eventually the distance of your anger and guilt. So I poured more champagne. As the gold mounted in your glass, so did your sense of pressure.

You thought I wanted to seduce you, so you treated me with the deference and the defiance due anyone coming on strong, any idol. I had just ordered champagne. You played along with the campaign you thought the champagne announced. You cooed and stroked and flattered and pampered and otherwise played the role of the seductee, the idol server. But you also resented the deference and resisted the demands you saw in the champagne. You stayed cool to any warmth your own stroking induced in me. You became wary of any moves toward intimacy. So, feeling distanced by the stroking and by the defiance and wariness, I poured more champagne. We became fellow prisoners of our unwitting and unwanted idol making.

*   *   *

I didn't want to be the untouchable sex goddess on a pedestal. I dieted and exercised and kept my figure trim and bought those bikinis and those frilly frocks just because that all seemed the thing to do and because you seemed to feel good about me looking that way. I didn't want to intimidate you into fearing that maybe I was too good for you, too much to handle. But I did. The attention from other men made you proud. But you also felt it as competition against which you measured yourself in your fantasies and found yourself wanting. I hoped you would like me with my nice figure and nice clothes. But you felt it all as expectation you couldn't measure up to. So you paid me homage and paid me court and kept me at a distance that we both resented.

*   *   *

When I suggested the vacation together, we seemed to be heading for a good time. We would explore and discover and play together; we would just *be* together in a relaxed and a pleasant place. But the vacation became fraught with tension because it became, in your eyes, *my* vacation. When I handed you the tickets and spread out the brochures with so much zest, I was warming to the vision of a private and tender interlude, you and me frolicking and cuddling on a lonely beach, you squeezing my arm and throwing me a flashing glance of delight over an exquisite piece of local pottery high on a back shelf of a tiny shop down an alley. This was to be a time we could be especially close to each other, especially open with each other. That's what I zested for. But you found my zest intimidating, offensive, selling you something you had to buy. So you felt in debt, owing; you paid and resented paying. "Whatever you want" was your theme all week. Swim? Hike? Concert? Breakfast in bed? "Whatever you want." Sometimes placid and compliant, sometimes sharp and resentful. Never there yourself, with your own wants, your frolicking, your cuddling, your squeezing, your delight. Somehow I, not we, became the focus of the week. I made too much of "we," and you made too much of me, somehow made pleasing me your main question, main task, main resentment. What happened to our tender interlude?

*   *   *

I was playing when I threw the frisbee, and you saw me displaying: displaying another accomplishment and setting up a task for you to fail. I was playing. I was unself-conscious about aiming and catching. I liked to see the frisbee soar, to be surprised by its dips and spurts, and I wanted to share that delight with you. If a dip put it beyond reach, or if it flew sideways into the bushes, that seemed to me part of the game, part of the freedom that frisbee is all about, part of the delight. But you said, "I'm sorry!" and gritted your teeth and tried all the harder to master the throw and to please me, now the coach. Because I thought the game was playful, I didn't know until it was too late that my chuckle of delight was to you a laugh of derision, my silence a sign of suppressed impatience, my forceful throw a rebuke and a dare, my gentle toss an impatient condescension, my leaping one-finger catch a rebuke for your wild throw or a norm to make you feel inadequate, my easy catch a complaint that you were making the game boring. If we kept playing, I was keeping you at the task, and you diligently persisted in the work of each throw and of each catch. If I suggested we quit, I was disappointed at your failing and you had to persevere all the more relentlessly at mastering the tasks of throwing and catching.

Finally, your "sorries" and your silent relentlessness got to me, and I did become self-conscious. Your grim anxiety became an idol of sorts for me to cater to. I did begin to gentle my throws, to count the catches and the misses (so as to meet you in your counting), to applaud your successes and reassure your misses, keeping score of them just as you had first supposed. In ten minutes, I was playing the role of the coach/wizard/ogre/idol into which you had cast me and I was doing it well, to your specifications. I somehow acquired—unwanted—the power to make you feel, by my looks and manner and words, either worthy or unworthy, pleased with yourself or displeased, one who sinned or one who was saved.

*   *   *

We were having a fine conversation there on the beach, you and I, warming to each other even as we laid back and opened ourselves to the deliciously warming sun, as delighted in our surprise encounter as in discovering this sheltered, private, smooth beach.

I only wanted to enjoy our new friendship, on this suddenly clear vacation morning, to share your dry comments on the day's news and my still resounding appreciation of last night's TV opera. When we got to talking about ourselves, that felt good too, tentative, then free and robust, a sharing of convictions, peeves, histories. As we pulled off jerseys, it was getting easy to open my life, too, to a stranger.

When I began talking about my work, I wanted that to move our conversation closer, deeper, not to end it. My work is important to me, important to others. I thought it would be important to you. I thought that talking about my work would fuel our talk about the dilemmas and delights of life, for that is what my work is about. But when I said "minister" I could see you, once leaning toward me, back away, your jaws slightly ajar, your smile suddenly frozen. It was as though I had said "single" or "I'm here alone this week." You raised up on your knees a little, as though you didn't know whether to stand up and salute or to crawl away backwards or to brace yourself for pushing me away. "That's interesting," you said. "I didn't realize," covering your feelings—and me—as much as the toe you had dug into the sand. You looked over to your towel as though you wanted to cover yourself up. No more uncovering, no more discovery.

"Minister" meant, to me, all the more approachable; to you, suddenly untouchable. To me, one intimately acquainted with grief and other poignancies of life; to you, one exempt from life, at a distance, on a pedestal. To me, "minister" claimed and craved common ground with you; to you, "minister" claimed and carved out higher ground. To me, it meant we could look all the more deeply, all the more companionably at the life around us; to you, it meant you needed to look at me in a new way, deferentially. To me, it meant one accustomed to and comfortable with exploring the roots of life, just as we had begun to do; to you, it meant someone threatening to route you in ways you didn't want to go. To me, a bonding of the friendship we had begun; to you, a power that threatened bondage. To me, a binding between us; to you, a potential binding of you.

I wanted "minister" to unclothe my anonymity and name me as ready and intimate companion, but it only made you clothe me in armor and halo and name me an alien species.

*   *   *

I never wanted to be your earth mother, growing you into a sturdy oak firm against all storms, endlessly replenishing your vitality against all droughts, nurturing your very marrow with deep, underground, ageless mysteries possessed only by me, receiving your fallen limbs and your used-up leaves, recycling them into an endless supply of new nurturance for you. I wanted you to grow tall and strong, reaching high and wide and flourishing. But I never wanted to be the one to make it happen; especially, I never wanted to be the one you relied on to make it happen.

I never wanted to be your earth mother. I wanted to be your lover, a gazelle prancing with you, sturdy elk. I wanted to come to you partly nurtured, partly hungry, both of us mingling our hungers and our fullness in a jumbled dance that would send us scurrying off to forage and prowl and play and to bound back again to mingle our new replenishments and our new yearnings.

When I pulled you to my breasts, it was because that felt good to me and I wanted you to feel how good that felt to me and to play with my breasts because that set up circuits of energy vibrating between us that sparkled and refreshed both of us. I wasn't doing you a favor. I didn't pull you to me just to please you, or just to offer a final resting place for your cares, just to revive you into life. Eagerly, I wanted you in me, but not in my womb.

I never wanted to be your earth mother, for that distorted both of us and our love. You resented it that you needed me, and you resented me as a reminder that you needed me. To look at me would be to look down at your nurturing, so you didn't look at me. You needed to keep the roots deeply hidden, even from yourself, even while you silently probed deeper into my being for still more nurturance. You looked only up and out, and reached only up and out.

You looked down at me only when I failed you, only when you felt the earth rumbling or when you felt your probing root unfed. Then you looked down and then quickly away—in fear, in terror, in resentment. It was in those moments that you released me as earth mother, but not only as earth mother. You dismissed me altogether: you hurt and me hurt, you guilty and me guilty, both angry at being abandoned, both angry at being loaded with guilt. Your turning away made me less able to open deeply and receive your searching hunger and to nurture you, which made you turn away the more. But I never wanted to be your earth mother, only your earthly partner.

I never wanted to be your earth mother, but I wanted to have you and I wanted you to have what you wanted, and something in me did want to be your earth mother. Your instincts, like your roots going for water, unerringly and re-lentlessly reached that part of me that did want to be your earth mother, and you lured me and taught me how to do it. I didn't want to be your earth mother, yet I did it gladly. And we suffered for it.

*   *   *

I am your father. I never wanted to be severe or cold or gruff or demanding; I wanted to reach out and embrace. I wanted to be your father. But you were standing there so stiffly that I was afraid to reach toward you. So I hid behind my gruffness and you did respond to that.

I never wanted to impose arbitrary requirements. I didn't want just to send you off on missions or to shape you. I didn't want just to say "go" or "do." But I wanted to say something. And busy talk is the easiest kind of talk.

I didn't want you in postures of deference or awe or fear or servitude. I really didn't, for it is harder to reach you and touch you when you are in those postures, and I did want to touch you. But you knelt so readily, and ran the errands so readily, and also defied even as you deified, and resisted so readily—all before you could hear the yearning in my words.

I was as frustrated by this impasse as you were. My own yearning made me lunge at you so quickly you thought you were being attacked. Maybe you were, but I didn't mean it that way. My yearning for you made me reach so suddenly and so closely to inner and private places your only response could be an instinctive coverup. You were not used to anybody, and especially not used to me, wanting to come so close and trying to know you so well. Wanting to stand close, I crowded you, and you had to push back. And your coverup and your pushing made me reach all the harder, which made me seem to be attacking all the harder, and the spiral went on and on.

I never wanted to make you feel inadequate and unable, tested and failed. I couched my hopes for you in such high terms that they seemed to be demands and probably were. My love probed so deeply inside you that I seemed invasive, domineering. I saw you as strong and warm at the core, but you weren't used to being seen at the core and my gaze seemed piercing and fearsome.

I didn't want to make you overly dependent on me, but we both wanted to relate to each other and that seemed to be the easiest way for it to happen.

Most of all, I didn't want to seem strong and self-sufficient and unneedy, an omnicompetent superman. I didn't want to seem to promise to save. I wanted my love to say that I wanted you saved. But I never wanted to promise to do it. I didn't want to be that aloof; I wanted to be your partner in the project. More, I didn't want the anger and the hurt that I foresaw would burst forth when you discovered that I could not deliver.

I wanted to be close and I wanted to be partner. But we were subtle prisoners, you and I, somehow cast in these roles of contracted adversaries. We were locked in and couldn't get out except by playing the game to the end. Pushing these roles until they exploded. Though we are covered with the debris, the game will probably start all over again, but I hope not.

I wanted my pointing finger to be singling you out and then beckoning you close. But you saw the pointing finger as jabbing with reproof. I wanted my sweeping arm to be pulling you closer in embrace, but I succeeded only in making it seem flaying. When I ran toward you full speed, I was trying to catch up with you. But you thought I was chasing you—away. If my eyes were narrowed, it was because I wanted to see you closely, so my love could be authentic and convincing. But instead the narrowed eyes seemed hostile. If I stripped my body, or even my soul, it was to be open to you in love. But my awkwardness and the novelty of such gestures made it seem more like a maneuver or manipulation or a stripping for battle.

When I wanted to say "I love you," or when I wanted to say "I hurt," it came out in my awkwardness, and earnestness, as advice-giving and pushiness—my advice was only meant to spare you the hurt I felt and knew so well. So you had no choice but to respond to it—necessarily with defiance and wariness—for the advice it was and not for the yearning and confession that it also was.

We—all of us—don't know how to say, or to hear just "Ouch" or "I hurt." We lurch past that to "You hurt me" and "You are bad." Attack and blame become the habitual overtones of "Ouch," so defense and counterattack become habitual response. Even when I feel down, you hold me up to knock me down.

Oh, how I wanted to be your father.

*   *   *

When I visited you in the hospital, I, too, was scared by your disease, and by all the busy people and machinery, and by wondering what we could talk about. But we did talk—and you did most of it—about these fears, and about your hopes and your memories and your disappointments. You opened up and let me share so much of your life, past, present, and future. I talked, too, sharing in more openness than most people ever find. It was an intimacy that both of us craved and treasured; we said so. That afternoon at the hospital promised something new in each of our lives, a lasting intimacy that would build on that precious breakthrough by your bed. That's what we said.

But something else happened. Was it because you were lying down and I was sitting up? Was it because such intimacy was so unfamiliar and unpracticed and more than a little fearsome? When we next met, for a drink, it seemed you didn't want to continue the intimacy but to avoid it. In fact you even seemed to want to avoid me. You no longer saw me as the partner in intimacy that I wanted to be and that I thought I was. Now you saw me as a power—the power, I guess, of one who knew so much about you and knew how to know more—a power to be coveted and a power to be feared. You had invited me close and then fended me off. You invited me to meet you and to talk of love and hate and fear and hopes and disapppointments. But when I arrived, you—we—spoke of politics and neighbors and baseball. You stuck to safe topics so as not to offend me and maybe also not to tempt me to use the powers of our more intimate knowing.

*   *   *

When you visited me in the hospital, we shared good talk. It was a private and special place, away from most of the distracting business of our lives. I had plenty of time to think long and deep thoughts, and you seemed able and willing and eager to share that time and those thoughts. There were interruptions and distractions: a nurse with a needle, another with a chart, buzzers down the hall, a beeping cardiac monitor across the hall, life-and-death urgencies thrust into our consciousness. It was a world of tension and scurry, but it was a world all its own, so different from the tension and scurry of our usual lives. It felt remote, isolated, special. It was like retreating to a monastery. It was like being six miles up in a speeding jet, or like drinking tea on the Champs Élysées. A moment out of space and time.

It was a birthing time. In that special moment, something was born that wouldn't have happend otherwise, a friendship. A friendship rooted in that moment, but also a friendship that freed us from that particular moment because it bound us to each other. A friendship that promised to transplant from that private greenhouse and make beautiful our everyday worlds. A friendship that touched something very deep in each of us and reminded us, even in a hospital, that we were rich, whole persons. A friendship that was important just because it was not a friendship between a hospital visitor and a hospital patient, but a friendship between you and me.

But something happened. It became hard for you to move our friendship into other places, out of the monastery into the world. It was as though you froze that hospital scene and wouldn't let the film roll on, as though you wanted me to stay the patient, sick, flat on my back, scared of what was going on, spilling my soul as fully as my veins threatened to spill. When I spoke not of my pain but of daily events, you shied and fell silent, numbed as though hurt. When I tried to speak of your hurt, you backed off and asked me again about mine. You idolized me as patient and fixed us in the hospital room. I wanted that time to be beginning, not end. If we could be close in the hospital, now could we be close over a drink? I wanted to be a partner in growth. Yet anything that moved from that moment—I would have said grown from it, but you would have said deteriorated—seemed so threatening that we both began treating that shared memory—which had once been precious just because it was so robust and fearless—as fragile and tender. We wrapped romantically and protectively our one golden moment, measuring all other moments against it and finding the others wanting. In any other role, and in any other posture, I was a disappointment to you.

I thought that hospital visit showed high promise of a growing, deepening relationship between us. I wanted to be your friend. I never wanted to stay the frightened hospital patient, stunted and motionless like an idol on an altar.

*   *   *

I worked hard at your committee meetings. I took them seriously and I wanted you to take me seriously, but not as intensely serious as you did. I threw myself into the committee work. I did my homework. I followed the discussions closely. I analyzed the issues deftly for you, and I proposed solutions that were well thought out and imaginative, solutions that reconciled differences adroitly and that you adopted enthusiastically. These offerings were to establish myself as member in good standing of the committee. I wanted to be one of you. Instead, they set me apart, or you set me apart. You set me apart with a great deal of ambivalence. You admired the energy and skill with which I worked. You even came to depend on them and on me—"Let's wait and see what *he* comes up with." There was a special attentiveness when I spoke. But you also came to disapprove, to avoid, to dislike, and maybe to fear my energy and my skill, and your dependence on them. You caucused without me. You clustered at the other end of the table. The hush when I spoke was exaggerated, like a protective blanketing, paying tribute to my words but also isolating them from the rest of your discussion. Sometimes I thought you paid more attention to whether I was frowning or smiling, intense or flustered, than to the analyses and arguments I was so earnestly attending to. You would say "You are always right" with appreciation and admiration, and with impatience and irritation. You welcomed it when I advanced the discussion, but you also felt judged and inadequate. When you murmured together cynically and wearily about the committee work and dropped the occasional acid remark about the tediousness and futility of it, you wouldn't let me join you, like the teacher's pet at recess on the playground. Somehow I became the champion or custodian or conscience of the committee and all it symbolized. You felt better about yourself and about the committe because I worked so hard at the business and so you needed me and catered to me. You identified me with the structures and with the demands and with the nuisances of the committee. You treated me the way we have always treated priests, set them apart as embodiments of the powers or the obligations we feel are necessary parts of our lives but from which we feel alienated: we admire the priests for playing this role but also find/make them strange and estranged.

My very desire, and the intensity of that desire, to be involved and close, a real part of the committee, and my effectiveness in doing that, made you make me remote and special.

*   *   *

When we went to the beach that day when you were six, I never wanted to be a policeman or to make you into a policeman. I meant, mostly, just the opposite when I called over from my blanket, "You be responsible for your own toys, okay?" I meant that I was not going to be a policeman, not wanting to hassle you. I really was so relaxed that day, and wanted to be so relaxed, that I was quite ready to let anything be. If toys got broken or lost that day, I wasn't going to worry. I wanted my words to signal and to share my sense of relaxation and peace. I wanted to take the pressure off, because I felt the pressure off. But, of course, you heard it as putting extra pressure on. You heard me giving you a job to do, with a Last Judgment waiting at the end of the day. I meant, at least that day, to be open, free, partner, playmate. And you heard another dose of closed, law, taskmaster, judge. I wanted that day to make me more of the kind of parent I wanted to be and you wanted and needed. But it only made me, perhaps finally and indelibly, the kind of parent—adversary—you most feared. You lived that day—and all the years thereafter, apparently— in apprehension of my wrath, building a script to avoid it.

*   *   *

I never wanted to be your savior, only your minister. I wanted to join with you, the congregation, in a covenant of search and trust in which we might together come closer to finding the sure roots and the clear directions for our lives. I needed that, and so did you. I had some gifts to bring to that covenant and that search, and so did you. I wanted to be your minister, not your God. I wanted to join with you in the search to find and trust and obey our God.

But you seemed to think that I was already on God's side. You seemed to treat me as someone who had already found God, securely and fully, as someone who lived the holy life, could answer all the hard questions, could guarantee God's presence and good will, if I would, could guarantee your salvation, if I would, and someone who pronounced the judgment of God on your life. When I came close to join you in search, you backed away and measured a distance between us, with your formality and deference and awkwardness, just as though I wore a dazzling halo or a damning scowl.

I wanted to be your partner and you made me your parent.

*   *   *

We in the congregation never wanted to be the ones to make good your vocation as minister and your spiritual pilgrimage. We never wanted to be the ones whose conduct and belief would be the means of vaulting you into heaven or dropping you into hell. We never wanted that power over you. We never wanted to be the ones you would look to so anxiously, constantly taking our temperature to see if our faith and biblical sensitivity and social responsibility and ecclesiastical loyalty was hot enough to fuel yours, rich enough to nurture yours. We never wanted you so dependent on us that our slightest stumbling out of step with you became interpreted as abandonment of the faith, and of you. We never wanted you to need us. We needed you, but we didn't want you to need us to need you.

*   *   *

God, I never wanted to be the place where you lodged, the place where you lodged your trust, your vision, your expectation that people can be free and healthy and loving. Couldn't you stay away and on high, as God is supposed to do, let us negotiate at a distance, and maybe even let me sometimes hide? I never wanted to be one that you counted on to be one of your adult people. It's easier to be a child, but you never seem content with that. I never wanted to be taken that seriously, that relentlessly. You don't let go. It is as though you *need* me, as though you have so much commitment to me and investment in me that it makes a crucial difference to you how I respond, how I behave. I never wanted to be taken that seriously, to be trusted that much, to be burdened with that unswerving love. It is almost like unmerited adoration. I feel as though I stand awkwardly on a pedestal, high and lifted up. You seem to mean it. But I am restless and wary. It feels like a setup for a fall, it feels like making me a visible target, it feels like mocking me. But when I try to climb down into the depths where I belong, you say it doesn't feel that way to you, and you keep lifting me up. I never wanted you to rely on me, to believe in me, to invest in me, to treat me as though I had power, as though I were so important to you that all other facts were less important, to you and to me, than that fact.

When you reach toward me, it is so determinedly, that I panic. You are so steady and firm in your reach that it makes me fear that you are punishing or judging me, crowding me, wanting to take something away. But you respond to my panic, to my testiness, to my unease, to my persistent resistance, with that same disturbing thereness. You are just looking at me, gently and steadily, waiting.

4. Yes-Men: The Empty Yes and the Masked Yes

"What do you think? A man had two sons; and he went to the first and said, 'Son, go and work in the vineyard today.' And he answered, 'I will not'; but afterward he repented and went. And he went to the second and said the same; and he answered, 'I go, sir,' but did not go. Which of the two did the will of his father?" (Matthew 21:28–31a)

What do you think? A certain woman invited guests to a dinner party. She called one and said, "Please come," and he said, "Of course I will come! I love dinner parties, and yours especially." And indeed he came, flourishing flowers, and conversing profusely, displaying a witty opinion on every subject raised, and otherwise magnificently going through the motions of playing the charming dinner guest—and he ruined the evening for several people, even while they enviously said to themselves: "I should be able to do that." And the woman called another and invited him also. He said, "You know how I dislike dinner parties!" He came anyway, but did not venture light repartee or pretend to be knowledgeable on every subject. Instead, he more or less turned his back on the party and talked quietly and closely with only three or four people, who later said to each other "That was a beautiful evening; I wish I could have more like that. Oh, yes, that man was nice, too." Which of these was truly present at the party and which did the will of the hostess?

What do you think? A certain man proposed marriage to a woman and promised to give her his all, and they were wed. He provided her a fine home and a high standard of living and was polite and proper and faithful and hardworking—the

model husband, everyone said so. But he withheld himself—
she never knew what he was thinking or feeling if anything.
And another man proposed marriage to another woman and
warned her that he could give her little and probably would
not be a "good husband." And, indeed, their standard of
living was low, and he was not always polite and proper—
sometimes they raged hard at each other—and on an occasion
or two he was not faithful. But she knew his zests and pains,
his dreams and frustrations, the loveliness of his bliss and the
swirls of his turmoil. And they became not just one flesh but
one spirit. Which of these was truly husband to his wife?

What do you think? A certain student had two teachers and
went to the class of one and said, "Teach me." And the teacher
lectured brilliantly, with erudition and wit. The class applauded frequently and admired the professor very much, from
a distance, of course, because the professor was much too
distinguished to be approached closely. And the student sitting
in the seventh row looked up at the professor and wondered
silently, "Where are you and where am I in all of this display?
Who are you and who am I? I wanted *you* to teach *me*." And
the student went to another class and said, "Teach me." And
the professor spoke haltingly, often breaking off his lecture to
sit with the students and to share musings and puzzlement.
The teacher offered more questions than answers. And the
student felt gripped by the contagion of the teacher's passion
and curiosity. Though teacher and student soon lost touch, the
student's grappling with the questions was unshakeable and
lifelong. Which of these truly taught?

What do you think? A certain personnel manager was asked
to comply with the affirmative action policies of his company.
He meticulously completed the questionnaires required for affirmative action review by the government. He showed that
each position was widely advertised and posted, that women
were in fact considered among the finalists, and then he explained in great detail how each of the women did not meet
the requirements of the job description as well as the men who

were appointed did. This demonstrated, precisely in accord with the affirmative action regulations, that it was not prejudice that kept women from the positions. Another personnel manager was impatient with these forms and these regulations, was always delinquent about completing them and was even careless about having all openings posted on all bulletin boards. Instead, he spent a lot of time at coffee breaks— "Doesn't he ever do any work?" people said—listening to men talk about their female colleagues and secretaries and getting acquainted with the women workers. When good jobs opened, he went to some of these women and urged them to apply for positions they had not even considered. Sometimes they got them. Which of these personnel directors engaged in affirmative action? Which filled the letter and which filled the spirit of the regulations?

What do you think? Some church people wanted their minister to be "more biblical," as they said. It was a kind of "affirmative action" to make the Bible and its messages more present and more meaningful in their lives. They wanted their minister to build sermons more explicitly from the Bible and to lead a group of them in weekly Bible study. The minister agreed, enthusiastically, for Bible had been his favorite subject in seminary, and he was expert in issues of biblical scholarship. He analyzed for the people the vagaries of the text, the problems of translation, and the dilemmas of trying to discover the authors' intentions—all in all, a resounding, scholarly, and astute display, emphasizing proper caution about formulating interpretations. Don't jump on any ideas. Know why you can't. (It was something like the personnel officer's complying with affirmative action regulations by explaining so carefully why it was impossible to hire a woman.) Another minister, similarly asked to be "biblical," said that he had been eager to get back to the biblical religion he had grown up in, and he moved easily into quoting the Bible with a verse-long answer for any question. (Maybe this is something like a personnel officer hiring a token woman for the front office.) A third minister said the request was a very difficult one, because the Bible had always been important but never very clear to him, and the scholarship of seminary even less clear, so that he found himself still in struggle with the Bible and careless about keeping up with biblical scholarship. He opened to his people his own struggles with the Bible, that is, his sense of the urgency of its message, coupled with his sense of its elusiveness and even sometimes the irrelevance or alienation of its message. He retold the Bible's stories and read its cadences in a way that dramatized the losing struggles of the Hebrew people to be faithful, and the failure of the disciples to comprehend, and the piercing way God touched the people in the midst of these failures. Which of these ministers met the people's need to reclaim the Bible?

What do you think? "Save our marrige," a couple said to a minister. So the minister reminded them of their commitments and obligations, told them to be less self-indulgent in their grievances, to recognize the importance of marriage. The minister had them come to his office for the usual series of three conferences, recommended a weekend retreat and some books that would fortify these lessons, and finally arranged a church service in which the couple could renew their vows. So the couple was soon asking another minister, "Save our marriage." This minister said she didn't know if she could. But she sat at their kitchen table patiently, listening to one and then the other tell of pains and angers seemingly without end, and then listened to still more outbursts of anger, and then listened as the couple finally began to hear each other. So there were moments of communication, and shreds of new trust, and maybe even some hope for the marriage. Which of these ministered to the marriage?

What do you think? Some committee members asked the chairman to help make their meetings more meaningful and effective. They thought, as he thought, that this meant making them more efficient. So he mobilized some techniques of administration, began calling members in advance of the meetings to ensure their attendance and to brief them on what would be discussed, drew up an agenda each time with a fixed number of minutes allocated to each item, posed the issues pro and con at the start of each discussion, intervened to cut off discussion when it began to stray and helped the committee get through its business in record time with a sense of accomplishment: many things had been checked off and many decisions reached. But when they were finished, one took a deep breath and said, "That was like a fast train ride, and I think I missed most of the scenery." And another told her husband when she got home, " I don't remember a thing we said but we must have said it really well, like in IBM meetings." Another committee asked their chairman to help make their meetings more meaningful and effective and were initially quite frustrated at the response, for he suggested that they move away from the conference table and into the lounge and spend more time at the beginning with coffee and snacks; he seemed to turn his back on the business at hand. The chairman actually pursued side tracks as they came up, and sometimes suggested that they abandon the agenda, and instead spend time with new issues that burst out now and then. And one member said afterward to her husband, "I'm sorry that I'm late home, but those meetings are so gripping. It's the one committee I go to where I feel something real is happening; we're not just going through the motions. We even care enough about things to get into arguments." Which of these chairmen helped make their meetings more meaningful?

THE EMPTY YES

The empty yes is the routine yes, the rootless yes, the route-less yes, the yes that goes nowhere, the bodiless yes, the thin yes, the cosmetic yes, the yes that washes away at first test, the yes that crumbles at first touch, and leaves the heartbreaking no. This is the yes that sabotages its promises by its own routineness, the yes that kills the spirit by feeding it the letter, the yes that defies by glibly complying. The empty yes—because it is yes—raises hopes, lulls guardedness, and lures vulnerable investment. The empty yes—because it is empty— shatters the hopes, refurbishes the guardedness, and withers the investment. The son with the ready but routine yes is seducing the father to expose his heart so it can be broken. The man with the routine readiness to answer people's needs and hopes is toying with these needs and hopes, sabotaging them, a friend more destructive than an enemy.

How does it feel to be victim of the empty yes? First it feels soothingly good—a dream come true. Then it is devastating— old disappointments now cutting more deeply. It is the excruciating pain of having and not having, at once, promises raised and dashed.

When the father says, "Go and work in the vineyard," and the son says, "I go," there is new spring in the father's step, new warmth in his breast. To be a father joined by a son is like falling in love in the spring or like having one's jokes laughed at or like being called by name by a celebrity; it is like having your arguments carry the vote in a committee meeting, or like having your hand held. You are joined, recognized, embraced, confirmed. It is an experience of grace.

When the answer is "yes," there is a freshening of spirit, an enlargement of self. You are jaunty, sprightly, and happy, more ready to join others because you feel joined, more ready to recognize others because you feel recognized. You are more giving because you have been received and more ready to receive because you feel given to. You are more unfolded, more present, more there. It is the opposite of being lonely. It is feeling a place and a belonging, fatherhood.

The son's "I go" answers questions, earnest, urgent, searching questions about the relations between you and him. You wouldn't have asked if it weren't gnawingly important. You relax, more at peace with yourself and the world because this son of yours is responding as you wish and not as you feared. The yes puts to rest the gnawing suspicions of alienation and unease. Past fears and annoyances are forgotten in this new blending of wills and persons.

But the son's yes promises more than it means. It promises a fulfillment, refreshment, replenishment, a nurturing of deep hungers, a salvation. But it doesn't mean any of these things. So it is an idol and dooms your heart to anguish. It is an idol so well placed and so well promised, and you are so needy that you eagerly welcome it, rejoice, grasp, rely on it again and again. So when the idol crumbles, the grief is sore, the heart emptier than before, and the scars thick.

The empty yes breeds the empty yes: the pain of this grief over this idol failed breeds wariness and caution that becomes your own empty yes, the withholding in the affirmation you offer to others. Fatherhood frustrated by a son aloof becomes aloof father. Men as victims of the empty yes become performers of the empty yes. Soothed and battered by these idols, men pose as the idols that become the soothers and batterers of others. This is man's story, the story of this book, this story of the empty yes.

THE MASKED YES

Men's story is also the story of the come-on no, the masked yes: No, I will not work in the fields . . . but I hint I might. If the empty yes lures a man into receiving, embracing as a savior, an idol that will fail him, then the hidden yes lures a man into fashioning the idol. This come-on no contains a promise, but obscure, a promise withheld. So the man is enticed into taking the responsibility for maturing the promise, nudging it to come true. He needs to rescue the yes from its masking no. The man is seduced into putting his energy into shaping the no into a yes. He rises to the challenge and builds an idol, pouring into it his own energy and trust and expectations: if it/she/he says no, I can make it/her/him say yes. It *will* say yes. I will get from it in exchange for what I give, in proportion to what I give. My effort to reshape the no guarantees the yes.

This too is men's story and the story of this book, this seduction into making "it" happen, and the painful grief when it doesn't, and then the grief-induced cautiousness with which the man subsequently utters his own yes, cloaking his own commitments in the seductive no.

The idol of the empty yes seduces the man into trusting, expecting, hoping; and its failure disappoints the man into hollowing out his own yes—he makes his promises glibly and smoothly—an idol that in turn, seduces, then fails, others.

The idol of the masked yes seduces the man into the effort to strip away the mask, to upgrade the no into its intended yes, (he's sure it is intended) and seduces him into trusting this effort, expecting, hoping; the failure of this idol disappoints the man into masking, armoring his own yes—winking when he says no—a lure that seduces others into their own upgrading effort, and hence their own disappointment.

This is men's experience, but if we are to believe Jesus and his editors, who told the story that began this chapter, it may also be God's experience. For the father in the story seems to be intended to portray the plight of God, a father who is so eager to hear our yes, who feels so gladdened by it, that he may hear the yes well before it is matured, and cannot take no as the last word, as the way people really are. If this is God's experience, the difference from men's experience is not that God does not suffer, but just the opposite. God appears capable of infinite grief—this may be what makes God in fact God—without needing to fend off the pain by closing up, closing out, without needing to mute, hide, withhold, blunt the hearty yes with which God continues to address us, without either hollowing or armoring the yes. God just persists in saying and perceiving yes, until it is so.

VICTIMS OF YES-MEN BECOME YES-MEN

How does it feel to be victim of the empty yes?

The father gazes contentedly down across the vineyard. It is not just that the vineyard work will be done, though that is important, and he is relieved to know that the backlog of weeding and pruning will be done by the end of the day. It is also that his son loves him. That was an unspoken question within the question, "Will you help me out in the vineyard?" Now the backlog of doubts about that can be laid to rest. They do have a future together—that was another question within the question—and the father is sweetly looking forward to working alongside his son at harvest time and in the seasons ahead. The son's ready yes has eased doubts and nurtured the father, who goes about his own chores with new zest.

These contented passions of the father are the passions—filled with sure hopes—of the voter whose candidate, the one who made just the right promises, wins; of the lover whose doubts and fears are dissolved by the consenting yes that promises all will be well; of the ethnic community whose struggles at last have yielded a favorable response from city hall, the way paved for a secure future; of the war veterans who march home wearily, but triumphantly happy in the knowledge that they have won the peace that will end wars, guarantee justice, and win the gratitude of their fellow citizens; of the teacher whose student has at last seen the point or the negotiator whose opponent has at last conceded the point; of the writer whose stubbornly slow subterranean thought processes have just yielded a plot that will now write itself; of the gardener whose patient, tender care is at last rewarded with a burst of healthy growth that will now flourish; of the distraught person whose alcoholic spouse has at last promised to go dry. All of these gaze contentedly with the father at the trusted stirrings among the vines. Patience and struggle have borne a response that buoys new covenants.

The father—each of these fathers—keeps casting his eyes down at the stirrings among the leaves and savoring the good feelings. But then towards the end of the day his eyes linger on the rustling, and a thought will not stay suppressed any longer. The father stares and stares, and the hard thought fixes in his mind. The rustling is the wind. The vineyard is empty and so was the promise and so is the father's heart, all the emptier for having burgeoned so fully. He lost a son and much more. He has lost that heartiness of self that he had invested in the son's yes. With the field empty, with the son's yes empty, part of himself is emptied, depleted, drained, hollowed.

We see the grief no more clearly than in the way the father now empties his own affirmations, the hollowness, the emptiness of his yes expressing the emptiness of self that grief is. (Maybe—no, probably—that's how the son's yes got empty, perfunctory—it was hollowed out by his own disappointment and grief.) The father promises himself to get out to the vineyard tomorrow, but he doesn't mean it, and doesn't do it. Even when he does get to the vineyards, or to any work, he does it in a routine, perfunctory way, frozen, going through the motions, dutifully doing what is required, or seeming to—man's work, done man's way—zestless and soulless, for his soul is depleted. A daughter asks a question and he grunts ready acquiescence, distracted—his emptiness seeking matching shallowness—by his century's equivalent of newspaper or beer or television or home computer; but that's all she gets. His wife asks for love and he goes through the motions of giving love and speaking love and making love. His neighbors, whose emptiness matches his and who are too depleted to ask anything of him except a casual yes, even a mocking yes, become his natural companions. Their tentativeness can withstand no more than his own tentativeness, whether at bar, cocktail party, carpool, locker room, or poker game. Poker game: the perfect symbol of the man's plight, with the false yes and the masked yes, high-stake bluff escalated to high art.

How does it feel to be victim of the come-on no, the masked yes?

The father gazes down across the vineyards, calculating the work that needs doing and deciding what has to be done first and what can be put off. But he is distracted, pulled back from

these thoughts about the vineyard to thoughts about the conversation with his son. There with his son, not in the vineyard, is where he feels called most urgently to labor. There's
something with his son that needs doing, needs his doing. Of
course he is disappointed and angry at his son's refusal, but
even more he is nagged by the sense that this was not the
final word. If the son's no was intended to draw attention to
himself and away from the vineyard, it succeeded. The refusal
was puzzling, demanding in its own way. Something was
amiss that needed correction, probably his correction. His son
was not himself. This was not the son the father knew, at least
not the son the father wanted, dreamed. "That just wasn't like
him!" The father ponders and wonders what to do. "He needs
something. He needs something from me. How may I have
offended him? How have I failed him? . . ." There is something wrong here and the father feels responsible, responsible
for making it wrong, responsible for making it right. The son's
refusal and his retreating back have left a vacuum that draws
the father in.

So the father gazes down across the vineyard, but he is
thinking about the work he must do with his son, not with
the vines, distracted by what the son has left unsaid more
than by what he has said, and feeling challenged to get it said.
What does he do? Jesus doesn't tell us, because Jesus wants
to teach us about a God who doesn't have to do anything, a
God who just perceives the yes that is hidden within the no,
takes it for granted, deems it as so. But the earthly father
needs to fill the emptiness in himself by filling the emptiness
he senses in his son.

Since we have each been that father, we know what he is
planning as he looks down across the vineyards. The father
wishes for the son's yes to be visible and the wishing becomes
so earnest that it becomes the urge to control, the urge to
cajole, command, plead, rebuke, whine, apologize, shame, scold,
all the arts of Pygmalion, determined to pump life into the
cold statue, determined to call forth his son's yes with a powerful

yes of his own. But if, like a man, he is lured into *making* the yes, he is also, like a man, being lured into shattering disappointment. After the disappointment, he will fall back onto imitating the son's maneuver, the seductive, come-and-find-me masked yes. Like a man, he will hide longing and effort behind the mask. He will veil his vulnerability and pretend a protective shrug. We sometimes suppose that it is the woman who lures and teases by hiding her own yes. But to believe that is not to notice that men's bluster is a coverup, a coverup of caring and longing, a coverup of "yes," even "please." It is men who cultivate an artistic array of veils to hide their caring; bluster and bluff, dullness and shallowness, preoccupation with sports, cars, business; the crippling and upmanship portrayed in the next two chapters . . . everything that utters the protective, resounding no, that says, this is as far as I can come out . . . please come in . . . the yes is inside. Meet me on my turf, behind my stockade of no. Please find me.

To be victim of the empty yes is to revel in a student's response to your teaching, a student who joins you in your passions and your views, extends them, lives them, confirms you. A year later when he visits the campus, you rearrange your schedule for a long conversation and another moment of his discipleship. But he's a different person now, mouthing new passions or none; your special array of ideas, code words, and symbols, which used to trigger animation and enthusiasm is now met with only blandness and blankness, and the conversation drags through perfunctories to its conclusion. You go back to your classroom more than a little gutted, reamed, hollowed; with passions subdued and views dulled; now it is more like going through the motions of teacher, playing the role, without that spark that has until now set you apart, made you vivid, present, colorful; without that depth that has kept students delaying you an hour after class. Now when they probe, they get only perfunctory mechanical "professorial" answers like "that sounds like a good idea, let's talk about it sometime" or "I think X has written about that." And they turn away, downed, new victims of your newly hollowed yes.

To be victim of the masked yes, the come-on no, is to respond energetically to those students who claim difficulty or disinterest. They make themselves prominent, so you know they are only taunting you and are ready to respond to your extra effort. So you make it, with lecture illustrations aimed at them, with long long comments on their papers, and with private tutoring. All that effort makes you ready to savor the payoff it must yield, these wooden Pinocchios come alive through your caring. But the payoff never comes, as their polite appreciation for the extra attention proves to be only that, polite and politic, and their engagement with you and your ideas is as tenuous as ever. Next time you think of making the extra effort, any effort even, you head it off, wrap it up, bury it. You adopt the same protective armoring of blasé indifference you learned from them while they learned nothing from you. Bury your yes and make them come to you. It's safer. Even though oh-so-impoverished.

To be victim of the empty yes is to respond to a woman's desperate "help": coach me and comfort me through this coming job interview, or school exam, or problem with my kids; teach me how to repair my car, how to manage finances, how to be more loving; help me through this crisis. You are unambiguously wanted, needed. There is a crucial place for you in her life. You are Somebody to her, the only one she turns to. You answer with energy, commitment, and imagination, filling that place, sure of your welcome and tenure. When she gets through the crisis, you are ready to claim that place, to have that welcome and tenure confirmed, to be warmly hugged in celebration, maybe even thanks. Now you say, "help" or "please" or "here I am." And she says, Why are you so demanding or so narcissistic? and Can't you understand I have a new crisis coming up? Or she turns against you, resenting your help and her dependence, and strides off. So it turns out after all that it wasn't you that she wanted, but just literally what she said, help through a crisis. So if she asks, you help with the new crisis, but it's more mechanical, more routine, more condescending—you act more like a business consultant. You miss your full-bodied zest and engagement, miss it more than she does.

To be victim of the masked yes is to stand by while the woman copes, announcing she is determined to do it herself, but never quite letting you get out of sight, looking at you furtively for reassurance, sneaking a request for advice. So you sneak your response, too. You let the assurance, the advice just "happen" indirectly, dropped into other conversations casually. Affirmation, praise, admiration offered, but never as though acknowledging her self-misgivings. Comments about finances or car repair are dropped into talk about other people. Neither of you honest about what is happening, so you learn to disguise yourself, to match her mask, in an arm's-length choreography. And soon you wonder where you disappeared to. It's like talking with your mouth closed, like making love with all of your clothes on. Pretending you are not there when you are becomes a pretense that you are there when you're not.

To be victim of the empty yes is to believe it when someone—boss, spouse, friend, parent, child, minister, someone—says, "Tell me what's troubling you. Let's talk about it." So you pour it out, the dam broken by this welcome, at last, for the long pent-up turmoil. And while the other listens, you pour and pour and pour, grateful for the offer of a listening that is attentive and sympathetic and supportive. You pour and pour and pour. You know it will all be embraced by a sympathetic hug or by a warm comment or by a penetrating insight. You know that the other's invitation means they want to know you and be with you, with all of this turmoil, not make you pretend any longer that this is not part of you, at least not with them. Then, just when you begin to run down and pause for a breath and maybe some comfort the other says, "That reminds me of when I . . ." or " I'm sure that it's going to get better soon . . ." or "I think what you should do is . . ." or "Your whole problem is . . ."—and you can't recognize yourself in any of these responses. So it turns out the other person, after all, like all of the rest, can't take you with all the turmoil, isn't really ready to know you as you are, wasn't seriously ready to take on all the overflow from the broken dam. So you sponge up what you can from everything that has spilled out, shore up the dam with whatever debris you can find—that is now going to take all the energy you have—and slog away.

The dam must now be stronger than ever. You don't permit yourself that many vulnerabilities to the empty yes—maybe the times you succumbed, really let go in abandon, are so long ago as to be lost. Now when people say "Tell me . . ." you go through the motions, but it's routine, it's empty. You are watching yourself, controlling the spilling, vigilant to keep the dam intact, managing the charade of sharing just enough to make the other feel helpful—because it is now the preservation of the hollowed roles and the other's self-esteem and comfort, not your own nurturance, that is important here. Energy is given to preserving the forms of the yes. The empty yes takes energy; the genuine yes would have given it. In this display of energy and skill in keeping things running smoothly and evenly, you have become a man again.

To be victim of the masked yes is to go to your lover or therapist or friend or parent or minister in distress, only to have them hide from it a little, but only a little. They don't turn you away cleanly; the no is not decisive but shallow, a come on. They should hear you out, can, want to, but seem to need a little coaxing. "Time is a little scarce right now"; "Oh, you probably understand yourself better than I do"; "Are you sure you can trust me?" So you give them the coaxing. You accommodate them on the time, you reassure them that your demands are not great, you find ways to dose out your distress so as not to be overwhelming. You control and manage yourself to help the others play their role. You find yourself needing to encourage, perhaps even manufacture, the other's attention, the other's caring, the other's support. "You can do it" you try to persuade them; and you persuade yourself: your own flood of energy that goes into making that so, makes it so, at least for you. Once you overcome their shyness and coyness, they really are yours—the delusion of every seducer. You count on the sympathetic ear and heart you have unmasked.

From there on, it is pretty much like being the victim of the empty yes, for the yes you have uncovered is a yes you surely count on, and a yes surely empty.

To be victim of the empty yes is to feel that special elation when things, at last, go your way at work. A promotion, a new boss, a move, a reorganization of the clerical staff . . . *finally* there is readiness for what you have to contribute. The persistent obstacles removed, the way is clear for you. There is your name on the desk, on the door, on the letterhead, on the book, in the paper, wherever it means most in recognition of your past and guarantee of your future. There is spring in your stride and zest in your voice as you dash home, phone home, write home to break the news of your new life. According to some myths, this is how men feel when they get married, when they have children, when they find God, when they quit drinking or quit smoking. But for you and the men you know, it is when the job goes right that you most ecstatically and deeply feel this elation. It has finally happened. They finally noticed you and said, "You are the one we want."

Their affirmation and your enthusiasm is contagious. You go to people you have responsibility for at work and encourage them. You say, "Let's be creative, let's think big, let's work on what can and should be done, not think about why it can't."

Throw the best of yourself into this new ideal work situation, and know that it's welcome: that is your expansive message to them, because it is the message you have received.

Then you discover—the "morning after," whether it comes weeks or months later—that they meant it, but they didn't mean it. They meant what they said, but didn't mean what you heard, in your long dammed-up zest and in the sudden release of that frustration. They meant the promotion and all the rest, but were valuing you for what they saw in you, not for what you saw in yourself. They meant the promotion and all the rest, but didn't mean that there was a sudden moratorium on the institution's standard quota of conflicting values and personalities and the struggle for survival and supremacy among them. They didn't mean that there was suddenly a moratorium on the powerful need of the institution to protect itself and to give priority to its survival over creativity and healthy change and the most productive use of individual talent. So, on the morning after, whenever it comes, there is a return to normalcy: the same old struggle for a niche and recognition, plus the hangover from the binge of celebration. And because of the hangover you walk all the more stiffly and carefully, the expansiveness and zest of the celebration turned upside down, inside out, and gutted. You don't withdraw the encouragement you gave the others: you are more wounded than that. You continue to say the encouraging things, but now your heart is not in it. It is a mood turned on and off quickly for just the opportune moments. It is manipulation. Even while talking with them and reading their reports, you are canvassing all the "realistic" reasons their ideas won't work in this business right now. But you still tease them along in the ongoing hearty charade in which—you now assume—everyone shares without speaking this appalling secret: there is no place and no payoff for talent or imagination or intense personal investment, but this truth is made more bearable by the pretense that there is. The naked emperor has clothes—let no one say otherwise. Quick and mechanical sex (premature ejaculation is the epitome of the empty yes) is satisfying and the real thing—let no one say otherwise.

You call committee meetings, you call for reports, you call for memoranda, you appoint new committees . . . you vigorously enlist and assign others' energies and efforts, just as though they would be heeded, just as though they would be honored, just as though they would make any difference, just as though they were not an elaborate charade—and let no one say otherwise. You rearrange organizational charts, you redesign job descriptions, you do what has been done to you, in an apparent attempt to give others the impression that there is something new, a new place, a new welcome for them in the organization. You learn anew the technique of listening and consulting and learn how to do this with great conviction, listening intently and attentively, with nods and responses, seemingly giving the impression that their thoughts are wanted and influential, every impression.

To be victim of the masked yes is to be hired with an unclear job description, ambiguous responsibilities and lines of authority, uncertain symbols and mandates. They must want you—it is clear to you that they need you—but they don't seem to quite know how to say it. So you help them. You work on a job definition, and you work on selling it to them, and you work on performing in a way to match and refine the description. You create the role the way an actor or opera singer does, and you await the applause. They give you a hint of recognition now and then, often enough to encourage what you have done but also to make you aware that more needs doing. So you redouble your efforts to please, impress, to make them want you and to know you are wanted, to unmask the yes. You see yourself succeeding. All your effort and imagination do give you greater assurance. And it doesn't take much imagination to see that they recognize this, too.

But that is imagination. At a meeting one day where new assignments are being discussed, it follows absolutely and logically from the job definition they have adopted and you have refined that you will get a particular assignment. You can see that clearly, of course, and so must they. But you go through the whole meeting, and your name is never mentioned, and the assignment is handled quite differently. Your idol, built entirely by your own efforts unilaterally, crumbles. This is your own doing—overly trustful of this idol of your own creation, expecting it to save you when you cannot save it. But it is their doing, too. In their ambiguity they have lured you, exploited you, tempted you by leaving you on your own to do what you just did. They have found and tapped an old male vulnerability, the readiness to hear and make the Joseph bargain: be a good boy and perform well and please us and we will love you and reward you.

So as victim you go into retreat and shelter your own enthusiasms and yearnings and commitments. You join in the coffee-break putdowns of the enterprise. You adopt a perpetual shrug, a charade of casualness. When something goes wrong, you say loudly, "What else do you expect around here?" burying deep the passion you actually feel to get the wrong remedied. Some may call it burn out, but it is more like a spark still waiting to be fueled and fanned into blaze. It is frozen power waiting to be thawed. It is limpness waiting to be aroused, coaxed into action. You wait to be discovered and called forth, giving off enough hints of your talents and commitments, your yes, for those with eyes to see. But mostly, in your numbed cautiousness, you display the mask of casualness and uncaring, hiding the yes.

5. Crippled Cripplers

Here is a story with a surprise in it. It's told, by John in Chapter 5, about Jesus and a crowd and a sick man. At least the crowd saw the man as "sick," but Jesus didn't.

"Near the Sheep Gate in Jerusalem there is a pool with five porches . . . A large crowd of sick people were lying on the porches—the blind, the lame, and the paralyzed. A man was there who had been sick for thirty-eight years. Jesus saw him lying there and he knew that the man had been sick for such a long time; so he asked, him, 'Do you want to get well?'

"The sick man answered, 'Sir, I don't have anyone here to put me in the pool when the water is stirred up; while I am trying to get in, somebody else gets there first.'

"Jesus said to him, 'Get up, pick up your mat, and walk.' Immediately the man got well; he picked up his mat and started walking.

"The day this happened was a Sabbath, so the Jewish authorities told the man who had been healed, 'This is the Sabbath, and it is against our Law for you to carry your mat.' "

What's the surprise? To you and to me and to the crowd and the authorities around the Sheep Gate, the surprise is that the sick man got well, and in a hurry. But to Jesus, the surprise was that the healthy man acted sick for so long—helpless, dependent, impotent.

Is this man crippled, or is he well? Is he a cripple who poses as a well man—to the crowd's dismay? Or is he a well man who poses as a cripple—to Jesus' dismay. The crowd and the authorities see him as a cripple, and so do we. When he acts well, stands on his own two feet, walks around, and carries his mat (instead of being carried on it), the authorities are astonished and upset and call it a sin. The crowd is astonished, as are we, and call it a miracle.

But Jesus sees the whole thing differently. He never sees the man as a cripple. He sees him as well and is astonished that he acts like a cripple: act as well as you are, he says. Get up, pick up your mat, and walk.

How does the man see himself? As others see him, of course; don't we all? As long as he is the creature of the crowds and the authorities and as long as we who are in the crowd and we who are the authorities are so ready to persuade him that he is a cripple—ready to challenge him if he gets up—he is. When Jesus stands there in front of the crowd, believing that the man is well, he is.

Does that make Jesus a liberated—and liberating—man? Precisely. That is just what makes any man or woman "liberated" in today's urgent sense of the term—not accepting crippledness as normal; impatient with crippledness, your own or anyone's; outraged at the posture of a person who lies inert, helpless, dependent, whining. Thirty-eight years paralyzed, indeed! Thirty-eight years waiting to be carried to healing! "Get up! Pick up your mat! Walk!" Liberating voices in our times—men's and women's, more often women's—are saying no more and no less than that: "Crippled? Oh yeah? Get up!" Startling words to those of us, like those around the Sheep Gate pool, who take crippledness as normal, and crippling, not healing, as the standard way that we relate to each other.

Seeing is believing—especially in the Gospel of John, especially in our experience, too—seeing is making it so: the power of regard. Whatever the man's history, whatever his posture, whatever labels people put on him, "crippled, lame, infirm, impotent, halt"—the various biblical translations give us a rich list of words that readily become flesh—Jesus perceives, unconditionally, the wholeness and health of the man. He signals this in no uncertain terms. Not the uncertain terms of diagnosis; not the uncertain terms of therapy; not the uncertain terms of class action litigation or welfare legislation; not even the uncertain terms of hope (hope was already symbolized by the remote nearby pool), which so readily emphasizes the despair, the gap between "is" and "could be". In no uncertain terms—you! here! now!—stand up and walk on your own two feet, as God intends you, as God regards you. Why lie here crippled, as this crowd regards you? That is false regard, crippling regard.

These days, too, we sometimes hear people tell of becoming uncrippled—women, so far, more often than men. Whatever postures they have accustomed themselves to in response to the expectations of infirmity imposed upon them, they simply discover that they are regarded—not by Jesus so much these days, usually by an intimate group of other women—as sturdy and as healthy. Finding themselves thus regarded, they find themselves sturdy and whole. It is not easy to trust this new regard and new posture in the face of the challenges it meets, as firm as the challenges met by the man Jesus uncrippled, as firm as the challenges that have done the crippling all along. It is not easy. But it happens. It can happen to any cripple. (More of this in chapter 7, "Paths of Liberation.")

It is women, so far, more than men, who have become clear how they are taught to be crippled. So it is not surprising that a lot of the crippling that has come to light is the crippling done by men. Men *are* cripplers; we are taught and induced to do it, so compellingly that it often becomes automatic and unthinking. This chapter will try to make clear how we do our crippling. But men-as-cripplers and women-as-crippled is not the whole story. Also, it is too simple just to turn it around to claim that men are crippled by women, though that often is true, too. Crippling is a pervasive way of life, a web we are all caught in. Each of us is a victim of crippling, made to feel less than we are by others' need to regard us that way, and each of us passes it on. Cripplers cripple because they themselves feel crippled.

Women are not the only group who have learned, and taught, how to uncripple themselves from others' crippling regard. A word needs to be said here in appreciation of another group, people who are physically "crippled," the victims of handicapping conditions. They are foremost among those who have discovered that whether you regard yourself as "crippled" in the sense of helpless, unfit, impotent, as used in this chapter, doesn't depend at all—any more than for the man by the Sheep Gate pool—on the actual physical state of limbs, but on how you let yourself be regarded by others. Their own uncrippling is another model for liberation, the tandem liberation from being crippled and from being crippler.

We know well the crowds and the authorities bustling around the Sheep Gate, teaching this man, for 38 years, that he is crippled. We are part of the crowd; we are the authorities. We don't *want* to be cripplers and would be appalled to think of ourselves as crippling him. We don't even want him crippled; but many of us *need* him crippled; and this has to do with our own crippledness. Few of the crowd, few of the authorities, are mean, some may be callous and indifferent, most are benign and sympathetic. But, however kind we are, we still find ways to convey decisively and persistently to him our conviction, making it his conviction, that we are healthy and he is sick, that we are sound and he is crippled. He is our kept cripple. We need him to measure our health by, just because we feel an inner limp and inner twitches, inner hints of our own crippledness.

Those of us by the Sheep Gate offer sympathetic words, alms, gifts, all very charitable, and all constant reminders to us and to the cripple that we are healthy and strong and he is not. Probably there is a special place for cripples, perhaps one side of the pool "where they will be more comfortable" and clearly segregated, even quarantined; for crippled cripplers, boundaries are important. Probably there are distinctive clothes for cripples to wear and standard deferential ways for them to behave. The expectations are probably codified in quite explicit rules. ("One at a time into the pool" and "Don't carry your bed on the Sabbath" are two that we know about.) Whatever the rules, the cripplers are the rule makers, to be clearly distinguished from the cripples, for whom the rules are made—for the cripplers' own good and well-being, of course.

It all could well have been much like an early version of what is now highly refined in the modern hospital, a place whose every detail seems intended to instruct—massively and unmistakably—some people that they are sick and therefore exiled from normal life, and that their lives are under the control of those who are designated by sharp caste distinctions as the health professionals, the professionally healthy.

But then modern hospitals are offshoots of the church, which has long been skilled at persuading people, sometimes gently, sometimes vigorously, that they are incomplete, infirm, delinquent, and wrong except as they accept their designated roles in acquiescent, dependent subordination to the church. But before you rush to join in this movement of liberation from the crippling of medicine and the clergy, let me ask you how your profession does its crippling. And how do you do your crippling at home?

Foremost, I bet, by hoarding privileged, private knowledge (though we will look at several other techniques in this chapter). Those at the Sheep Gate do their crippling especially by knowing. They know about health and about crippledness and about what makes the difference. They diagnose and appraise and analyze and prescribe. They know. Whatever happens, they already have a system for explaining and judging it. Even when the man jumps up and strides away, uncrippled, they still know—systematically and thoroughly—with a leverage that keeps them on top and him down: back down on your mat. We know better than you do what happened to you. Explain it away, or co-opt it, explain it they will, in their own terms, and in their system, in their matrix, but they will not learn from it. They know.

We can imagine what the cripple experienced with 38 years

from the crowds and the authorities around the Sheep Gate, because we have been there. We know how we have become crippled in the eyes of others, and therefore in our own eyes, even as we have been in the crowds and among the authorities, doing the crippling.

We have learned—and we have taught—how to read and how to add, how to drive cars or how to sail boats, how to tie knots or how to pound nails, how to make love and how to choose clothes, how to pray and how to read the Bible. We have learned these things from instructors who have made us know two things; first, we must do these things well, and second, we couldn't do these things well, at least not without persistent, ever-so-patient coaching and monitoring from them. They have sat beside us on the car seat, stood beside us at the workbench, stood up in front of us in the classroom or the church. They have peppered us with information, riddled us with questions, blasted us with our mistakes, until we feel befuddled. They have surrounded us with warnings of our mistakes and reminders of their prowess until we feel totally subdued in inadequacy. They have brushed off our questions or restated them oh-so-gently and helpfully, until we feel stupid. We have finally learned the basic lesson in all these lessons, the lesson that we are crippled and inept.

It can happen the other way. When teachers are told that their class has a high average IQ, even when it doesn't, a year later the class does. When the teachers perceive the students as bright, the students come to share and embody that perception. We can all remember those delightful moments when we have been with a teacher who has conveyed foremost the trust that we could and would achieve. But for most of us, those have been the rare experiences. Mostly, we have been among teachers who salvaged their own sense of mastery and accomplishment by conveying their conviction of our own inadequacy and our need for their prowess. And, so, we have become such teachers.

Men and women alike are crippled—and cripplers. But

women's awakened awareness of men's pernicious crippling of them can alert us all. Here is what women have helped me notice:

I walk up to the airport baggage check-in with a complex itinerary involving a couple of plane changes and a stopover. I am white, male, middle-aged, and well-dressed, so the agent assumes that I know what I am doing and addresses me companionably, like an equal, "Check it through to Louisville for you today, sir?" A white-haired woman—later my seat partner—steps up to the same agent with the same itinerary. She also knows what she is doing. But he doesn't treat her that way. He starts patronizing her, "You are going to take one plane to Buffalo, and then you are going to change planes and take another plane to Louisville, but you are not going on to Chicago today. So when you get to Louisville this afternoon this suitcase will be there waiting for you." He so overloads her with information and with relentless caring, all conveying the impression that the situation is really too much for her to handle, that she finally is persuaded that there must be some complication that she doesn't understand—or he wouldn't be carrying on this way—and she lets herself become befuddled by this overload. The crippler scores again. He has, at least temporarily, made her into the image he holds of her—and needs to hold—to confirm his own (tenuous) status and authority.

By 5:30, a woman has the house in order, the kids quiet, herself attractive, and the meal ready and tasty. She has earned her man's approval, a need which has already badly crippled her posture. But this day at 5:30, his greeting is, "Who left the trash cans on the curb all day?" "I can't ever get it right. I'm a hopeless cripple," is the lesson she learns—because it is the lesson he needs to teach—because it is the lesson he has learned about himself, all that day, and all his life.

The four-year-old girl has just spent her dollar in gift money. She had insisted on going into the store all by herself and she now comes out proudly bearing her choice, a miniature red-and-yellow oil tank car from a train set. She has picked it for its colors and for its smooth round shape and for the funny clink the brass wheels make when they turn, and maybe also because she half remembers her father pointing to the oil tank cars on a passing train. Her father had let her go into the store alone but with some misgivings. "Remember you only have one dollar. Hold it carefully, buy something you really like . . ." She doesn't remember any of that now when she comes out with her choice to show him. But his mood is not much different: "What are you going to do with *that*? You don't have a track for it to run on. That's supposed to be part of a train with an engine pulling it. Didn't you find the doll shelf? . . ."

She gets confused trying to deal with his questions and still hang onto her delight, because they don't have much to do with each other, and soon she lets go of the delight. She starts to say, "But I like it," but he and his questions are overwhelming. She is soon floundering, "Well . . . I didn't think of that . . ." His cross-examination has wrung from her a confession of the crime he had convicted her of before she even began: being foolish, untrustworthy, and unsatisfactory.

No one will ever see that oil tank car again, and never again for the rest of her life will anyone see her indulge in a gesture quite so impulsive or display a smile of such unalloyed delight. She has now learned to know herself as an unsatisfactory person, as a cripple, as an invalid, as invalid. She is down on her mat, separated from the vitality of the healing water. Any move to stand on her feet and carry her stretcher will be rebuffed and turned against her and made into further evidence of her lameness.

She could try to make good her blunder—get carried into the healing water—by making the oil tank car an idol to save her; she could court it—save money, buy the track, buy the engine, buy the rest of the train, buy dolls to ride in it, meet all her father's oh-so-reasonable, oh-so-patient objections, and please this male parent by getting her whole life "on track." But more likely her efforts would still be painted as all the more bizarre and eccentric. For his objections, though couched in reasonable and logical remarks about the train, are not that at all. In fact they are his prejudice—his pre-view—or his culture's prejudice against her vitality as a person. She is a cripple. This is the message he conveyed, and will insist on conveying and this is the message she received. He is a crippler.

Undoubtedly he is a crippler because, once upon a time, probably many times, he was on the receiving end of the crippling message. Maybe it happened when he was four and fell off the back seat of the car. His father or mother—already crippled—was so frightened, upset, and guilty about his or her driving that he or she yelled sharply, "Can't you hang on back there?" The message, unspoken but unmistakable was there: "Dolt, clod, nuisance, drain, failure, cripple—you can't do anything right, you can't do anything for yourself." Maybe it happened this morning when his wife put a teakettle on the stove, went off to the shower, and then yelled at him for letting it go dry. "Do I have to do everything in the kitchen? Can't you do anything right?" Or maybe it happened yesterday when the bus driver gave him a studied, crippling sneer as he juggled umbrella and package while trying to fish out change.

This chapter is mostly about men as cripplers. But we can't talk about men as cripplers without also talking about men as crippled.

JENNY AND BRYAN TAKE THE KIDS CAMPING

It had been Jenny's idea to go camping, because she had dreamed of some carefree, relaxed family time away from the hustle of the city and the TV, and away from the chores of home and yard, and away from the neighbor kids that seemed to make it so much harder to deal with hers. Bryan hadn't shown any enthusiasm for the idea, but he hadn't opposed it either. He just took over. He began checking out the sites and routes, measuring packing space in the car, telling family members how much they could take, and giving Tad (but not

Kim) lessons on how to build a fire. There was a right way to do these things; he knew what it was, and though they didn't, if they would pay attention to him, they would: that was the clear message.

Camping day comes. Even before starting out Bryan is anxious about finding a good campsite, because he has assumed the responsibility for providing it. But he would never talk about being anxious, because he is much more skilled in being the crippler than in showing any lameness himself. So what he talks about is "I thought sure, Jenny, that you would have the icebox cleaned out last night." And, "I already explained to Kim that there was no room to take the teddy bear this trip" blaming the victim, who needs the teddy to comfort her because of her father's management. (That battle takes half an hour and a lot of tears and tense, patient "explaining.") And so it goes through the day until they get the tent pitched, and it is time, part of the required routine, to take a picture. "Don't look so stiff," Bryan demands; the picture is to record the happy family he presides over. But they just stand there, looking as numbed as they feel. So he takes the picture anyhow, disgruntled, but "forgiving." "I guess you all are just not used to camping yet." (Blaming the victim again: he has created that stiffness, and he now explains and forgives it.)

Bryan the crippler, however, doesn't get into high gear until that night. After the kids are asleep, Jenny starts a conversation. She is still dreaming of the relaxed vacation and feels it being crippled by Bryan. "I know how you do everything with care and want it to go right, and I appreciate that. But sometimes it seems that you make the camping awfully formidable to the kids. I think the whole thing got to be such a big project, so that Kim got scared, for example, and wanted her teddy and that's why we all couldn't loosen up beside the tent. You really did a good job in getting us here. Now can't we just relax and enjoy it?" Bryan isn't defensive. He doesn't need to be. He already has his response at the ready, really a nonresponse, not factoring in what she has said, but only taking the occasion for some more management. "No, you don't understand. It's because you don't expect enough of the children. They are old enough to take some responsibility, and that is what I'm trying to teach them."

Jenny can only sigh. "Sometimes I think we just talk past each other; we really need to find some way to talk better so we can understand each other better." Jenny wants to go on to explain what she understands of this talking past each other, and how she thinks it can be remedied. She really means the "we." It is not a disguised apologetic "I" or a disguised attacking "you." But she doesn't get a chance to go on. Bryan is right there with his answer, as always. Again he is not defensive, at least not overtly. He doesn't need to be, because the best defense is a good offense; the most effective aggression is passive aggression. "Yes, I understand"—ironically, he co-opts her word—"how you need to feel in close touch with people. I think that's one reason you have so much trouble setting limits on the children. I wish these dratted sleeping bags weren't so awkward. I think you could use a little close holding right now. It's been a tough day for you." He's so helpful, trying so hard to meet her needs and, of course, he knows exactly what they are.

Again, she makes the double effort of trying to acknowledge him at the same time that she tries to express her own point of view (that's twice as much effort as he is making) accepting the responsibility, as long taught (even as Bryan insists now) for how things go. "That is sweet of you to want to help. You're always there, available. Sometimes, though, I think maybe you don't need to try so hard. It might be all right just to relax and let us get along as best we can."

He cuts her off again and deflects the focus of the conversation back to her, smothering her with his solicitousness. "Don't back away or be so recessive or apologetic. It's all right to admit your needs and ask for what you want."

"I thought that's what I was doing!" Her voice now rises in frustration at trying to break into his marshmallow fortress. "I was only trying to say . . ."

"Do you hear your voice now?" He cuts her off again, and cuts her down. "This has been a frustrating day. That need you have for comfort always turns to anger and irritation if we don't catch it in time to do something about it. I almost wish I had let Kim bring her teddy bear, so you could borrow it now. She's sleeping peacefully, but you could use it. Can you take me, sleeping bag and all, as a substitute teddy bear?"

"I feel like I just can't get through to you."

"Well, you don't have to try. I'm right here. Just relax. Remember, that's what you said you wanted to do. I understand that you just want me to be with you. And that's what I'm going to do now. I'm sorry that I was distracted today about the trip, and neglected you a bit."

"No, I wish you wouldn't try so hard. I wish you'd back away and give me some room." Her voice is tense because she is determined she will not sound like the Hysterical Woman, which she is fast feeling herself being fashioned into.

"Well, I wish you would make up your mind." He now permits himself a touch of self-righteous anger, (1) because he has so energetically and visibly and patiently been going the extra miles for her, and (2) because he has now isolated and targeted an identifiable flaw, her "inconsistency." "It isn't easy to take you seriously when you aren't being reasonable. You wanted attention and closeness, and now you don't."

"I can't do anything right, can I!" She has given up the battle against sounding "hysterical."

"You said it—I didn't."

The sleeping bag pillow talk is over. He goes off to sleep easily: triumphant, self-righteous. In his eyes he is reasonable, generous, caring, sensitive, and—above all—right. He has done his best for his crippled wife. In the morning he will be energetic and ready to greet all with a hearty attitude of "Come unto me all you who are upset. I am big enough to take care of all you little people." To Kim it will be, "You slept just fine, after all, didn't you, without the teddy. You are going to be daddy's big girl on this camping trip." To Tad it will be, "Let's see you start the fire the way I taught you." And to Jenny, of course, it will be "Feeling better this morning, honey?" Still impervious, still imperious, this crippler.

Jenny will sleep with an all-too-familiar fitfulness, her knees pulled up close under her chin. She now feels exactly as she said, "I can't do anything right, can I?" She has antagonized Bryan and made herself, as she sees it, look stupid and irrational, whining and needy. She feels inept, of course, because she couldn't keep her own in the conversation or make a point with Bryan; he kept the initiative and scored all the points. She feels as though she has no mind of her own right now, but has only been trying miserably to share his mind. She feels crippled.

She feels crippled because Bryan has practiced skillfully and expertly, even though entirely unconsciously, the arts of the crippler. He has learned these skills, as all men learn them, from watching other men working this craft with finesse, sometimes on him, all of this mixed in the cauldron of his own desperate need to stay on top and keep her down. Bryan has learned the skill of crippling so well that it might seem as if he's taken a course in crippling. If he had, the course might have had a textbook like the manual beginning on the next page.

MANUAL FOR CRIPPLERS

YOU-ING

You-ing is sometimes known as U-ing or as U-turning. It is as though you are holding a large double funnel with spouts that connect, both open ends pointing at the other person. Whatever the other person says is collected in the funnel and deflected back to him or her, without the words ever touching you. Sometimes it is called mirroring, because one of the very best shields is a large mirror. You become the mirror, never letting the other see you or touch you. The harder you are reached for, the more vigorously you point back. Keep attention at all times focused on the cripple-to-be. This is charitable and generous and sacrificial: I won't demand attention now; we can talk about you.

What you deflect or reflect back is never a direct response to what has been said or done. To do that is to make the mistake of engaging in direct confrontation when the point of this strategy is to stay above confrontation, to claim the high ground. For the same reason, the best response is never an uncomplimentary one. In fact, a primitive form of this strategy is to become excessively complimentary: a leering "You've got great legs" or "You've got a terrific shape" in response to whatever a woman says, or the slightly more artful "Your eyes flash beautifully when you're angry." This form is practically obsolete now, except in its most sophisticated version, "You excite me when you rage like that." (But this is the most dangerous version because it risks exposing too much of one's own reactions.)

An older and well-established technique, still practiced especially among older men, as it was by the Sheep Gate authorities who confronted the healthy man they saw as crippled, is the technique of dismissal-by-categorization: "There you are, showing yourself to be the X you are." X can be shrew, nag, castrator, hysteric, neurotic, cripple . . . These words are intended to be last words. They are used to dismiss the woman from your presence. One does this bit of mirroring while walking away. Dismissing while turning one's back and walking away is an accomplished act of bravado, like the bullfighter turning his back as a final insult to the crippled and vanquished bull, displaying not vulnerability but mastery and conquest.

As useful as you-ing is in personal relations, it has become massively established and rationalized in the professions; it is often combined with "helping" (see the next section). Think of the physician peering/leering at you from behind his bedside manner, a counselor from behind his nondirective counseling, a teacher from behind rules of discipline. The patient/client/student, the helpee by whatever label, must never see or touch you.

There are paradoxes and dangers involved in the art of you-ing. For one thing, you must be willing to risk what could seem like a disappearance of self. To use mirrors as shields, to keep initiative and attention focused on the woman is to keep attention from you; you do have to be willing to fade away from immediate visibility—all for the sake, of course, of remaining all the more hauntingly an imposing, if elusive, presence. Actually, you do have a kind of derived existence, a standing point that is always relative to her. In pushing against her, you are in a posture that is somewhat off balance and does depend on her. This kind of dependence is not necessarily damaging, so long as you can keep persistently pushing up against her. But that continuing need of someone to push against makes this behavior addictive. The crippler *needs* the crippled and needs the crippled to stay crippled. Who am I? I'm the reflector, the helper—that's not much identity unless there is always someone to reflect, someone to help. Not much more than: I'm a drinker, a junkie, a workaholic. (Of course, this self-denial helps you pose as the benign, sacrificial, even martyred hero: "Look, I'm not trying to get anything out of this. I'm only thinking about you." That is quintessential you-ing.)

The other paradox that needs to be understood by the artful practitioner of you-ing might at first seem inconsistent with the last paragraph, because it requires an emphasis on keeping your own point of view. It is important never to respond to anything in terms of what it means to the person who says it, but only in terms of what it means, or can be made to mean, to you. If she says, "I prefer a chocolate ice cream cone," you simply must not take this at face value; you don't just order a chocolate ice cream cone for her or let her do it unmolested. You must make it mean something to you: a challenge of your preference for vanilla; a commission to search out a better quality chocolate at another store; a challenge to your memory ("I *know* you like chocolate"); an occasion for a lecture on the process of producing chocolate, or a monologue on the greater calories and fat content of chocolate; an offer to help her change her unhealthy food choices; or an analysis of the peculiar psychological meanings of her preference; or some combination of these or other responses. All this must take her by surprise, have nothing to do with what she meant, and issue from you only as the basis for leverage against her. Keep some independent, even irrelevant perspectives as a solid bastion from which to assail her.

It helps to be right in you-ing, but that is by no means essential. The point, remember, is to maintain the initiative, the high ground, and the advantage without ever pressing for a showdown. One of the risks of permitting a showdown is that the other will employ some of these arts against you. The spectacle of two people you-ing each other is a living monument to talking-past, the initiative ricocheting back and forth in midair without ever coming to light on either side, a perpetual exile from sanity and human relating.

HELPING

Help her. You have the resources, the strength; she has the needs, the weaknesses. How better to claim the high ground and to define her as disadvantaged, as crippled?

She doesn't ask for help? Of course not. That is the point. She doesn't yet define herself as needy, as crippled. She needs to be taught to do that. That is precisely why you help—to teach her she needs help. The helping is what defines her need, your advantage and her disadvantage. Offer a crutch, a wheelchair, a lift into healing waters, and the other must therefore be a cripple, thereby is crippled. The prescription implies the diagnosis, solution defines the problem. Alms, unsought or sought, define and measure the poverty; explanation, the ignorance; forgiveness, the guilt; reassurance, the anxiety; help defines the need and neediness.

To the man thirty-eight years crippled by the Sheep Gate, Jesus' first words were "Do you want to get well?" These were uncrippling words, liberating words. They were such unfamiliar words—the opposite of crippling words, which the man had been hearing for thirty-eight years—that he didn't know how to respond to the question directly. They were uncrippling—and startling to the crippled—because they asked the man to define himself, to decide whether he was weak or strong, needy or resourceful, crippled or well. The uncrippler liberates by giving this choice to the crippled: you can decide. The crippler must never leave this choice to the crippled. The crippler helps *without asking*.

The cripplers by the Sheep Gate provided the water and the legend of healing that went with it and the lift into it and the porches to await the lift, all the helping paraphernalia for cripples. Physician, clergy, father, lawyer, psychotherapist, husband—all of these, all of us, define our roles in terms of the helping paraphernalia we offer, the technology of crippling: "Here's what I will do for you because you can't or you won't or you don't do it for yourself, or you bungle if you try."

In the perverse patter of our time, "You need help!" has become the angry putdown. That's the message the crippler wants to give, but never directly or explicitly. To diagnose need directly (You are delinquent in the way you drive . . . manage kids . . . think about politics . . .) would invite challenge and encourage defiance. The good crippler bypasses this risk by just giving the help. Same message—you need help—but wrapped up in a sweet, self-righteous, and unassailable cloak. Bryan smothered Jenny with his relentless helping, smothering just because he gave her no opportunity to confront directly the assault that his helping was. Bryan was a skilled, artistic helper.

The diagnosis implied in the crippler's help may be accurate or false. Some cripplers think it more devastating and unassailable to be sure to be on target, a precise rapier hit. The cripple feels the blow more keenly for recognizing its accuracy. But other cripplers prefer what is more like a club blow, feeling an inaccurate diagnosis is more damaging and more unassailable simply because more disconcerting. Any attempt to parry ("But I don't *need* more money. . . more hugging . . . more driving lessons . . . more advice . . .") just opens up more targets for helping: this newly displayed "petulance" or "resistance."

Here is the ambiguity that sabotages and saps the liberal's (for that is precisely what a helper is—a liberal) abundant energy and goodwill, the ambiguity that draws the huge line between being liberal and liberating, the ambiguity that, to the utter dismay and surprise of the liberal, eventually draws the attack of the very ones the liberal has been so steadfastly helping. The liberal parent, the liberal white, the liberal employer, the liberal middle-class, the liberal male, the liberal Westerner: the liberal needs a label for self and needs a target to contrast self with: child, black, employee, lower-class, woman, Third World inhabitant. That target, which shapes and defines the liberal's actions and role, must be needy or lower status. The liberal acts vigorously and with the best of intentions, and often with genuinely helpful effect, but this very activity, the very initiative is precisely what retains the power; it defines the liberal as up and the target as down, as crippled, as needy. The liberal may be absolutely accurate in defining the need, may be delivering precisely what the "target" does need and would ask for if given the chance. But, not given the chance to define self and needs, not given the initiative, the target is kept dependent, down, disadvantaged, crippled. In this ecology, liberal and target need each other, are in a mutual bond of dependence; whatever the target needs and gets, the liberal needs to retain the initiative, the power, the superiority and needs the target in order to define and retain these badges of identity. The liberal's identity—as is any crippler's, any man's—is so inextricably tied to this initiative ("I see what needs to be done and I do it!"), that the liberal is crushed and uncomprehending when the target finally rises up and says, "You liberals are our worst enemy because you undercut our initiative, keep us lying on the mats by soothing our pain."

The unrepentant liberal—the one who wants to stay "liberal" and not liberating—needs to be ready for this uprising by having some solicitous putdowns ready. The crippler must not heed and learn from this rebellion of the target but must be ready to define the rebellion as a further problem to be understood and the rebel as a cripple to be helped; it is the genuine liberator, the liberal's worst enemy, who would encourage the target to take the initiative. So the well-meaning, thoroughly religious authorities by the Sheep Gate, those whose life was structured in some part by having cripples to help, were quick to recognize the threat Jesus offered to them and were quick to find a new problem—carrying the mat on the Sabbath—in the crippled's uncrippling. They were ready to help the man get right with God by properly observing the Sabbath, in other words to remind him—as their alms and other acts of helping had done—that he was not now right. So the true crippler needs to have ready a repertory of responses to help the cripple quickly recover from any spontaneous uncrippling. "There, there, I know you're upset. Let me comfort you. You'll get over it." This is the infuriating but effectively smothering prototype for how to maneuver quickly onto higher ground again any time the crippled tries to rise up.

The most efficient and most effective form of crippling

probably is this technique of helping the other deal with you. "Admit" that your ideas may be hard to follow, your emotional reactions deep and complicated, your point of view unusual, or in some other way you are just too much. But you are willing and able to be oh-so-patient, oh-so-solicitous, oh-so-helpful in assisting her in catching up. This technique stakes out high ground twice, once as you innocently and gallantly "admit" to being part of the problem, and again as you offer to provide the solution. Bryan showed his mastery as a crippler with his artistic use of this "Oh I'm so sorry; I'll help you catch up" device.

A man's characteristic helping is insistent and imperious and vigorous—"Watch what I am doing to you and for you . . . and be grateful." It is more explicit than the woman's form of helping, which is usually more concealed. The man says out loud, in so many words and with visible gestures, "Your problem is . . . and I will help you get over it." The woman helper-crippler says much the same thing but says it to herself: "He is angry (or whatever) and I will do what I can to reduce his anger (or whatever)." So she may appease or defy or placate or apologize or reassure or counter-attack or in some other way treat him as she has learned to treat an angry man. Eventually he realizes he is being regarded as angry (or whatever) and, sooner or later, the treatment makes him so.

CON-DESCENDING

Establish your high ground by dramatizing the strenuous effort it takes to move down to where she is. You belong to the larger agendas of life, to the high realm, and she belongs to the lesser, the more trivial, and this can be made evident by the display of strenuous effort it costs you to bridge the distance. Your descent from on high is the opposite of the Christian's understanding of God's entry into human life, which comes quietly, effortlessly, as a surprise and as a gift. Instead, take as your model an Olympian deity arriving at the doorstep of a lucky chosen one, arriving weary and disgruntled, preoccupied with the journey and with the glories left behind, sitting down, pulling off boots laboriously, needing food and drink and a foot soak and a back rub, talking incessantly about how far he has come, the labors of his trip, requiring constant attention and grateful pampering.

You screech to a stop beside the stalled car, brandishing—even as you relinquish it—your car's power and headway. You reassure the woman inside, patiently. You flourish your own jumper cables (declining hers because "we need heavier cables" to carry the power your car has to give) and attach them with much further information about how important it is to make the right connections and make them tight. You impart more elaborate instructions on when and how to start the car at your signal. You lend calm reassurance when it fails at first, and more detailed instructions, then, after the car starts, still more instructions and reassurance about how to handle it from here on. It's a big deal to deliver the power from your car to hers even though, or maybe especially because, it looks so simple when the two cars are just sitting there side-by-side, equal. Your stop is a gift from on high.

You are part of the crowd by the Sheep Gate displaying your own upper-caste status of wellness, confirming the cripples as cripples by the elaborate way you measure the differences, all in the guise of coming closer, condescending. You sympathize, you offer alms with a flourish, you provide, benignly, special places for the cripples. You arrange systems, the more elaborate the better, for the cripples to be carried to the healing waters. Best, because most effortful, you do some of the carrying yourself. If the cripple shows any signs of walking or even crawling, trying to bridge the distance from that side and move toward your high ground, you bring in more insistent techniques of putting down. You provide better beds, more thorough segregation, more elaborate and more helpful regulations and instructions for care and for access to the healing waters.

You are Bryan coming down from the important business of

running the camping trip to attend to Jenny's concerns, and doing so with extreme patience and extreme solicitousness and extreme vigor.

You are slowly laying the papers on your desk, taking off your glasses, turning in your chair with great deliberate kindness to attend to the interrupter—all the gestures calculated to cast the other *as* interrupter in the elaborately gentle and sweet way you receive her.

You are the physician turning from the esoteric huddle at the foot of the bed to explain excessively elaborate half-truths and to withhold others. "Now, little lady, here's what we think is happening and what we will do . . ." You are the keeper of the last things, the first things, the best things. The tracks down from on high must be very visible but not accessible. This is one-way traffic. There is no invitation back up.

You are professor, lawyer, engineer, minister, automobile mechanic, skilled in the arts of explaining, elaborately explaining, never in ways that admit the other as a partner in the information but in ways that establish yourself as the custodian and expert and keep the other crippled, succumbed.

You help your young protégé get a job or initiate the newcomer at your place of work, but never behind the scenes, always right on stage, always in ways that insist on the message: you are the protégé. You are the newcomer. You are the one needing my coaching.

It is never enough just to be absent from home to participate in the higher realm of the bowling league, or even to talk enthusiastically about the bowling game. It is necessary, as a condescender, to explain, patiently and laboriously, the rules for scoring. It is not enough to keep the TV sports on, or even enough to cheer, in her hearing, names and events she can't recognize. It is necessary to teach her about these, patiently of course, to make clear her difficulty in understanding.

It is important, at the end of the day, to talk about your world of work or politics or whatever. But never as you would at the bar, trading quips and gossip and complaints as fellow members of the club. It is necessary to teach her about the mechanisms of work and explain the significance of events, as one would to a novice or an outsider—which, of course, is the intention and the message.

KNOWING

Knowing, explaining, having an answer—always, even when questions are not asked—having the last word: these, like all crippling, are basically defensive strategies, protecting yourself, displaying control of yourself. No good general defending high ground is ever taken by surprise, or at least never admits to it. Whatever happens, you have a word for it, a category, an explanation. Something in your head, in your ken, can absorb, package, wrap, control. You are unassailable because your understanding is never at a loss. You know.

As with any defensive strategy, however, this knowing, suitably refined, can readily become aggressive; it can belittle, cripple, down. Knowing becomes no-ing. Just add to the message "I know" the simple putdown "You should know and you don't know."

Like jiujitsu, like all the crippling devices, your move is to receive and absorb any energy of hers and change it into your energy in order to keep her off balance. She exclaims with delight, "Listen to that lovely bird call!" You answer, patiently, "Yes, it's a warbler." It's that simple.

Or perhaps the model is the chess player who knows how to absorb your moves and make them work against you. Or perhaps the model is simply the habitual liar who, once launched on a private perception of reality, undertakes to explain away all possible contradictions, in ways to make you feel wrong for your contradiction.

The light touch is best. As with the skillful practice of all the crippling arts, make your move unobtrusively, delicately; keep your move from becoming visible and hence less challengeable. Your own moves as crippler must be as stealthy as possible so that the attention, the onus, the burden of proof remains on the crippled one. She (or he, if you are dealing with an employee or son or other male cripple-to-be) must remain center stage, defects under constant scrutiny, a clear target. You remain sheltered by heavy cover and protected by fast footwork. So the knowing remark is always given in as off-hand a way as possible, while gazing distractedly into space (demonstrating that you have been distracted by her from something more remote and more important). Use as drab, as droning, as matter-of-fact a tone as possible (making clear, without resorting to a sneer, that the information is something everybody has except, apparently, her). Snap back just as quickly as possible after her remark (again illustrating the ordinariness of the knowledge—if it doesn't require any reflection, of course it's something everybody knows). Speak slowly and deliberately (so that such teaching or coaching can further deliver the message that she does not yet know something you do know).

She looks out the airplane window and blurts, "We're coming down. The trees are getting bigger!" You reply—immediately, patiently, and matter-of-factly—"The pilot lowered the wheels about five minutes ago" or "Right on schedule; we're suppose to land in eight minutes." Her delight and her discovery must be immediately absorbed and neutralized and somehow made cause for mild discomfort and humiliation.

If you need coaching or modeling of these techniques, visit the nearest mental hospital and try to talk to a diagnosed paranoid schizophrenic. This person has an airtight, foolproof system of ideas, and whatever you say gets absorbed into it and fed back to you in some way shaped by this system of ideas. Everything that you say is taken for what it is made to mean to that person, not for what it means to you. Even your casual remarks about the weather or about the route you took to get to the hospital may be answered in some knowing, private way ("Yes, I expected clouds today" or "You know why they number that road Route 66, don't you?"). This person knows something about these matters and conveys this in a way that vaguely expects you should know it too, but you don't and can't. Uncomfortable as you feel, trying to run to catch up, you are saved from feeling stupid only by your knowing that this person is crazy and locked up, and you are not. Suppose you met this person on the plane or at work or at home and could not readily discount this talking-past as this person's craziness; you might eventually come to suppose it was your craziness. That's the idea: know another into crippledness.

She says, "I feel tired," and you say, "I noticed those vitamin pills were getting out of date."

She says, "Nuts. The milk is going sour in the refrigerator . . . everything's warm in here!" You reply calmly and matter-of-factly, "Those coils get clogged up with dust and grime and need to be vacuumed off." To know is to discount and to dismiss immediately and fully whatever meaning and importance her remarks have for her.

She says, "I wish we could get away for a week at Christmas." It doesn't matter whether you approve or disapprove of her idea. What does matter is that you immediately reclaim the initiative by knowing, by advancing considerations she should have thought of but didn't. "That will be a good time because we'll have that extra check in December." Or, "Don't you remember how crowded things get then?" Rejecting her idea for reasons she should have thought of is an elementary form of knowing. More advanced cripplers can endorse her idea but still make her feel chagrined, incomplete, and humiliated about the way she introduced it. It is a real art to utter what could sound like supporting partnership—"We'll have an extra check in December"—in a way that snatches away ownership of the proposal and belittles her form of it.

The crippler has an instant retort ready for any intrusion of another's spontaneity or surprise, whether despair or delight, discovery or loss.

BLAMING THE VICTIM

What could keep a man lying flat on his mat for thirty-eight years within yards of swirling healing waters, apparently resigned to living out his life in that posture? (That's a question you don't even ask until you come, like Jesus, to see health as the norm and crippledness as the surprise, the mystery, the puzzle.) He must feel, at bottom, that this is what he deserves, his fate. He *is* a cripple. Anything else is wrong for him—an internalized form of the crippling challenge the man in fact encountered from the Sheep Gate authorities as soon as he dared to walk upright. He must have a low view of himself, which his posture acts out, the same low view that keeps people fearful and uncomfortable with success, with love, with health. "I wouldn't want to belong to a club that would have me as a member." I am so low I must be suspicious of and keep my distance from anyone that would reach down to me, even to pick me up. (Notice that Jesus did no such thing. He merely said Get up.)

This is the cripple's state of mind, a self-image that accepts, even welcomes, even seeks crippledness. This is the state of mind that the crippler wants to induce, the state of mind that can do the work of crippling, all by itself.

In the litany of self-abuse that cripplers teach and cripples learn, "sick" and "bad" are closely linked. The ill are sinners, and so are the unemployed, the raped, the bombed, the exiled, and all other victims. "Whose sin caused him to be born blind? Was it his own or his parents' sin?" This was the only question Jesus' disciples had about a blind man they saw in an incident told a few chapters after the encounter at the Sheep Gate was told (John 9:2). Jesus' answer ("His blindness has nothing to do with his sins or his parents' sins," John 9:3) was no more welcome to that crowd of cripplers than was his abrupt permission to the cripple by the Sheep Gate to get off his mat. The uncrippler uncouples the plight and the person. The crippler welds them. Bad plights: bad persons. Not just You are crippled, but You are a cripple. Any low blow proves the person's low estate. The crippler must always blame the victim.

The unemployed are lazy; the raped, provocative; the bombed, enemies; the injured child, careless; the exiled, troublemakers; the unfinished typist, inefficient. A carton of milk going sour? You should have checked the date before you bought it, or you should have defrosted the refrigerator so it would work properly. Faucet still dripping? Why didn't you tell me when I had my tools out? Annoyed by the kids' noise? You need to get used to it or plan schedules better. Not getting well fast enough? You must not have been taking the pills the way the doctor told you.

Simple and straightforward—whatever befalls, however it might be legitimately attributed, the good crippler must promptly attribute it to the blameworthiness of the victim: blame the victim.

But the genuinely artful crippler specializes not just in blaming *the* victim. Instead, blame *your* victim! Don't wait for something else to befall. Do it all yourself, in a two-stage process: first you injure or threaten or intimidate or squelch or overpower or otherwise cripple, then you blame your victim.

Bryan frightened Kim into wanting her teddy, then scolded her for this symptom of her fright. He frightened his family stiff, then blamed them for their stiffness when they posed for their photograph. Make a person feel baffled, cornered by your bluster, unsure how to move, how to respond. Then blast them for their unsureness, their befuddlement. Make a woman too defensive, too angry, too frightened to be warm or attentive, then blast her for her coldness. Victimize, cripple. Blame the victim. Soon she will be blaming herself and victimizing, crippling herself.

The general principle in all of this is that you are big and the other is little, that you are trustworthy and the other is not, that you are up and the other is down, that you are strong and the other is weak, that you are right and the other is wrong.

It is best not to be too inventive, but rather use familiar and well-tested devices, because these get the message across best. Do not be embarrassed about using the identical phrases and techniques over and over again, every day, or even in the same conversation. The fact that they have worked once only adds to their effectiveness: the other remembers that she has crumbled before and so has no reason not to crumble again. Innovative practices might make her hesitate. Better to keep the automatic, knee-jerk reactions, once she is trained. Anyway, remember that you are the master, and what you say goes.

Above all, keep the high ground. The goal is not to win— that would bring things into focus and bring about an overt confrontation and resolution. The goal is to claim and defend the high ground. The other must feel disadvantaged, looking up, fearing that she would lose if she pressed the attack. (In fact she might not lose, and that is one reason you must avoid the direct confrontation.) Your cool aplomb, your staying above the fray, avoiding the direct confrontation, is one of the ways of establishing the high ground. You need to make clear that you are not in the arena where the grubby contests go on, but in the emperor's box, chief among the spectators, appraising the combat, delivering a thumbs-up or thumbs-down judgment about the performances and the fate of a combatant.

Keep the contest constantly at game point, with you holding the "advantage." The dis-advantaged one dare not make a single mistake—and because of the pressure probably will— or the game will be over and she will lose. The advantaged one has no such risk. That *is* the advantage, the high ground. Keep the long volley going, with you advantaged and she disadvantaged.

6. Up-manship

"Maybe I'm just not a good parent." Judith is looking at the floor, not at me. "Maybe I just should never have had children. I can't seem to get in touch with them. I can't seem to give them what they need, whatever that is."

Everything deep within me wants to surrender my place behind the desk, sit beside her, maybe on the floor with my head in her lap, and moan, "Me too. I know, I know." Her words speak my mood, my mood more often than I care to admit. Her words call up scenes with my daughters, scenes from which I have turned away with the same anguish she now dares to speak aloud. Her words call up that head-down feeling I often have at the end of an hour conversation like this, when I feel I am sending people away as needy as they were when they came. Something tugs in me, urging me to let go of my posture as helper and to share, at least for the moment, her posture of helplessness. Something tugs in me, urging me to honor the honest despair in me that her despair touches. Something tugs in me, urging me to break out and admire her strengths, her honesty, her courage, her caring.

But I dare not. There are rules and scripts. Her part is to break down. My part is to hold up, to stay on top of things, to stay together. Her helplessness assigns me to be the helper— unless (banish the thought) it is the other way around: could it be that my helping assigns her to be helpless? Or is it that we are both cast in these fixed complementary roles by coercions prior to, and stronger than, the assignments we give each other?

I remember the impatience of the customers, mine foremost, the barely subdued rage of those in line at the bank this morning. "The computer is down," the teller shrugged. "There's nothing we can do." The computer is down. But the computer should be up, so that we can go away with what we came for, our passbooks updated and our wallets replenished. When the computer is down, we are cheated and we fume. Judith is down, but I must be up. Judith is down, *so* I must be up (unless—that haunting fear again—I am up, so Judith must be down). I dare not cause Judith to fume or to go away unreplenished. So the very fear I yearn to speak—that *I* may be an inadequate "parent" to Judith—keeps me mute.

Not just mute, but really hiding myself and faking my feelings. Not just not-down, but up: competent, insightful, helpful, on top of everything, performing, performing well; all of the promises that I suppose she supposes I have made to her. All of the promises that I suppose my teachers and mentors and role models suppose I have made to them in joining their profession. All of the promises I suppose that God supposes I have made in accepting this calling. These are not rules of my making. They are not rules I would make. They are rules that I barely accept. But I do obey them: perform coolly and competently. Be an effective helper.

For the promises exacted as a professional helper are only updated renewals of the promises long since exacted of me as a man. Long before the gauntlet of the down Judiths supposedly demanding an up helper, and long before the gauntlet of teachers, mentors, and role models summoning me to professional competence, there was the gauntlet, to be run from infancy through adolescence and still, clamoring "Be a man." And that means very simply "Be up."

Their voices are now my own. "Batter up: You're up, kid! Look 'em over! Make him pitch to you! Take your cuts! Lean into it! Score!" Either score or walk away, suddenly invisible, shrouded by masked disappointment, the shun that passes as a shrug. There was no middle ground between being up and being downed. In fact there was nothing except being up. Either fling yourself off that high diving board with the rest or slink away humiliated. "Now try to get your speed up."

It's just a blending of the voices of Mr. Cornell, my track coach, and Mrs. Simpson, my piano teacher. But the message is the same: your performance is not good enough, get it up. So blend in all the other voices: "You're too old for training wheels, you can keep the bike up." "Stand up and recite." "Keep your grades up." "Get up there in front and speak your piece in a loud voice." "Tighten your lips, get up to those high notes on the trumpet." "Can you stay up on that horse, like John Wayne?" "Do your push-ups!" "Wake up!" "Chin up!" "Grow up." "Measure up."

I want to level with Judith. I want to mingle my despair and my fear with hers in common search and in a blend of emerging mood of trust. But the faces in her face, the voices in her voice don't permit leveling. It is either up or out. (Interesting that I work for an institution that makes "up or out" the cardinal career principle: either perform and get promoted or disappear.)

A memory: I am at a carnival, and all the boys are lined up to do combat with a machine. You conquer a spring-loaded steel lever, pressing it down, all the way down to its platform, and you ring a bell. If you are a man, you do that. The girls are ringed around, a relentless jury. When the bell rings, the eyes are alight and the bodies aquiver and the voices warm and seductive. When not, the eyes are narrow, the bodies stiff, the voices silent, masking a giggle. Or, more cruel, the voices are "comforting." On top or else. Prove. Win. Perform.

I don't want to be bewitched by that quivering circle of bobbed hair and bobbing halter tops into supposing that my mission now is to ring Judith's chimes. But they cast a strong spell, they and whomever it is they speak for, whatever powers they serve as priestesses. I think of Jesus in the wilderness, tempted three times by the devil to perform; he was able to say simply, There is more to life than such performance. I think of Jesus' stern reply when Peter urged him to stay away from the risks of Jeruselem (Peter who was so quick later to be coward and also so quick to brandish his sword—is there a connection?) Peter's voice joins the chorus of my adolescence, Don't let failure or death happen to you. I want to join Jesus in his reply, "Get away from me, Satan! You are an obstacle in my way, because these thoughts of yours don't come from God, but from man." (Matthew 16:23) Did Jesus have Coach Cornell and Mrs. Simpson and the bevy of quivering priestesses to contend with? Is that who he was talking to while he was looking at Peter and calling him Satan? Could I do that? Where is the Peter I can tell off and break the spell? It probably has to be a woman. But it can't be Judith. The spell is strong, and in my conversation with Judith, I live it out. I stay up. I perform, cleverly and smoothly and helpfully.

I will show you how.

But first there is one more memory to confess—a deep, primitive memory—for it too is present, powerfully present, in the room with Judith, keeping me up. Or maybe it's only the memory of a fantasy, or maybe the memory of other's stories and fantasies, or maybe a memory somehow planted in my manhood at my conception—it's the paradigm, the persistent haunting paradigm, the plot of all the scripts, all the more excruciating and unmitigated, all the more potent, for being a memory even before it happened. Except that it did happen, over and over again, in my head and eventually, I guess, in a bed. For it is in bed, it is in sex, sex with a woman, that the stakes are exquisitely high, as every boy senses long before he knows what he is supposed to do about it; up or out, perform or disappear. Performance is measured against competition never seen and by standards mysterious, elusive, and totally in possession of the woman. Standards never known, so never attained. "How was it?" of course, means "How did I do?" Did I reach, did I fill, did I last—enough? How did I do? Was I tender enough? Passionate enough? How did I do? With manhood always on test and never proven—no wonder the attempts to prove manhood go on and on.

STAYING UP BY TAKING CHARGE AND COACHING

"Maybe I'm just not a good parent," Judith says. "Maybe I just should never have had children. I can't seem to get in touch with them. I can't seem to give them what they need, whatever that is." Something in me wants to level with Judith, to honor her despair and my own. Much in me wants to honor the strength in her honesty and caring. Get behind me, Satan. But I dare not, not this time at least. I stay up, up in the habitual way, stiffly behind my desk, in charge of myself, of her, and of the situation. Something deeper in me than the best of me, more sovereign than rational, like knocking on wood, or any other magical ritual or superstition or compulsion. I feel anxious—God knows I wish I didn't—if I don't keep to the habit, to the ritual, to the script.

There are lots of scripts for staying up, for staying in charge, for performing visibly and well. I could reassure: "I'm sure you're a good parent." I could pronounce: "All parents of teenagers feel that way." I could diagnose: "Your children are getting so tall, it may begin to make you feel insignificant." I could prescribe: "Maybe you need to get better acquainted, maybe with a regular family time together before supper." I could refer: "I know a counselor who is good with helping parents of teenagers." I could capture and absorb: "I'm planning to lecture about this in three weeks. Why don't you come?" Maybe I'll use one or more of these devices later. But for now I choose a more subtle prescription, *my* tested, impervious up-posture, "Why don't you tell me about it." Not: "Why don't you talk about it." The "me" is important.

Whatever else any of these remarks may or may not do, they all are part of the repertory for getting across one message: "You need me." But the message of that message, like all men's strutting, is: I'm not impotent, not an imposter, not a cripple, not a little kid. Or, perhaps more precisely: Don't think me so. And undoubtedly the message behind that message is: I too often fear myself to be impotent, imposter, cripple, little kid.

For all those messages drilled in through the years were really a double message: (1) You must measure up; and (2) You can't measure up. You *must* play well, prove, perform, win the race, ring the chimes; but of course *you* won't. The inevitable, insidious oppressing (up-pressing) of the "law," with its impossible scripts. How pathetic the irony that I, victim of such oppression, now pass it along to Judith. Struggling to prove myself, to get up, as the scripts require, and as the scripts prevent, I struggle against her. I must *push* myself up—the scripts' expectations are too unreachable for them to help me *pull* myself up—and I must push down against whoever is at hand. This time it happens to be Judith. Not grossly, not cruelly, hardly even noticeably, so accustomed are we to the standard ways for men to treat women, and—what often amounts to the same thing—the standard ways for professionals to treat clients. I push Judith down, so I can be up. I stake out the highest ground I can find over her. I will be the helper, *her* helper.

I could have foresaken the high ground. I could have shared, genuinely shared her feelings. ("I think I know that helpless feeling, when you think there's something to be done and you're just not doing it, because I have that feeling a lot, too.") I could have admired her vigor and honesty. ("It must take a lot of guts to say those things about yourself. You must really care and you must have been thinking about this a lot.") Sometimes I can do that. But this time I seem determined to stay up and be her helper: "Why don't you tell me about it."

"Richard, my oldest, has been cutting school a lot. I can't sem to get him to understand his responsibilities. He's good at school, but he just seems to like to thumb his nose at school authorities, the way he does at me sometimes."

"How long has this been going on?" To follow a script, to accumulate points to check, to nurture the feeling of getting somewhere, getting ahead, I go for the easy data, the quick kill: probing instead of listening, facts instead of feelings. I focus on Richard, the more remote one, and hence available to talk about, instead of Judith who is right here, hurting. Both master and victim of my checklist agenda, I know I am coming on strong, and I regret it as I say it, yet I can't help myself. It's like making the trivial dinner party small talk that you hate yourself for later, because it is small talk instead of a more meaningful encounter, but it generates its own momentum just because it is small talk, refuge from the more risky big talk or the anonymity of silence. Some part of me feels on the spot with Judith, like I feel on the spot at such a dinner party. Some part of me feels on the spot with any problem about being a parent. Some part of me feels on the spot with any problem about relations with authority. Some part of me feels helplessly on the spot with any problem as large as Richard's sounds. So I narrow down the problem to make it manageable and claim the initative, "How long has this been going on?"

"Well, the school called me about the cutting just last week. But I have never been sure that I have had his respect, even when he was very little." Her two-part answer gives me clear choices: I can be open to the searching and the starkly unanswerable pain of being a parent, gnawing at her for years. Or I can stick to the more immediate and narrow practical problem, something more manageable, and therefore something I can be up on. I can be open, or I can be up on. The best in me wants to be open. But those voices that gnaw at me—"Be a man"; "Are you a man?"—not at all unlike the eroding demands and questions she feels—make me move to stay up and aim at what is most solvable.

The best in me, that in me which trusts in God's healing sovereignty over all of these impossible and painful dilemmas, hers and mine, wants to be as open and as vulnerable and as honest and as reflective as I am expressing in the writing of these pages. But that in me which, with Judith and on the spot, feels the need to prove (to whom?) my manhood, and somehow still chronically mistrusts it, that part of me which still needs to be my own man, has to focus on what I can manage, what I can be up on. The best in me wants to invite, "I know how painful it is to be haunted, all the time, 24 hours a day, by that question of whether you're a good enough parent, whether your child respects you." But to do that is to throw myself into a void, which is more than I dare risk. So I hang on and manage. I stay up. Instead of inviting, I pronounce, "Maybe there's something going on in school these days that particularly upsets him. Have you talked with him or the teachers?"

Instead of staying with her feelings of inadequacy, I further challenge her. Instead of confessing my own fear of crippledness, as I am trying to do in these pages, as an offering toward her healing, I don my own mask of wholeness in a move that only confirms and engorges her fear of crippledness. Judith's tentative unfolding of her own fears and vulnerability is like a delicate butterfly, just emerging, to be admired and encouraged. In spite of myself, I pinion it for my collection—"See what I have!" ". . . something going on in school . . . talked with him or the teachers . . ."

But the life and trust in her is not so easily quenched. She gives me another chance. Despite my refusal of her offer to share herself and her fears deeply, she makes the offer again. Despite my need to make a project out of Richard's immediate school problems, she is still willing to venture into the chronic and unsolvable dilemmas of living out her role and responsibility under fear and harassment. "It's not easy to talk to those teachers. I don't think they think I'm such a hot parent either. They keep asking me questions—like you just did: Have you talked to Richard about this? Or have you tried that?"

Again she gives me a choice of being open, risky, responsive, vulnerable, genuinely helpful—dealing with her gnawing fears—or of playing it close and safe—dealing with my project. I can lose myself in my attempt to be of service to her. Or I can lose

Judith and her yearnings and fears. I can try to respond to her remark in terms of what it most deeply means to her, or I can respond on my own terms. My attention now is on my project of solving, by remote control, Richard's truancy. "Oh, I'm sure the teachers would be glad to talk with you. I know they must recognize you as an intelligent and concerned parent. You won't have any trouble; you can do it." Salvation (mine) by project (mine). The infantry captain leading the charge. The football coach at halftime.

How quickly have I become committed to—hooked on—this project of analyzing and solving Richard's truancy. I seem to need a fix, at least daily, of being a fixer. And in this case I need Judith's cooperation to do my fixing and get my fix. So compelled, I compel her on. Admiral Richard E. Byrd relentlessly driving on his dogs and his men, with single-minded intensity. The Kennedy family closing ranks and narrowing all energies toward the triumphant election. Rocky or the Raging Bull training, training, training, driving, driving, driving toward the prizefight. The detective mobilizing all his wits to solve the crime. The good shepherd leaving all to save the one lost lamb. The cowboy recklessly risking all in the leap onto the runaway stagecoach horses. The professor absent-minded to all save one idea, one concept. Are these not the heroes who have shaped my life, and all men's? Is it any wonder that this is how I play the role with Judith, no matter how much I know—as I am trying to remind myself in these pages—that true helping is not in these heroics, and real manhood is not in being seduced by the anxious siren calls of America's frontier culture.

I cannot wrest free from the harness of "manhood" to achieve an honestly helping relationship with Judith. My enlistment of Judith in my project—gentle, supportive, well-intentioned as my enlistment is, masquerading as it does in the guise of enlisting myself in her service—is still just what it is: my enlistment of Judith in my project. This is what I have learned that a man, a leader, does. This is the male model of success.

This is what people admire and expect. This is what I—that part of me shaped by these people—admire and expect of myself. This is *man*aging, *man*ipulating, *man*euvering. Bring me a problem; I bring you the solution. What else?

What else, indeed? There could be a helping response that stood with Judith, not over her, joined her, a response modeled by one—the God of the New Testament—who surrendered the conventional macho notions of Godhood and manhood and priesthood, and became incarnate in the lives of people as they are.

"FOLLOW ME"

My words—"you can do it"—masquerade as support, as putting Judith up. And they would be if talking with the teachers were her proposal, something she wanted to do but felt timid about. But talking with the teachers was not her proposal, it was mine. That is the slight difference that makes all the difference in the world. It is so slight that my coaching can masquerade as being in her service, as enabling her and her goals. If you would interrupt at this point in the conversation and ask Judith and me, both of us might really believe that talking with the teachers was her idea, her goal. I would believe and remember it that way because I need to disguise my own manipulation and play the humble servant. And Judith, for her own reasons, also needs to disguise my manipulation, needs to retain some sense of initiative. She also may well need to preserve the illusion that I, the counselor, am different from other men and more genuinely helpful and less manipulative—even as the subtle choreography in which we both are so well trained casts us in the traditional roles. Saviors, when they are mere men, do need to be saved, and women do spend a lot of energy, mental and otherwise, endowing and preserving their saving qualities. So both of us might now think of talking to teachers as her task, a task in which I am assisting her.

But in fact it is not a task of her choosing. Slight as the difference is, and slight as both Judith and I may need to try to keep it, there is a crucial difference between her wanting to talk to the teachers and my suggesting it. It puts me out in front—up—as the leader, and puts her behind—down—as the follower. Choosing Judith's task for her is just as primitive a custom as the custom that the woman walk behind the man . . . or follow the man's lead in dancing, be the passenger in the car he is driving, cook and serve what he likes to eat, live near where he works, adapt her conversation and way of life to his, defer to his wisdom and follow his advice on important questions.

For me to take the lead gives her only two options: she can follow or she can resist. But in either case the question has now subtly shifted to become one of her capacity and willingness to follow my lead. Now the question is not about her relationship with Richard or her relationship with the teachers, but about her relationship with me. We have begun to negotiate and jockey about our relative positions, hers and mine. She has come in to talk about being a good parent, a good leader, and somehow in a few exchanges with me it has become a question of how well and whether she follows me. As a counselor I am like that, because men are like that. We cast others, especially women, in follower roles, because we are cast in leader roles. Then we coach them to be good followers and diagnose bad following as a problem. (I wrote a whole book recently, doing just that, defining bad following as a problem, *When the People Say No*; it is a good book, a helpful book, but a book that does just that.) Neither of us wants this when we stop to think about it. But the casting is as though in bronze.

Judith has a choice of following, in effect abandoning the concerns she came to me with, and adopting my agenda, assuming the concerns and needs I attribute to her—or of feeling guilty for not following. This will give her one more instance of the kind of experiences she has had all of her life, the kind of experiences that contribute precisely to any reluctance to assume initiative with schoolteachers or to assume a confident parental role. She will be reinforced in the all-too-familiar posture of being down, because of my all-too-familiar posture of being up.

The best in me really wants to intervene in a way that will allow her to break her restricting harness and change her crippled posture. But I am in harness and am cast in a hobbled posture myself.

In fact, Judith does find room to assert a shred of autonomy. What she says next is, "I'm not sure that's really the move I want to make next." This is the second time she has backed off from my suggestion that she talk to the teachers. Perhaps she chooses not to follow because something in her recognizes that following me at this point would be bad for her, just as something in me recognizes that leading is bad for me. I am reminded of a small kitten (even the analogy is a putdown) who is being "taught" to play with a string. And the kitten, far from throwing its energies into this new realization of its "kittenhood," uses all its energies to resist, to pull away from this manipulation—as though something in it recognizes that its kittenhood depends far more on its autonomy than on its refinement right now of the skill of batting at a dangling string. I am reminded of the Little League baseball player who shuts his ears to the coach's harangue—"Choke up on the bat, stand farther back in the box, keep your eye on the ball, hold your bat off the shoulder! . . ."—because he recognizes that learning to bat, not to mention learning to be, is going to be better achieved by solving each of these problems at his own pace, even at the risk of blunders and humiliation, rather than by shaping himself immediately to the coach's specifications; in one case he will learn to bat, and in the other case he will learn to shape himself to another's specifications.

By pushing my project I have compelled her to deal with me and my pushing as a new problem in her life, not a big problem, but the one she now has to deal with here and now; she deals with it effectively by gently pushing back. What she most needs to hear from me now is some support for this courageous and resilient bid for autonomy.

Perhaps Judith chooses not to follow because she is aware that she knows more about the situation and the people involved, and may very well have better intuitions about its dynamics than I do. This, despite the fact that it is hard for either of us to acknowledge her basically greater wisdom in this regard, because she is cast in the helpee's role and I am cast in the helper role, down and up, woman and man.

HER RELUCTANCE: WEAKNESS OR STRENGTH?

So when Judith says that she doesn't wish to talk with the teachers, this could be a simple statement of her own preference and judgment. But in my helper—up—role, I take it as a confession of timidity, the plea of a cripple. So I say, "Do you generally have trouble taking this kind of initiative with others, maybe especially with people in authority that you don't know well?" This seems a plausible and natural inference, given the basic "up" assumptions which I am so ready to make, assumptions that (1) the strategy I suggest is a good one, and (2) any difficulties that arise are due to her inadequacies.

But consider a very different possibility. Suppose it is like a man asking a woman to a dinner date she doesn't really want. She is trained, of course, to decline diplomatically and gratefully, so as not to offend him. "I have too much work to do." "I haven't a thing to wear." Or the all-purpose "I'm too tired." Or, as Judith actually said, "I'm not sure that is the move I want to make next." In a social situation that is usually enough, and the man backs off. Only the most macho boor would persist to help her out of her difficulty so she can make good his plans for her to have dinner with him. "I'll help you with your work." "Here's some money to buy a dress." or "Let's have coffee before dinner; that will revive you."

Only the most macho boor would persist in that way. But that is what I do with Judith. My responses have followed easily and naturally from the assumption that I am up and she is down. My responses have tragically reinforced that assumption. My responses have followed naturally from the way that men most easily and most often perceive women: as lesser, as crippled, as defective, as needing men to complete and heal, as the poor drivers, the poor thinkers, the passive and untutored sex partners.

That men are up and women are down is an idea as fixed, pervasive, and ineradicable as, once, were the ideas that the world is flat, that the sun revolves around the earth, and that each species is created fully evolved. These firm impressions as to how things are, are impressions that religionists have been the last to hold onto. Here I am, in spite of "knowing better," giving full voice and vigor to male up-ness and female down-ness. The attitude is planted in the genes by a sociological DNA and needs some recombinant gene splicer to undo and redo. Might as well try to train the cat not to pounce on the mouse. Or try to train the mother cat not to wash and nurse her helpless kittens, fight to protect them, and carry them off to a safe place if she feels threatened. Men treat women with some combination of the pouncing and the protecting. And so professionals treat their people: I am up and you are down. Whatever happens, you will be the needy one, the crippled one, and I will be the helper, the savior. You the consumer, I the provider; you the receiver, I the transmitter. It is as though I cannot see you—us—any other way. It is a kind of scapegoating, blaming the victim. Whatever happens, you are to blame. Whatever happens, it is, of course, due to your neediness, crippledness, deficiencies. But that's all right, because whatever happens I can remedy.

Or is it the other way around: whatever happens I can remedy, therefore whatever happens must be a sign of your crippledness. Whatever a woman does gets the response, "Here, let me help you." Whatever a client does gets a professional response, "Here, let me help you." Servanthood converted to the needs of the helper. Like the flourish, the self-conscious and self-attentive and self-serving flourish, with which men (used to?) scurry to open doors, help off trains, or steer along sidewalks—breaking step, interrupting conversations, dropping a companionable interlocking of arms, sometimes even shouldering the woman—just so the man can maintain himself in the right place, and keep her in her place. Abandoning the natural relationship, he has to lead, to protect, to stay in charge.

This is what I do with Judith. I know better than this. I really do. But I still do this. Is it some anger in me that makes me attempt to degrade others, strip them of initiative and common sense and strength and parity with me, the subtle, mean, jealous, castrating father? Is it, more plainly, gnawing insecurities in me that compel me to exaggerate and distort whatever real talents and legitimate mission I have to help? Am I simply wearing blinders and harnessed up to the lumbering social machinery that requires me, if I am to belong at all, to be one of those cogs that behaves this way? Is this machinery fueled by entrenched hates and fears?

THE UP ADDICT

What does go on inside the head of the man in these moments of up-manship? How does it feel to be so addicted to being up? Getting up is like getting a fix, a drug high after feeling down or tense. It's like coming home to the familiar, the comfortable, the safe, after a time abroad where one felt among aliens, unplaced and unrecognized. That moment when she acknowledges the relative postures: "Yes, you are right, I am weak or needy or at fault"—that's a moment of harboring, relaxation, back in role again, home. Without his up-ness acknowledged, the up-addict feels unknown, at sea, stripped of identity, feels like he is walking alone in a mob of strangers, or walking into a party without recognizing anyone, or like reading a book upside down or through foggy glasses. Like playing in a ball game or a card game with unknown rules, like playing music without a recognizable meter. It feels jarring, it feels like "not me." Then when she plays the role that gives me my familiar role, that *is* like getting a fix, like suddenly surfacing from under water and gulping air, like stumbling out of a dark cave into sunlight. As soon as she confesses her weakness, makes herself vulnerable, opens herself, then there is a place for me—the sexual overtones are hardly accidental—and until she does, there isn't.

As I think on how I felt talking to Judith, I half-remember—or perhaps I am inventing a myth to express my own fears of humiliation—a cartoon joke of a Boy Scout offering to help an old lady across the street, and she replies with an indignant, withering swing of her purse, "Keep your hands off of me, you masher!" I suppose I fear feeling like that Boy Scout, rejected from playing that role which is habitual, assigned, comfortable, required, responsible, "me": helping Judith with her problems. My role requires her to play a reciprocal role— it takes two to play "helping"—and if she declines, then I am left stranded, feeling "not me," rejected and rebuked simply for doing what seemed my natural duty. It feels like being called out while I am standing safely on the assigned base. I want to defend myself by attacking the attacker; "Why are you so unfairly attacking me?" Among good helpers, this takes the form of diagnosing her reaction as a new problem, and offering to help with it—as though the Boy Scout whips out a straitjacket to help this insane, raging woman. What else is one to do when stripped of role, and therefore stripped of identity?

As I reflect on how I felt in this conversation with Judith— and also on how she must have felt—I remember how my conversations with lawyers usually go. Whether the question concerns real estate, or taxes, or a will, or whatever, the conversation almost always falters in the same way: I have a specific and well-defined question about which I need advice. I do not want to review the whole transaction and all the legal issues concerned with the real estate or will or whatever, because I do not want to pay high hourly rates for the lawyer to discuss questions I already understand, and because I am quite ready to take responsibility for the overall transaction. But the lawyer seems to have a fixed agenda and check-list for handling any case like mine, "Give me all the papers, and we will start from the beginning and go over this." "No," I say, "just answer my question." So, we have an impasse, as men often do, as clients increasingly do with professionals, each wanting to be up, to be in charge of the proceedings.

It is my legal problem and my money paying the lawyer's fees, and my responsibility for the final decision, so I will not yield control of the discussion, nor accept the degree of helplessnesss implied by the lawyer, nor pretend that I don't understand the basic transaction as well as I do. I am determined to free myself from the oppression of the relentless legal machinery, to make it work for me, not vice versa. These memories of me in lawyers' offices help me sense more of how Judith must have been feeling—Judith, whom I was so quick to see as crippled and needy.

But the memories also help me sense my own feelings in the conversation with Judith, by reminding me of how the lawyers must feel. They must experience genuine frustation, genuinely hostile threat, in my attitude. They *are* professionals, after all, proud professionals, ready to accept responsibility for my legal well-being and masters of procedures intended to meet that responsibility, procedures established in training and custom, procedures sanctioned by the scrutiny of peers and by the usually unchallenged acceptance of clients. This is the way to be a lawyer. If I don't want these procedures, as one lawyer told me, I don't want *him*. The rejection is that completely personal. Without such badges of identity the professional feels as naked and unprofessional as the lifelong priest without a clerical collar, or the baseball player without a chew of tobacco, or the hospital resident without a white coat and stethoscope, or any of them without a compliant client, parishioner, fan, patient, to work on.

My restlessness with Judith really was the restlessness of one who felt naked, roleless, unarmed, even unrecognized, because I felt I was not enrolled as her healer or helper or protector. When I walk into a party or a meeting, I feel myself comfortably eloquent or else subdued, according to whether or not I feel recognized and enrolled, given a place. It is as though each of us has a particular pattern of gears, and we function—like a key in a lock—when we are offered a set of gears that ours can engage. Otherwise, we spin or clash and grind. We require complementary partners of a particular kind. If a partner doesn't fit us, we must either try to reshape our partner or reshape ourself. Men and professionals usually feel that they are in the business of reshaping others. "Men" require "women."

I can understand how I felt with Judith, if I remember the teachers at a recent PTA meeting I attended. They had their script set—their standard and "professional" way of reporting on school and on students. It didn't make any difference, so far as I could tell, what conerns the parents had. We were instructed first on what kinds of questions we should have about children and then what the answers were. Other questions were dismissed, sometimes even with a scoff, or converted into one of the preordained standard questions. I wonder if Judith feels as dismissed as I did at that PTA meeting, and whether I am as hardened against sensing that as were the teachers, who are really quite fine, sensitive, and warm persons, just professionalized.

The choreography of professional and client is not so different from the choreography between sexual partners. There may be just as much mutual dependence, just as much need for the partner to play a role that acknowledges and encourages your role, just as much hurt when that doesn't happen, just as much sense of rejection when these unspoken expectations and frustrations are not met, and just as seldom a chance to talk out loud about these expectations and frustration of expectations. "I feel rejected and lost and even helpless when you don't . . ." becomes the angry attack, "Why don't you . . . you bad person" or "Why can't you . . . you crippled person." That isn't very different from how it was between Judith and me.

"Do you generally have trouble taking this kind of initiative with others, maybe especially with people in authority that you don't know well?"

It is such a slight but crucial difference whether we see people for what they are or for what they are not. Like the question of whether the glass is half full or half empty (optimists versus pessimists), like the examples of visual gestalts (Do you see white faces against a black background or do you see black vases against a white background? Is the staircase going up or down?), whichever gestalt snaps into view controls the scene and your responses.

The marvel of the Christian message, as I understand it, has to do with the fact that whatever the configuration of our lives, God still sees people as whole. The tragedy of male and professional narrowing of life is that whatever the configuration, men and professionals see people as partial and crippled.

Whatever my limits or partialness, God, securely up, comes down, regards me as up and whole, and in so regarding me, lifts me up and makes me whole. Whatever your soundness and wholeness, I, a man and a professional, insecurely up, regard you as down and in so regarding, push you down. God trusts, habitually. Maybe sometimes you find a Little League coach who trusts, with a pat on the fanny, "You're going to be all right out there." But most of us Little League coaches mistrust and fill in the gap—is the gap in them or in us?—with our constant coaching ("Choke up on the bat, remember what I told you . . . ."). Maybe if we were Big League coaches it would be different, or maybe that wouldn't be enough. Maybe we would have to *feel* like Big League coaches. Maybe we would have to be *champion* Big League coaches. Maybe nothing would make us feel safely enough arrived.

Somehow we seem to need the other as a partner to make us look like a successful coach—in a way that God does not need us. Like trying to signal and control a bridge partner—or a sex partner—what to play so as to fit and justify your own play, rather than trusting them to play their own hand out of their own wisdom and trusting the game is at its best when both partners, equals, are playing their own hands for what they are. If we spend a lot of energies and earn a lot of frustration manipulating others as puppets, shoving our hands inside of them to move them as we want and need, it must be because we often feel hollowed like a puppet and need the others filling the empty spaces inside of us to make us move. This is the bizarre male symbol—which it would take an Escher or a Steinberg to draw—an arm reaching inside a puppet to make it move, but that arm is itself part of a puppet that is being filled and moved by an arm from the puppet that it is moving.

SEEING POWER IN CHAOS

The possibility of perceiving either strength or weakness in the same events is illustrated by the biblical story of Pentecost in the second chapter of Acts. "When the day of Pentecost came, all the believers were gathered together in one place" and then there was a great commotion. Some people heard in this commotion a sensible meaning and power: "Yet all of us hear them speaking in our own languages about the great things that God has done" (Verse 11). Others heard in this same commotion something else: "These people are drunk" (Verse 13). We hear what we want and need to hear, what we are prepared to hear, that which fits something already in us. The people who heard sensible and powerful speech, even though it left them "amazed and confused," had in them something (some trust, some openness) that was ready to be engaged by the power they heard. Those who heard a drunkenness had something in them (some fear, some emptiness) that needed to control this power, needed to dominate it, needed to be up over it. They needed to fit the event to a label, a familiar label, a disparaging label, and most of all, a label they knew how to deal with. I can imagine a vanguard of the Moral Majority moving among the commotion at Pentecost, ducking the tongues of flame, passing out temperance tracts and pledge cards or maybe collecting signatures on a petition for Prohibition. We see what we need to see, and when we see the other as wrong or needy it is because we need to be judge or helper. If being judge or helper is all we know how to be, and if we desperately need something to be, then we hear drunkenness even at Pentecost. Or maybe especially at Pentecost, when the power of God is breaking in and disrupting.

Or look at the next chapter of Acts, chapter 3: There was a man at the gate of the temple whom everybody perceived as crippled—and therefore he perceived himself as crippled. If he was crippled, people knew what to do: they could give him alms. "Every day he was carried to the gate to beg for money from the people who were going into the temple" (Acts 3:21). To be sure, the alms giving only defines and confirms the crippledness, not heals it. But that is the point. Alms giving makes cripples because alms givers need cripples. If high stakes have been attached to my giving alms, if I may not walk through the courtyard into the temple with my head up unless I have done my alms giving, then I need cripples and beggars, and I create them if necessary.

Being manly happens that way, too, far more often than we men care to acknowledge. To be a man, I must control or manage or help, so I search out and create people to control or manage, or help, often women. Men are taught that high stakes are attached to bossing or helping or completing a woman.

They dare not hold their heads up and walk across the court-yard unless they are dominating, making good a woman. So we need to perceive women needy, helpless, partial, void.

Professionals have been trained—in the same way that males are trained to be "men"—that they are not professionals, that they cannot walk across the courtyard with their head up, unless they are visibly and unambiguously helping or bossing or otherwise controlling. So they—we—therefore need to search out and cajole and coerce and seduce and batter and badger, but mostly just perceive, others to be helpless and needy.

But Peter and John were not such addicted alms givers when they confronted the man by the gate of the temple. For one thing, they did not have the alms to give. For another, they did not need to give alms. Perhaps they had been lucky enough to be kept on the margins of the crowd of men milling in the temple courtyard, and never fully initiated into these ranks of "real men"—barroom men, locker room men, courthouse men, courtyard men, manly alms givers all. Perhaps something had happened to them, at Pentecost or before, that gave them other reasons for holding up their heads as they walked across the temple courtyard. In any case, they had no trouble showing the man their empty pockets and, *as a consequence of this liberation*, they did not see the man as a cripple. They saw him whole. They took him by the hand. "He jumped up, stood on his feet, and started walking around." (Acts 2:28).

What if at the beginning I had dared turn my pockets inside out and expose my despair to Judith?

That is dangerous business, disrupting the settled and trusted, tried and true behavioral badges of identity. The authorities did not welcome this sort of thing—which is a a decisive clue, if any more were needed, as to what the alms giving was for, or rather who it was for. No fury is as great as that of the man stopped from beating his woman, or otherwise downing her. In the locker room, defend homosexuality or Puerto Ricans or communists before you defend women from stereotyping as targets, sexual targets, derogatory targets, instructional tar-gets. Don't take away what we need to be men.

Don't take away from helpers, especially professional, habitual helpers, what they need to be helpers, that is, someone to help. Social change runs into resistance when the cripples are put back on their feet and made unneedy of alms, whether the cripples are homosexuals, single parents, slow readers, adolescents, the aging, the endless stream of Judiths, or any of the other targets of helpers. To try to redefine these groups as sturdy and unneedy is to risk the disdain of helpers, a disdain as fierce and immediate as the wrath of the man whose fist is caught in midair as he is about to strike his woman. Peter and John found that out when they upset the ecological balance between alms givers and cripples. By the fourth chapter of Acts, the authorities—alms givers all—are so offended at this healing, Peter and John are in jail.

Listen to ministers sitting around disdaining the spiritual insensitivity of their congregation and their disloyalty to the church. Listen to faculty members sitting around disdaining the illiteracy of their students and their disloyalty to the academic enterprise. (I mention only the two groups of professionals I have listened to the most. How do they say it in your profession?) It's not so different from bullies sitting around the locker room plotting, at least in their talk, sexual conquests. They are all creating convenient targets, the simple macho remedies, remedies that are to be ad-ministered—like medicine or like a beating. For the faculty: change the admissions standards or the admissions committee; require a remedial course; prepare, distribute, and enforce a manual for literacy. Ministers find similar targets to shoot at, always by defining the congregations' need to conform to the ministers' remedies: attend church, attend committee meetings, give money, know the Bible. It's like the locker room crowd complaining about women running around when they should be back in their place, that is, when they should be sustaining the men's notion of their own place. Woe to anyone who interrupts this ritual putdown of students or congregations or women, anyone who robs the war dancers of their targets, and hence of their remedies and hence of their "manhood," their up-ness.

REHEARING THE POWER IN JUDITH

That's how I treated Judith. I transformed her and the complex situation she brought to me and her own understanding of it into an easy target, so I could be a good marksman. I heard her Pentecostal commotion and quickly labeled her "drunk." Just as some people heard wisdom pouring forth from the commotion at Pentecost, I could have heard each of Judith's remarks as a mark of power, as evidence of her own capacity to perceive and analyze and cope with what was happening. I could have admired this in her, supported her in the skills and determination she was showing in dealing with Richard and appraising the situation. I could have admired the courage she showed just in opening up with me. I could have seen that someone coming to a counselor with an astute appraisal of her situation is displaying strength, sturdiness, courage, and trust; she is not begging for alms like a cripple. I could have seen her as an adult inviting me to join her for a moment as an adult partner in her growth. For those with eyes to see, each of her remarks—go back and look at them— invites just that kind of understanding, that she is a person of wisdom and power, that she is a whole adult. But to see her differently, I would have had to see myself differently. To see her as whole, not needing me, I would have had to see myself as whole, not needing her.

It is clear from my remarks that I saw her precisely as lacking wisdom and power and wholeness and adulthood, and that these were to be supplied by me. I focused on what I could supply, which, in the poverty of my own understanding of the situation, was not much. I focused on narrow fact finding and on a quick programmatic remedy (talking with the teachers) and on analyzing her crippledness.

I could have stood with her, as Peter and John stood with the former beggar in the temple. Instead I stood over her, as the alms giver does to the squatting beggar.

If I had perceived her as a person of wisdom and power and

wholeness and adulthood, I would have behaved differently. I would have admired out loud her wisdom and power: "I can see you've been thinking about this carefully and sensitively." "I admire the way you can sum things up. 'Thumb his nose' is a powerful image for how it must feel." "You're working hard to be a good parent to Richard." "It takes resilience to bounce back from the hurt and disappointment you must feel over Richard and his struggles."

I could have shown her the respect of listening to her story as she wanted to tell it, rather than trying to find some target within her first words. When she resisted my agenda, I could have credited this as a sign of the very strength I accused her of lacking in dealing with the teachers, rather than a sign of crippledness or weakness.

I could have asked her honest questions, as real inquirer, to help myself get further inside of her experience and her thinking about it, rather than asking questions like a cross-examiner or an interrogator, questions intended to lead her inside of my perception of her experience, and to help me propose a remedy of my devising.

(Up in the saddle, John Wayne. Get your fists up, Muhammad Ali.)

Above all, I could have listened to her as though she knew what she was talking about, rather than listening to her as though I knew what she was talking about better than she did. If there is any one thing that characterizes a man's habitual treatment of a woman, a professional's habitual treatment of people, it is this: in my own expertise and authority, in my own posture over you—in my own insecurity? my own fear that I don't really understand or that I don't really have a posture?—I understand better than you do what you want to say. Bluff. Swagger. Manhood.

I think women are more ready to assume strength in others, and men more ready to diagnose weakness. In my own experience with male ministers and female ministers, I find that the women are readier to be with the Judiths (and Edwards) in those ways that trust them as whole, as possessed of wisdom and power and adulthood and capacity. (Perhaps you find yourself reacting at this point by supposing that such empathy and trust derives from women's greater passivity and inexperience, that is, that this is a virtue that springs from weakness, rather than strength. If so, I suspect you are a man, just exactly one of the men I am talking about, and among whom I count myself.) Female ministers, at least in my experience, have the strength in themselves to permit others to show strength. They are not constantly and habitually forced to measure their prowess by the unattainable standards that compel men to look for new ways to flex their muscles, to get it up.

I think of ministry as the art of making space for others to grow. That seems an apt metaphor for ministry in the name of one who so relentlessly creates and recreates supporting life around us, whose own self-revelation leaves healthy enigma, who, as the supreme act of salvation, "emptied himself . . . humbled himself and became obedient unto death, even death on a cross" (Philemon 2:7, 8). Ministry often requires a radical move, requires becoming a vacuum that enables others to loom large. Ministry is the constant sharpening and shaping of questions, more than the giving of answers. Ministry is the giving up of authority and status and acclaim in ways that help others to discover their own authority and status and claims. Ministry is in moving beyond the assumption of roles—recognized, defined patterns and guidelines, agendas for popularity and checklists for accomplishment—into raw encounters with people at their growing edges, where there is chaos before there is form. Ministry is in renouncing self and in renouncing all the structures that define ministry, because the structures ultimately falsify and impede ministry. Ministry is in going, radically, to the people as they are, rather than insisting that the people come to the minister.

It seems to be the case that women more often and more

comfortably practice the ministry of making space, leaving space, for others to move into and grow, while men as ministers more often and more comfortably make space in others' lives, a space to be penetrated. So in all professions.

Why is this so? The difference in sexual roles—making space to receive, and making space to penetrate—is a deliberate metaphor, but it is only a metaphor.

Women's openness and "servanthood" might be attributed to a socially imposed passivity. But socially required meekness is, of course, quite different from the voluntary choice of yielding space and power. There is no saving, there is no art, there is no ministry in enforced docility, no more health in anxiety about feeling "up" than in male anxiety for not feeling "up." When women are denied power, they are quite right to claim vigorously the right to power, the option to do with it what they will, including the option to relinquish it in favor of the empowerment of others, an act and art of ministry.

Women are freed to pursue space-making ministry, I believe, because they are less harnessed into performance, solo performance, less required to be up. All the ways of eroding others' selfhood, whether by coaching or by targeting or by crippling, are the patterns that men lapse into or are driven into by the relentless pressures to perform and to perform well, pressures that are imposed upon us and that we impose upon ourselves and then impose on all within range. A man can never be up enough to satisfy these demanding voices. One living with this lifelong low-grade anxiety, constantly falling short, constantly falling down, can only envy those who have not been coached into the demands to be up, unfailingly up.

7. Paths of Liberation: Women and Men in Tandem and in Conflict

Men can and do wrest free from their tightly confining "manly" roles—relentless helper/crippler, humble Good Scout, quiet hero, and all the rest—in favor of more authentic, self-chosen modes of manhood, often modes yielding both greater assertiveness and greater vulnerability at the same time. This chapter will describe how that can happen, mostly by tracking some episodes in the personal and professional life of one man.

Then the final chapter will explore a more delicate kind of liberation—a release from the tyranny of roles even while choosing to stay in the roles, the discovery that a role can serve a man's purposes; it needn't be vice versa. Perhaps that is a style of liberation with which men are more free to experiment than are women. In any case, the final chapter "Joseph: Father Nevertheless" proposes such experiments, in great hope.

But first, in this chapter: the strategies of breaking loose from roles, something about which men can learn much from what women have learned in recent decades, the benefits of close self-conscious attention to the roles and the role-makers, the freedom and light-heartedness that accompanies an emboldened self-confidence to make choices and to direct one's own life. What can men learn from women about the arts of liberation? This chapter, in the first half, answers that question by telling the story of a woman and a man finding themselves emerging in tandem, encouraging each other.

But there are differences, too, in the paths of liberation that men and women must follow. This chapter, in the last half, explores those differences, and how it is that a man and a woman, each on a path of liberation, will at times run athwart each other.

EMERGING, WOMEN FIRST

The church clock began striking just as she pulled up to the curb in front. She said she would be here at nine, and the morning chores had dissolved before her newfound zest. So had David's usual fussiness at the nursery school dropoff. He must have found her own surge of self-confidence contagious and reassuring; he had marched right into school just as though he belonged there. That's how Marilyn wanted to feel here at the church. Maybe she did.

Her first encounter was with the parking sign. It said in bold red letters No Parking, Except on Church Business—Police Order. To Marilyn, chronic outsider, that usually meant simply Keep Out. So she looked around for a metered space; she would leave this place for one of the insiders, someone on real church business—"one of the real people," she almost thought—the two older women who came on Monday mornings to sort donated food and clothing, or the man who came to count the Sunday offering. But with another surge of resolve she made herself decide that trying to sort out the church library was real church business and that she was a real person. She felt like it this morning—or wanted to.

So she huddled her Honda up against the sign, two wheels a foot up on the sidewalk, in fact. She didn't have one of those cards that said "On Church Business" to put in her window— no one had offered her one—but maybe if she parked close to the sign, it would be the same thing. Besides, that way she wouldn't be taking so much of the street; people would see she was trying to be helpful. Also, the new Honda wouldn't be quite so exposed.

Her own wheels, at last. Walter had asked her at breakfast,

jokingly she hoped, "Do you want me to drop you off at the church this morning?" She had answered with what she hoped had been a convincing jauntiness suitably qualified with a note of appreciation, "No thank you, sir, I think I will drive *my* car." At least she had felt jaunty and exuberant when she said it, but not after Walter's reply, "Well, drive carefully, it's the shiniest car we have." She wished he had been joking about that; but if she really thought he had, she wouldn't feel so deflated about the issue. Anyway, better to park the car away from traffic as far as possible and not risk scratches and up-setting Walter.

Not that this particular light-green finish, which she loved so much, was something Walter cared much about. "Pick out whatever color you want, baby," Walter had said, seeming enthusiastic and supportive about her move to emerge. So she had picked a pastel green. And Walter had said—how she had searched for a twinkle in his eye—"That color will be awfully hard to keep clean, and you can't touch up the scratches if you get any. They had so many real car colors to choose from." That had been the point, she guessed, of picking the light green. But Walter hadn't gotten the point, or hadn't liked it. But he would like scratches less. So she snuggled the car into refuge on the curb even as she boldly—sort of—claimed the privileged parking space. As she locked the car door she pulled herself in close to the car to let a couple of men with briefcases walk by. At the same time her eyes roamed up and down the street and around to the church door, half-idly, half-apprehen-sively. Like a man urinating in public, she mused, a man trying to look around nonchalantly and casually, even while he is checking out the environs to allay his uneasiness, and maybe also—as male animals have marked boundaries for eons—claiming turf. Part of the sweep of her gaze was a kind of jaunty claim to sovereignty over the terrain, just a delight in herself starting the week by doing something of her choos-ing in her way and in her style. Part of the sweep was the wariness that she had learned, through most of her 34 years, should accompany any such boldness; when breaking out of the cocoon move very cautiously. Would somebody come and scold her for parking here, or take the space away? Was she trespassing?—her habitual question. But she didn't ask herself the question this time, because this was a special day of new and bold beginnings, and she was feeling jaunty. But then again, something inside her did ask the question automatically, unavoidably, insistently, because feelings of jauntiness were always wrapped in such fears.

She thought back to another spring Monday, but in the evening, a little more than twenty years ago, just at the end of her triumphant seventh grade. When she had started junior high school her father had made a big thing out of it: this was now beginning a new important part of her life, school was important, grades were important, it made a big difference in how you lived the rest of your life, and he really expected her to do well. She would never forget that September conversation, just the two of them, under the trees with the air turning crisp. It had been like they were mentally shaking hands, partners making a deal, Daddy and his Merry. She had kept to that deal all year. Though the conversation had never been repeated or even mentioned, she had known how important it was to her father. His occasional questions, "How is school?" may have seemed casual to the rest of the family, but she had known they were booster shots, renewing the September commission, reminding her how important school was to her and how important she was to him. And when he had seemed casual about her midyear report card, she had known that this was his way of keeping the bargain of the partnership, his way of saying that this part was up to her and he was trusting her. She had perceived these conversational winks, even if no one else had; they had put the wind in her sails as she had breezed, even gusted, through the year.

At last had come the day of the final report card, all As, the commissioned voyage triumphantly ended, time for harboring at home. She hadn't mentioned the report card to anyone else, hadn't even let on that she had it—though once during supper her mother had said that she was chattering away so happily that she must have swallowed a canary—because her father was the one with whom she was in partnership. So after supper, her father enthroned in his green armchair, she had approached, almost floating, with a quietly bursting joy, and had made her offering, still in its envelope. And he had said, "Marilyn, let's do this later. The Red Sox game is just starting." And she had shriveled, and so had her joy.

He never did see that report card, and she never again felt such unguarded, billowing joy.

As she walked away from the car she tugged down the overblouse that had crept up while she was driving. She was wearing rose slacks, a white sleeveless jersey, and a filmy overblouse, which had been a matter of some hesitation at the closet this morning, because she felt daring and therefore felt both exhilarated and apologetic. "Maybe this is more like party clothes than work clothes," she had mused in front of the mirror, letting her hands stroke the overblouse down so it tightened and emphasized her figure, then gathered the material and curtained it, then decided—in a burst of confidence—to wear it because it was pretty.

The whole weekend had been like that, a series of experiments in emerging.

With mixed results, she had experimented with asking David to play by himself for an hour after his nap on Saturday. "Be a grown-up boy," was what she had told him. But what she had meant was more like, "Maybe I can be a grown-up mother and make some claims for myself." She had really wanted that extra hour in her garden. It hadn't been so much that the plants had needed to be set out as that she needed that time crawling around in the earth getting her soul back to basics for a bit. David had seemed to sense that, too, and had happily ridden his plastic bike up and down the sidewalk, making loud motor noises and waving over at her now and then. "Maybe there really is a place even for me in this family," she had begun to ponder. But that night after supper when she went to look at her plants she noticed that David had stepped on most of them, and she had felt guilty, collapsed her resolve, and had promised herself to spend more time with David.

But the plants had left a legacy of sorts. They had helped her to get Walter to recognize her emerging and to understand and encourage it—at least a little—maybe. She had been trying, off and on, to get in the church library a couple of mornings a week. He had said that he understood that the library needed sorting out and she would be good at that. He had said that he understood that she needed a break out of the house now and then, and he really did seem supportive of that move. But she had still not been able to get him to understand why she wanted to do it. She had thought the plants gave her a good chance. "It's not that the plants really need doing, and I certainly don't mind doing things around the house. It's just that I need some place, some time that is just mine, for me, just as though I'm really a person put on this earth too." Her eloquence, her passion had surprised even her, and had also itself been an experiment in emerging. And Walter had responded as though the eloquence had reached him. "Of course you want to be someone other than just my wife and David's mother, and you are, and we love you for who you really are." He had kissed her solidly and had held her gently for a long time, and she had basked in this sense of recognition and response. She had made a speech about how she felt and how she saw things, and it had been heard. "That's what I've been trying to tell you for a long time," he had broken the silence. "You really should take up some hobby. Do you want to golf? I could teach you and then we could play together." Back to square one. And worse: "If you had just told me, I could have helped get those plants in while David was sleeping, and then he wouldn't have gotten annoyed and undone all that work you did." He just could not seem to let her go and let her be. ("Of course your orgasm is important; I'll give you a big one.")

But the big thing that had happened over the weekend had

been Roger's sermon. (And how surprised he would have been to hear that, because unknown to her he was feeling let down in his own way, feeling that he had invested labor and soul in a sermon that had received no serious response.) The sermon had touched her so closely it was eerie. How could he know what was going on in her life better than she did?

Roger had preached about the story of Jesus encountering a crippled man lying beside a pool of water. He had been there for 38 years, even longer than Marilyn had been living her life, on the edge of things. The water in the pool was healing and if the man could just get somebody to carry him into that water at a certain time, he would be healed. But he could never make it. So close so long and yet so far, just because other people wouldn't cooperate. "Living an almost-life" Roger had called the sermon. And that's exactly how Marilyn felt, living—almost. On the verge, thinking "Just around the corner," "As soon as I get my life organized," "Just past the present crisis," "As soon as David is in school," and so on. Roger knew that. She had always been blaming circumstances, other people, just like the man by the pool ("just as soon as they cooperate") and Roger seemed to know all about that, too. Then there was Jesus who seemed to believe in the man more than he believed in himself. Roger didn't make it sound like scolding, and it probably wasn't. Just directly and simply, "Get up . . . and walk." You can do it. You don't have to wait any longer. Roger had talked mostly about men, men who closed their eyes to shady business practices, or men who knew that they needed to make a job change, or to get up from bad habits, or even go in and ask the boss for a raise. Jesus believes in you, get on those two feet that God has given you. It was mostly about men, but Marilyn felt that Roger and Jesus were both saying to her, "I believe in you. You can do it."

What was "it"? Marilyn wasn't quite sure, and Roger hadn't helped with that. It had something to do with making longings come true, with getting out of the cocoon, with taking all of these steps, or at least one of them, which she had taken in her head so many times. Dive in, don't wait to be carried. It was exhilarating and it was scary. But it was not so scary as it would be if she had to do it completely on her own. It really did make a difference that it was at the church that she was taking this Monday morning big first step, and she knew Roger would probably be around part of the day. It was sort of like going to school the first day and being very proud you were doing it on your own and very glad your mother was going along with you.

It wasn't just Roger's sermon yesterday that made her feel that he really knew and understood and stood by her. It was also the knowing way he sometimes said things that gave voice to a depth of feeling that otherwise would have gone unheard and unrecognized. It was as though he were verbally winking at her. Like the night she and Walter were leaving what had been a heated discussion at a church committee meeting, and someone had warned Walter, "Don't keep up this fight all night in your sleep." Walter had bragged, "Don't worry. I don't lose sleep over things like this." And then Roger had snapped, "You must be hard to live with if you drop off right away after getting that worked up." Marilyn had felt a gush of warmth at Roger's remark, flushed at having a piece of her own intimate experience suddenly discovered, and flushed at how much she welcomed that. Roger really did know, maybe better than she did herself, what it was like to live with such a cool machine. Remembering the incident, she felt a flash of gratitude. What did people do when they didn't have a minister like Roger to carry them along.?

(There was one time, in about the fourth grade—she gets her memory mixed up with her reading of Cinderella and the Sleeping Beauty and their rescuing princes—when some boys thought it would be fun to ambush her and her friend Margaret with snowballs. The pelting had just started and they had been really scared and mad and helpless when all of a sudden her father had driven up alongside—he had thought it might be too cold for them to walk. They had dashed for his car, and the boys had disappeared. Her father had seemed to know just when to come.)

So, this Monday morning of emerging, Marilyn walked up to the front door of the church parish house, seeing it as a kind of sheltered workshop for liberation, a cocoon for breaking out of cocoons, a cocoon fashioned by and guaranteed by Roger. Battered by life-long demanding put-downs, lured by a vision of a life not on hold, a life not deferring to men's needs to keep her in thrall and subdued, Marilyn was testing ways to emerge into a life guided by her own choices.

But men are no less captive to demands that deflect their dreams, no less battered by judgments of having fallen short, no less marking time, on hold, sidelined. Even though many men stay content in such captivity, Roger is trying, in his own way, to cut loose, to heed others less and the inner voice more. He can preach to Marilyn's tentative emerging, because he is preaching out of his own.

A MAN EMERGING

While Marilyn was parking, diffidently, on the street in front, Roger was parking defiantly, in his spot behind the church and was winning, more or less, his own skirmish against expectations, claiming (reclaiming) space, in his own way. As he turned off the key, there dangling in front of him was what he had for years called his "Monday morning name tag." Almost upside down and hanging literally by a thin wire from the wall of the church was a sign that said Reverend Anderson. This morning he stared at it, precisely because it did not fit this particular Monday morning mood. In fact, he left his papers on the seat of the car while he went into the church to dig around for hammer, nail, screwdriver, and wire. He soon had Reverend Anderson upright and securely attached to the church. The mild pangs of annoyance he felt at having to do the repair work himself was nothing compared with the glow he felt inside, that occasional glow of hope and firm newness that comes with New Year's, a job change, peacemaking after a quarrel, the arrival of children, the departure of children for college, a new love, a fresh spring morning, that feeling that was supposed to come—and sometimes did, perhaps, to some people—Sunday morning after the confession and absolution: a fresh start. Roger felt some combination of all of these moods. This Monday morning did seem to be a fresh start, not a morning after.

The weekend had been a time of mild rebellion, maybe not so mild really, and therefore a time of reaffirming, re-firming. He had wiped the steam off the bathroom mirror this morning with a vigorous flourish, determined to get his own face out of the mist and into clear focus. He had not been conscious of this rebellion, this liberation, not conscious of how much his sermon had been addressed to himself—take up your mat and walk—until last night while he was idly sitting in front of the television. Suddenly a battered pickup truck was being forced off the road by a flashy sports car. He was driving that truck. He was that truck. Deflected, shouldered, elbowed, thwarted, stymied, sidelined, shunned—beside the pool and never in it—pushed out of the action, by the voices, clamoring or whining, by the eyes, piercing or downcast, by the events, rushing or stalling, to which he had to defer—well, to which he did defer. Doing it *their* way, being *their* man, *their* minister, not his own, not God's. Sermons shaped, or misshaped, time schedules rearranged, energies immobilized and enthusiasms blunted, other enthusiasms feebly and falsely fabricated, all to accommodate those voices lurking in the dark fringes of the crowd milling around him or his mat; they gave him space, but a space made by them, not by him. He felt like an actor ringed by a small, bright spotlight, his performance shaped not by commitment to the author's script but by anxiety over what *they* wanted, out front in the dark. He was driving that battered pickup truck, being shouldered off the road.

On the playground in fifth grade he had been shouldered

out, shouldered out of the huddle of boys around the baseball cards and dirty stories, a lynch mob more deadly in their turned backs than in outright attack, a lynch mob drawing a mob's usual sharp boundaries between the accepted in group and the discarded out group. Admission was by performance (and exclusion was for nonperformance), performance of the limited he-man, nonwimp repertory: swapping baseball cards and dirty stories, being willing to call one teacher a fag and another a whore, always coming late for music class, joining the under-the-desk pencil tapping for substitute teachers, throwing snowballs at cars and girls, and catching baseballs one-handed in the pocket of the glove. These were the pre-scribed rites of admission, and Roger had never been able to bring himself to perform them with the proper enthusiasm. The actions had seemed too much of a sellout to the mob's shallow notions of authenticity, and, besides, he was just scared. He had tried all these things, but only halfheartedly and half-successfully. He had never persuaded them or himself. In-stead, doing what came naturally, he had performed other rituals, had followed the script written for admission to an-other group, the group convened under the patronage and sponsorship of adults. He had cut his losses with the play-ground mob and had obeyed, instead, parents, teachers, and ministers. He had imitated parents, teachers, and ministers. He had pleased parents, teachers, and ministers. He had put on the badges and carrried the banners of the school safety patrol, policing crosswalks and playgrounds, and had found this a way to shoulder back the rejecting mob. He had sharp-ened pencils, not tapped them, had reported baseball scores to the gym teacher instead of playing, and, once, had even reported a snowball thrower to the principal—a sellout, too, to others' scripts, but it came more naturally. In the name of breaking the claims of the schoolyard mob, he had acceded to the claims of the adult authorities. He had been shouldered off the road onto a path he tried to make the best of. Maybe he still felt like a kid pleasing the adults in charge of his world.

Ten years later on another kind of playground, when he stood at the open bar of a wedding reception not knowing what to order, he had felt the foolish blush in his breast, perceived the barely disguised impatience of the bartender, and seen the embarrassed turnings of the backs around him. Again, a right way to perform, and he didn't know what it was—what scriptholder would prompt him? At first he had felt he would rather not drink at all, not even go to parties, rather than endure such intimidation. Then he learned to say quickly, "Gin and tonic, please," with a surge of confidence from clutching this token—until he overheard that this was only a summer drink, overheard that this was not really a man's drink.

Back in front of the TV, indignation at the truck's fate had welled up and then took over. He had fought back. Half-dozing, half-watching, he had simply willed that the truck regain the road, musing wryly how much easier it was to rescue and to coach another. But he had been the truck, too, and even as he had willed it, the truck had used the shoulder as a shortcut across a bend in the road, had emerged to hit the sports car broadside with a satisfying shudder, and had jauntily resumed the road, now its road.

Twice yesterday, he had reclaimed the road like that, and both times it had felt as wrenchingly violent—and as fully satisfying—as had the truck's impact on the Jaguar.

First, while the greeting line had filed out after church, old Mrs. Wilson, as usual, had been slouching impatiently by the wall, announcing herself and her claim on turf, time, and minister with noisy snappings of her purse, open and shut. As the snaps had accelerated, he had readied himself for the icy, whiny reassurance—"Oh I know you have so many important people to talk to." Just as he had begun to hurry the line, make more glib his greeting, and prepare his apology to forestall her blast, he had caught himself short, almost like feeling a hand on his shoulder (Jesus: "Pick up your mat, and walk.") Maybe he had heard his own sermon. Sally Jenkins had wanted to talk about the sermon. She really had, and had engaged him in a very personal conversation as to how the sermon had engaged her life. He had savored that encounter, they both had, and he had let it run its natural course, a moment of pastoral intimacy and a moment of pastoral seriousness; he and Sally took each other seriously. Buoyed up by the genuine intimacy and the seriousness of his talk with Sally and by his unabashed decision to indulge in it, he had turned to Mrs. Wilson with head high and feet firm. He had never realized quite how apprehensive, off-balance, cowering, and annoyed he usually was with Mrs. Wilson until he had felt the contrast that morning. His hearty "Good Morning" had disarmed her far more effectively than his usual apology, bypassed the whine, and begun a pastoral conversation on his terms, not on hers. He had been sensitive to her—"It's a long wait for you some mornings, isn't it?" But he had not been defensive, with an "I'm sorry I took so long." Strength speaking to strength, not weakness speaking to weakness. Mrs. Wilson had been startled, pleasantly startled out of her whine and had even found her own heartiness, "Don't these ladies look pretty today?" without a detectable trace of bitterness or sarcasm.

"Why not just assume people are sturdy, and I can be too?" Roger thought. "Perceive them as so, as God does, as Jesus did the man on the mat, not try to make them so."

For Roger to perceive Mrs. Wilson as essentially sturdy and whole is for Roger to be free to see himself as independent from her—and vice versa—as free to approach on his own feet, on his own terms. To perceive her as needy, deficient is to set himself up to feel responsible for her welfare, to make himself vulnerable to the guilt she wants to engender in him, to define and script his relationship to her to a narrow role of taking care of her and appeasing her.

"Taking care" of the Mrs. Wilsons is, of course, a kind of controlling that may be the most characteristic "masculine" behavior there is; and here we see it in Roger as in Marilyn's

Walter: I'll make good things happen for you! You just play along with my script. But the man caught up in "taking care of" is just as thoroughly controlled and scripted, trying to cramp and squeeze himself into fitting a woman's needs and expectations (at least his perception of them) as he is scripting, squeezing her into an object to be cared for. Roger has been just as accustomed to letting—no, making—his life be shaped by the important women in his life as Marilyn has been accustomed to letting—no, making—her life be shaped by the important men in her life.

But this day is different from other days, for both Roger and Marilyn, a day of halting liberation, a day of seeing self and others as sturdily self-derived, not parasitic or symbiotic. (Well, almost, and in some ways: the biggest obstacle will be that these two companions in liberation rely on each other, and rely on each other to follow certain scripts, to assist their liberation.)

Roger's second moment of liberation on Sunday had come in the afternoon when he had called on the Morrisons. They had missed church, obviously still upset over Ruth Morrison's brother's death the morning before. Larry had been very close to Ruth, had even lived with the Morrisons for much of the time since his own wife had died. Ruth's son Tom had greeted Roger at the door with obvious relief. "Thank God you're here. We can't get Mother calmed down. She thinks she'll never see Uncle Larry again, but she'll believe you if you tell her differently." Roger had taken a deep breath. The minister's job is to rescue, to console the upset, to pronounce reassurance, to suppress the grief and the doubt and the anger—at least that was the Morrison's expectations, as it was most everyone's. They would sit around watching him do his tricks and be ready to spread the legend of how he had "helped Ruth."

But as he walked into the Morrison's house, Roger had also felt a startling surge of "so what," a defiant, calm confidence that his own sense of ministry was surer than theirs. They had wanted a freeze on feelings and he had dared to know better, to know that Ruth needed to expose and explore and maybe even explode feelings. So Roger had encouraged Ruth's moans of enormous loss, of loneliness, of unfairness, of bewilderment, of anger. He had urged her to talk about Larry, to say the things she wanted to say to Larry when he was alive. He had asked—the family had practically gasped—to see some pictures of Larry and had paused over the album, asking for recollections about each scene. He had acted as though Larry was a real person, and Ruth, and himself. When he had left, there had been no fawning gratitude—"Thank you, thank you." In fact, some of the family were still stunned. Ruth had not clung to him as people sometimes do after getting doses of ministerial reassurance and calming. Instead, she had looked him in the eye. She had seemed centered. She had seemed "there." And Roger had felt the same way. He had left, head up, striding. "People are wonderful if you give them a chance."

Roger's head was still high and his stride was still vigorous and his mood was still upbeat as he arrived at church Monday morning. People could be real people and he could be a real minister. From now on.

How long he had spent—how persistent the habits had been—treating people as less than whole, needing him to make them whole, as papier-mâché figures needing him to hold them up and breathe life into them, as overwhelmed people unable to deal with the trouble in their lives without him. People may have felt his response was one of strength. But he had felt himself to be chronically overpowered, constantly deflected from his own sense of vocation by the claims he perceived they made on him.

Often their claims were indeed demanding. He was supposed to see Elmer Kimball this morning. He had an uncanny way of making Roger feel responsible, guilty, compelled to find a remedy, any remedy. Today it might be Elmer's painful back, his noisy neighbors, the high grocery prices, but it would all be connected somehow with the Sunday service, the "hymns you have us singing these days," the new assistant minister, or something else under Roger's control—as though all of Elmer's complaints were. Somehow he had a way of making Roger feel indicted, convicted and sentenced, without ever quite knowing what the charges were. It was the kind of no-win feeling he had had when his mother would call from the kitchen "Oh, fiddlesticks! Roger!" and he would dash out to find her sucking a finger she had burned on the oven door and looking at him as though he was supposed to do something about it. So he would end up giving her a stiff, perfunctory hug, or washing the dishes, or rearranging the oven racks. Later on he came to limit himself to advice—the kind of thing Marilyn heard from Walter—"Why don't you use those hot pads we got you?" or "Run your finger under the cold water." It reminded him of his mother now every week going over and over the same question on the phone: Should she get her house painted? Just as though Roger were responsible for her indecision, and at first he had acted as if he were, calling around getting estimates from contractors, until he realized the futility of all that: She was going to feel upset and helpless and abandoned by him, no matter what he did. Could he just let her be that way, without trying to make her different, better, happier by making a cure? Could he just let Elmer Kimball be the way he was, a little lonely, a little abandoned, a little angry, a little confused, without assuming that this was all his to mend? Old habits of "ministering" die hard; old habits of being a "man" are not laid to rest quickly. Could he minister to Elmer as he wanted, hearty person to hearty person, by treating him as the growling lion that he was, rather than the whining, bleating lamb that Roger had made him so he could rush to the rescue?

He recalled his wife's response when he had impulsively called her the other day from the office just for a midday chat and telephone hug. Her response, an eager and delighted "I'm so glad you called," had given him just what he had wanted and had lifted his soul. But immediately the rest of her sentence had crumbled it. Why was she glad he called? "If you would bring some milk on the way home, it would save me a trip out . . . I didn't want to call you, but . . ."

She wants him in her life! What he most craves: Wants! Him!

She wants him as chore boy—what he most hears. Be quietly useful, on-call problem solver, the good Scout, the good boy—with the subtle evolution to cold controller—this is all *their* idea as much as his.

A WOMAN AND A MAN: LIBERATION IN TANDEM

The paths of women's liberation are fairly clear to most of us these days, and Marilyn is following them. So is Roger, venturing a very similar liberation.

Marilyn is freeing herself from the posture of living a life that is managed by someone else, the pattern of deriving identity from someone else's needs and expectations; in this case, from the posture of being taken care of, the posture of being helpless or at least being the helpee, the rescued. It is a habitual posture, one which she is comfortable with. But ultimately it is utterly destructive. For one thing, any person she thinks she is pleasing by playing out this script comes to feel trapped and controlled by her, the partner in it. This is an idol that fails. (Walter might admit to feeling that her helplessness, her need to be taken care of, constricted and eroded and consumed him.) Worse, though, is what it does to her; this is not only an idol that fails, it is only an idol; it deflects her from directions and posture of selfhood she would prefer if she chose freely, different ways of being herself, a woman, a mother . . . These are new ways she is trying to act out this Monday morning.

Roger too is freeing himself from the posture of living a life that is managed by someone else, the pattern of deriving identity from someone else's needs and expectations. In this case it is the posture of taking care of, the posture of being helper, rescuer. It is a habitual posture, one with which he is comfortable. But ultimately it is utterly destructive. For one thing, any person he thinks he is pleasing by playing out this script comes to feel trapped and controlled by him. This is an idol that fails. (Mother, wife, Elmer Kimball, Mrs. Wilson . . . All would admit to feelings of being constricted, consumed, eroded, overpowered by his relentless caretaking . . . Off my back!) Worse, though, is what it does to him; this is not only an idol that fails, it is only an idol; it deflects him from directions and postures of selfhood he would prefer if he chose freely, different ways of being himself, a man, a minister . . . These are new ways he is trying to act out this Monday morning. Off my back and walk!

Roger is trying to come out from under the demands to be Joseph, the golden bull, the passive, compliant, frozen, impotent, battered doer of other people's chores, the superficial meeter of their needs, hero in reins. He is discovering he can pick up his mat and walk. He can be self-directing, and meet other people at deeper levels, the real Roger confronting the real people.

Monday morning, then, finds both Marilyn and Roger experimenting with a fresh, exultant mood of liberation. Both have had their consciousness raised. Both have become increasingly aware of and resistant to the way their lives have been derived from and managed by others' wants and expectations. They have both been performing in scripts they never chose and performing in roles that were trivial, even humiliating, supporting roles to other persons. Both have challenged, at least for themselves, the authority and power that they had accorded to others—husband and children, parishioners and families—and in the challenging have found resilience and self-command. Energies once spent in discerning and obeying or rebelling are now at their own command. They are helping each other make these discoveries.

A WOMAN AND A MAN: LIBERATION IN CONFLICT

But as they emerge, they are also going to impede each other. Men's liberation and women's liberation, with so much in common and so much in need of each other, inevitably thwart each other. Because the liberation is new and tender, Marilyn and Roger each needs the help, for now at least, of a particular kind of partner in liberation. So they script each other into the partner they need. Though the roles they script are new, the process of imposing expectations and resisting expectations and being disappointed by expectations—that process is all too painfully familiar, the more painful for having been, so they thought, left behind.

Marilyn needs Roger's total and discerning support. Roger needs free and strong partners, people who don't "need" him—paradoxical as that may be for a minister. So, with Marilyn needing closeness with Roger, and Roger needing distance from any "neediness," they are destined to disappoint each other.

Because the liberation is new and tender, both are supersensitive to demands that pull them backwards; both are extremely vigilant to signals that other people want to hold them hostage to special scripts. Both are destined to feel as if that is exactly what the other is doing.

Because the liberation is new and tender, both are at risk of falling back into old patterns. Not so much old patterns of compliance, but old patters of half-rebellious, ineffective noncompliance, and stubbornness. Marilyn's favorite device is to retreat into polite, cool, superficial chatter, distancing and even offending, but safely and sweetly so. Roger's favorite device, all men's favorite device, is a mild counterattack, manipulating and shaping people oh-so-tenderly and politely, even as he feels manipulated and shaped. (They are destined to call forth these old skills in each other.)

But most importantly in the way the two liberations—Marilyn's and Roger's, woman's and man's—play against each other, impede each other is this: Roger—any man—is destined to mistake the "new," liberated woman for the "old" demanding, threatening woman; to mistake her solid strength, standing firmly on her own ground for assault on his ground; to mistake the emerging Marilyn for the submerging mother, wife, Elmer, Mrs. Wilson. And Marilyn—any woman—is destined to mistake Roger's emerging self-reliance for the angry, sullen withholding of father and Walter.

So what does happen when a man and woman, emerging in tandem and in conflict, get together? Let us resume the story.

DUSTING OFF

The parish house was unlocked when Marilyn got to the door. Who would have gotten here before nine o'clock? But she got down to the library alcove without having to encounter Joanne, the church secretary, or anyone else. That preserved her feeling of sovereignty and freshness—queen for a day—because it avoided the need for making old small talk on a morning when she felt new and big. Today she felt "caught up" not running to catch up, catapulted by Roger's sermon into an unfamiliar energy, into an exuberance of confidence that seemed unshakable. Instead of standing there, hands on hips, befuddled by the task ahead, feeling it bigger than she was, and unsure how to begin, she just dived in—into the pool?—pulling all the books off the shelves and sorting them into piles on the table.

When Roger showed up, she didn't have the time—and maybe not even the need—to think what she might say to him. Her heart didn't skip a beat, nor was she even self-conscious. Somehow the old hero-helpless distance had disappeared, replaced by a new sense of partnership: Roger understood her, and she understood Roger. The verbal wink had taken flesh. Roger opened, of course. "You beat me this morning. You're here before anybody." That could have been a routine silence breaker, conversation filler. But Marilyn heard it as his jauntiness and his affirmation of hers, her new specialness. He did recognize how this library job fit into her life, just as his sermon had talked about.

"Well, I can't wait around for someone to carry me into the pool, because nobody will do it." She was seldom this witty or imaginative, daring to stray so far from safe small talk. But she really did feel that she was in a comfortable partnership with Roger, a partnership that was symbolized by this shorthand talk, the almost private language of his sermon applied to her life. With this kind of bond her words just flowed, without self-consciousness and with a kind of zing that was fed by and fed her radiantly emerging self. Here was the happy, long-sought paradox of the mutuality that nourished independence. It was all right here in their opening exchange of remarks, better than she might have hoped.

"Those books have been needing attention for a long time." Roger felt her coming on strong, all right, but felt her coming on strong to him. He felt, as was his habit, that her adoption of the sermon language was somehow an attempt to adopt him, to ask him for something. She was coming in close to set him up ("You know about death and grief; make us all feel better." "You know the old house well; should I get it painted?" "As long as you're going by the store, could you get some milk?") Her remark signaled that she was moving awfully close, even intimately close. People who got that close to Roger were always on the make, on the way to asking him for something. Better keep the distance, in the way that men know so well how to do, by pronouncing about things. He froze.

Marilyn froze, her hand resting on the next book she was about to take. It seemed more like her hand was clutching a report card in front of her father. Was Roger really more interested in the books than in her? Did he really think that she was more interested in the books than in herself and the way he was helping her to think about herself as emerging. Maybe she hadn't correctly heard what he had said. Maybe he hadn't heard her. She stood frozen because there was nothing else to do. She had invested everything, the momentum of the past 24 hours and more, in this one move, invested unguardedly—that's why it had flowed with such welcome ease. And the move had been rebuffed. She had plunged into the healing pool and found it suddenly drained.

She remembered the time Walter had got her out playing frisbee. After struggling with how to twist her wrist and twist her body and getting the thing to sail at all, then in the right direction, then far enough, she had finally thrown one Walter wouldn't have to chase into the tall grass. It had been sailing right for his head when he had heard David call, and he had turned. And the frisbee had gone sailing on past his head, uncaught and unnoticed. When he had turned back, he had said, "Well, where did it go this time?"

She stood there frozen, stunned, for there was nothing else to do.

Then she knew what to do, not out of her new energy, but out of old habit, not her new emerging self, but her old well-tried self. She relapsed into small talk. "Some of these books have been here a long time, but they are interesting." It was part of the old habitual self to be cheerful, a graceful martyr if necessary. But then there was silence. She didn't have the energy for more than the gesture.

Meanwhile, Roger, too, felt stunned, stymied. He filled the frozen silence with his own instant memories.

He saw the heavy brick wall of the church rising over his windshield, with the Monday morning "Reverend Anderson" hanging upside down by a thin wire. Monday morning had been test time all through seventh grade. Every week, start the week by seeing if you could measure up, pass the test. Monday morning continued to be test time now that he was a minister. Sunday mornings he was up, full of energy, performing to his own satisfaction and to some acclaim. Monday morning was test time, the test he gave himself: could he measure up to the mood of Sunday, maintain it, set the pace for taking seriously his own sermon and liturgical assurances? Was this how the emperor felt just before the boy called out, "He has no clothes!"

There had been that piano teacher on Mondays also. Roger would work hard on the piece all week and feel really proud about how he could sail through it. But she had never seemed to see it that way. She would say, "Now let's work on the fingering," or, worse, that devastating day when she said, "Let's work this up for the public recital in June."

Then there had been that shattering day of the yo-yo. He had been lured into joining the bragging in the schoolyard about doing tricks—"Sure, I can 'walk the dog,' " when he had never even heard of "walking the dog," a safely idle boast because that had been November and summer yo-yos were all put away—until suddenly somebody had brought out that yo-yo! That had happened to him once with cigarettes, too.

Then there had been that time in the spring, bantering with Louise at the picnic table: "You better not take a chance out in the woods with me" and other heady seventh-grade bravado and testing, when suddenly he had felt her hand on his knee, and the testing had become serious. Can you perform? For me? He had been deadly silent then too.

Marilyn tried once more. "Your sermon said some things to me yesterday that have really got me going. I've been going over and over them since yesterday morning." She was trying to break through Roger's Monday morning wall.

"I'm glad. I really worked on that one, and I wanted to get it across." Slam! The Monday morning wall won, to the distress of both of them. To Roger, it was like her invitation was Louise's hand on his knee. To Marilyn, it was like one more partner who needed to retreat into his own program (on TV or whatever). So there was more loaded, disappointed silence. Both knew how to break the silence, from past practice: be busy. Marilyn started moving books, and Roger wisecracked— still struggling to *act* comfortably intimate—and maybe revealing more about his inner state than he knew—"Well, before you show me up, I guess I'd better get to work, too." And he was gone.

A WOMAN STRUGGLES WITH TRESPASSING AND PEDESTALS

The encounter, as risky encounters of liberation seem sure to do, provoked the worst of Marilyn's fears and old postures. She had trusted and been rejected, so she felt at fault. She felt she had offended a man whom she had endowed with power. So—one old posture—she felt trespasser; and—another old posture—she was tempted to set the man even higher on a pedestal, and therefore also all the more angrily determined to bring him down.

Vigorously blowing dust and banging books together hard, she brooded.

"What did I do wrong?" "How did I fail? How did I offend?" Always the first thought of all, suggested by those years of father and teachers and husband and sometimes minister telling her she was to blame when things went wrong; suggested by the years in which her culture told her that women were responsible for smooth relations between men and women; suggested by the relief she habitually felt when she absorbed the blame and avoided confrontation.

"Forgive us our trespasses." That languge had always seemed archaic and out of touch with modern experience. But now it spoke precisely of those devastating feelings that flooded— swamped—any move she made toward self-assertion. Stand on your own two feet and walk, yes, but always at the risk, almost guarantee that you are treading on someone else's turf. Was it really true that the greatest sin of all was to trespass? (Or if the word was "debts," it was pretty much the same message: you owe, you owe value to another, you owe duty to another, you belong among those who are second class, servant class.) Do not presume, do not stray across the line that separates you from the real people, the big leagues, the owners who are trespassed on and indebted to. Apartheid by color was only the visible way of posting limits. Whatever color you have in your life, keep it within the lines.

Had she trespassed at the curb? Had she trespassed in moving so directly to the library without checking in at the office? It was the abiding, eroding question that monitored and tempered and maybe stifled any move. Nobody had appeared at curb or in hallway to enforce No Trespassing rules; it was only that inner gnawing. Had she trespassed in venturing to talk in the language of the sermon with the minister, to talk about herself with the minister, to treat the minister as a partner? He had brushed her aside—disapproving?—so she must have trespassed. She had offended him. Should she find some way to apologize? Or should she find some way to appease him, a friendly, well-placed stroke, and regain his friendliness?

She didn't like being back in these postures. It was like lying beside the pool. It smarted. Em-balming the hurt by blaming herself still was part of the hurt.

But then, as the blame swirled around, some of it began to land on Roger. Obliquely and glancing, of course. When she picked up volume 8 of the Interpreters' Bible (Luke-John) she threw it on the pile—hard! It completed the set of the 12 volumes, and she remembered Roger assuring her the other week, "You probably won't find a whole set of things such as the Interpreters' Bible. Don't expect too much." (Did that mean "I don't expect too much of you"?) Anyway, what she did right now was to sit down and scratch out a quick note to Roger: "If you wish to consult *any* of the volumes of the Interpreters' Bible, please refer to the church library, or the librarian." A playful note? Perhaps. A helpful note? Seemingly. A defiant note? Definitely. She felt the "Ha!" in her throat as she etched the line under "any." But then she thought that he might not even remember that conversation, and she would feel foolish. So she tore up that note and instead arranged the volumes in order on the eye-level shelf.

She was nursing an edginess. Joanne came down the hall and said, "Roger and I wonder if you want to join us for coffee," and Marilyn found herself answering stiffly and politely, "I'm much obliged, but no thank you." She wondered why she didn't accept or didn't answer with her natural breeziness.

She didn't want coffee-time talk. She wanted big talk. Like the sermon, like the sermon-talk she had tried. She wanted him like yesterday, up there in the pulpit, beaming down knowingly, knowing her through his high eagle-vision. She didn't want him face-to-face here in the parish house. She wanted him in the pulpit, so she could look up to him, so he could look down into her . . . So it could be like yesteday . . . She wanted him in the pulpit? "Listen to what I'm thinking." Did she mean it? Was that what she had been doing this morning, trying to get him back into the pulpit, saving hero, instead of the friendly neighbor he wanted to be, small talk, coffee, and all?

But to lift him up was to demean herself. (Prince Charmings need their beauties sleeping or in cinders or otherwise helpless.) So to lift him up, even in her own mind, was to need to bring him down. Anger rose. She was miffed, miffed at the way he had turned her aside, miffed at the way he had not been true to his own big talk. "Shyster," she thought, like the lawyer who uses professional skills and status not to help people but just to be coldly and ruthlessly professional and work for narrow self-interest. Not the hero who rushes in to save, "I'll pay the rent!" but the villain who is not on her side at all. Shy stirrer. Get somebody stirred up, worked up, then back away. When women do that, it's called teasing or frigid or castrating. Why should men get away with it? Or think that they can? Lead on then pull away. Set up and then put down. It was as though he thought saying it was enough without having to mean it. Just say it on Sunday and leave her stuck with it. Like "treating" a child to a tour past all of the buckets of a Baskins-Robbins store—and out again, empty-handed.

She felt empty-handed, as though she had reached for something offered her, and it had been pulled away. Her empty hand became a fist. And she lunged at another book on the shelf. Roger the dodger.

Or was it dodging? Had Roger done anything? Had he promised her anything? Or was it only her hunger that had made him appear in her daydreams, like a mirage in the desert, beckoning and nurturing, offering food and shelter to her soul? Had she put into his mouth the promises on which he was now reneging? After all, he had only preached a sermon.

Blowing the dust off—in the direction of the church office, she noted wryly—she started chanting to herself, "Ashes to ashes, dust to dust . . . ashes, ashes, all fall down." It suited her mood of bleakness. "Shake the dust off your feet, and move on." This had been another of Roger's sermons, about a month ago, and the message suddenly came back—in spite of Roger. It had been about Jesus sending his disciples out to tell the good news, tell the truth. If they were received in a village, they were to stay. If they were rejected, they were to shake the dust off their feet and move along. Roger had talked about feeling the hurt of that rejection. If you feel that hurt, then you really have to feel it and not pretend you don't. The dust may have gotten into the machinery so that it doesn't work. The dust may have gotten in your clothing and made you feel uncomfortable and grimy. The hurt may last a lot longer than a simple shake of the leg. (And just as Marilyn had let her hurt catapult into anger, she could now begin to feel some of the anger drift away and reveal the hurt.) Too many people leapfrog over the hurt into the dust shaking, blaming themselves and others. Jesus didn't say anything about scolding the resistant villagers. Just let them be as they are; you have done what you can and must. Blaming the self or others usually merely covers over the hurt. It closes off communication. It makes other people defensive. Brush the dust off yourself. But if you try to clean off the other—brushing the dust off their eyes or out of their ears—your reaching will only seem to them an intrusion and an attack. Tell your message, tell the truth, and then tell how you feel about the rejection. That's all you can do, and that is a lot. That takes the courage that Jesus was talking about when he sent out his disciples.

The sermon fit here. Why was she so testy about the coffee invitation? Well, she had been swiping at the dust, but not really coming clean about the rejection and the hurt. "Let the hurt be heard," Roger had said. It might not be so hard to tell Roger that she had felt let down by his response to her attempt to talk about the sermon and her life. She could hear herself saying that to him, not complaining or accusing or angry, just a straightforward "ouch!"

Roger had said something else about the hurt that fit here. He had said that the rejection, of course, would hurt most if you were a member of that village—and he had talked about how that had happened to Jesus, who had returned to his hometown and been scorned and turned out. It would also hurt the more you wanted to be a member of that village. If you want city hall to like you and accept you and reward you, then you can't tell the truth to city hall—much less fight city hall—because you have an investment you can't risk losing. Roger had said that was what was good about the disciples depending on Jesus and on the truth and not on the people to whom they talked. He had said that is the bad spot children are in: we say that truth comes out of the mouths of children, but we don't really give them the freedom to express it, because we make the stakes so high for them. They feel a strong need to belong to our village—until they suddenly and dramatically decide they can't stand it any longer and then shake off the accumulated dust of the years with a flurry and vengeance. He had said that women often feel so dependent because they live in a man's village. They feel they can't risk rejection and when they do feel rejection, it is so anguishing that they overreact. It is very hard just to do the straightforward shaking off of the dust when the rejection is by those on whom you are dependent. "Where your treasure is, there your heart will be also," (Matthew 6:21) and also your heartbreak. So often the treasure we are attached to is a buried treasure, the possibilities and the daydreams and the maybes and the somedays—what the marriage or the spouse or the job or the club or the church or the political party or the president or the vacation might be or could be. If we are hooked on the treasure, we are hooked all the more when it is buried and we can't find it, but feel sure we should. So instead of shaking off the dust, we keep digging through it frantically and energetically, sure that it is our fault for not finding it. Giving up is hard when we have fallen hard—and our overinvestment, our overtreasuring, our yearning to belong to a village that is not really our village—all of this is a "fall," our yearnings nurturing their idols, the idols nurturing the yearnings.

If it is hard to shake off the dust of the rejecting village, it is harder to shake off the dust of the rejecting village we so fervently want to belong to. It is disappointing enough that the village cannot recognize you; it is far more disappointing for you not to be able to recognize the village as what you had thought it was.

It is hardest to shake off the dust that is the debris of dreams, hopes, and, illusions. To leave, actually to shake off this dust, is to turn one's back not only on the disappointment, but also on the dreams. It is to leave the treasure buried forever, and therefore maybe it never even existed. To stay is to accept your own pain, the disappointment, maybe the blame for the failure. But to leave is to accept the even greater anguish of the flaws in the other, on whom you had depended to be flawless, to accept the incompleteness in the other, on whom you had depended to be complete. If the village just disappears back into the mist, like Brigadoon, then you can keep your dreams of its real perfection, now simply lost. But if you actually have to shake off its dust, vigorously slap your own feet to rid yourself of the dust, then you have to face the fact that you are really leaving—and, worse, for good reason— the village, the lover, the marriage, the church, the minister, whatever and whomever. Do not turn back to bury the dead, Jesus said, let them bury themselves. That hard saying makes sense, the same gracious, liberating sense as the assurance that you can shake off the dust. You don't have to look back, because you don't really need them as much as as you had thought.

To lose a loved one is to grieve. To lose that one's love is to grieve harder. To lose your love for that one and to know that the loss is justified is to grieve hardest.

To lose a beloved leather purse is to grieve. To suffer the insult of having the purse snatched is to grieve harder. To discover the purse is imitation leather is to grieve hardest.

To have the adolescent child move away from home is to grieve. To have the child belligerently slam the door is to grieve harder. To have the child lie about where he or she is going is to grieve hardest.

For the adolescent to have a parent who doesn't talk is to grieve. To have a parent who won't talk is to grieve harder. To have a parent who mouths meaningless clichés is to grieve hardest.

To be out of work is to grieve. To be fired from the company to which you have long been committed is to grieve harder. To find that company abandoning you and your commitment by dumping pollutants at night or making false bookkeeping entries is to grieve hardest.

To have her husband die would be to grieve, Marilyn had realized. To have him leave her would be to grieve harder. But to find him as human, as boring, and as boorish, sometimes as mean and petty, as any other man, was to grieve hardest.

To find Roger absent from church this morning, she realized, would be to grieve. To find him turning away from her was to grieve harder. To find him not just unwilling but unable to pick up her leads from his sermons, to find him only a Sunday morning minister, a once-a-week front, was to grieve hardest.

Marilyn hesistated to confront Roger partly because she feared she had brought on his rejection by her own blundering or

trespass. But what also held her back was that greater gnawing that hinted not at her inferiority but at his, the hint that
he was backing away from her from fear, that if she pressed,
he might crumble all the more or disappear. Then she would
be without a minister, and she would be to blame. The most
devastating discovery would be to test him and find him unmistakably not there, not because he wouldn't, but because he
couldn't.

That day that her brother Timmy had slipped off the edge
of the pool into deep water stayed in her memory with just
one face haunting her, her father's. Everything else was a fast,
fast blur: Timmy reaching out for a ball in the pool and falling
forward, Marilyn screaming "Daddy," three or four people
suddenly right there grabbing Timmy and setting him up on
the edge of the pool, wiping the water from his face, and
Timmy still reaching for the ball—and her father standing
stock still, paralyzed, on the other side of the pool, face showing terror, and body frozen.

It was this hardest grief, the risk of the idol crumbling, that
kept her back in the library now and not up front with Roger;
that's what kept her putting Roger up front.

This stubborn idolizing of Roger—and the well-founded fear
of the idol's collapse—is what kept her in thrall, crippled, on
her mat, timid. This same stubborn idolizing, as long as he
discerned it—or even thought he did—lurking in her approach to him, is what kept Roger distant and defensive,
shunning, with new vigor in fact, this burdensome expectation. In the course of mutual idol making and idol fearing,
each fed the other's fears.

EMERGING NEVERTHELESS

What is needed is a Marilyn standing sturdy, on her own,
without triggering Roger's fears of demands to perform—and
a Roger standing sturdy, on his own, without triggering Marilyn's fears of abandonment. What is needed is a Marilyn and

a Roger who both trust their conversation as a dialogue between equals, two persons, at least for this moment, of equivalent status and power—rather than assuming a difference,
assuming her whiny and needy—an assumption that keeps
both off-balance.

In the miracle of mutual liberation, it happened, his approx-
imations encouraging hers, and hers, his. Her example had
encouraged his sermon, his sermon, her new moves. Her moves
gradually marshalled his trust that she could be her own
strong person, not leaning on him, so he could relent his
guard and stand straight, not leaning away from her.

Marilyn simply decided to blow away this cloying dust: so
what if Roger only was a Sunday morning preacher? So what
if he was not spiritual Superman, who knew all, understood
all, loved all? So what if those sermon ideas were great ideas
that he himself couldn't live by? That was disappointing and
lonely and even scary. But the ideas were still great and she
still wanted to live by them. And this time she was willing to
let the rage be heard, willing to speak the truth, willing to
shake off the dust. That's all you have to do. What he does
with it is his business; you don't have to plan that ahead for
him. Dethrone the idol before he crumbles, he is safe from
you. She was different from the Marilyn who had feared his
crumbling, just as she was different from the Marilyn who had
feared her own crumbling under rejection. Maybe she could
stand on her own feet without a protective layer of dust.

As she heard the coffee break ending, Marilyn slapped the
library dust off her hands and walked back to Roger's office.
He was standing at his bookshelf. "Have you got time to let
me shake some dust off my feet?" It was forward—maybe
trespassing—to try to talk with Roger in the language of
another of his sermons. It was also risky, because in their most
recent encounter, that language hadn't worked. But forward
was her motion, and risk was only risk, not disaster.

"You bring my sermons back to haunt me." It was a wariness

but not a rejection, a hand up but not a back turned. As part of the wariness, he kept things more literal than Marilyn had intended. "Don't tell me you've been off preaching in some village somewhere."

"No I won't tell you I'm a preacher." Did she sense a threat to Roger that she wanted to allay? "But I do take your sermons home and work with them."

"I'm sure that they can use some reworking." Roger was still sparring and mildly defensive, and not really ready yet to hear what Marilyn was saying in the way that she meant it. So far he had dealt with emerging women who were emerging by his script, not their own. He was still in that defensive posture of responding to her remarks for what they had meant to him, and what they meant seemed to be some kind of criticism (expectation about the past) or a dream (expectation about the present).

"I wanted to say that I've been thinking about that sermon about rejection and hurt and how to deal with it. I decided that I just wanted to put it behind me, and not carry that hurt around all day. I thought you would be the right person to help me put it behind me. 'Let the hurt be heard,' you said."

Her casting him as helper was more familiar and comfortable, and he dropped his guard and fitted into that role of gracious helper. "Sit down and let's talk."

"Actually, you're the person I'm talking about." She kept her own footing. "Because I've decided that I need you to know that I'm disappointed with our earlier conversation—or maybe I even mean non-conversation." She had a quick flash of herself parking at the curb and looking around. She added a cushion here too. "But I certainly don't give up on having converstions with you, or I wouldn't be here now."

The sting got to Roger, even with the cushion, and he winced with a bit of bluster, maybe even splutter, "I certainly didn't mean to upset you. I'm sorry. Tell me what happened." Sting and bluster, but not entirely closed off either. So Marilyn told him of the momentum and help and hope she had felt from his sermon yesterday and of how she had thought she was telling him that in the library encounter and of how she had felt put down by his response. It was a direct and clear statement, more direct than people are used to, and maybe even more direct than Roger could handle at first, "Well, I guess I just can't get started in the morning until I have my coffee." And, a bit later on, "I can see why you would be especially sensitive." Certainly easier and more customary responses than facing directly what she had said so directly. He was mildly defensive and he was gently practicing the man's art, the minister's art, of turning the tables and blaming the victim: you are too sensitive.

Marilyn was undismayed and undaunted. She told her story, about how she had built up her father and other men and in so doing had set herself up to be disappointed, and that it was nobody's fault. It was just the way it had been. But no more, if she could help it. And part of the story was how Roger had played parts on both sides, part of the old patterns, and part of the emerging new life. "And thanks for all of that. You don't even have to answer. I just wanted to tell you."

At first, Roger thought he was falling in love with Marilyn. Warm, glowing, opening, melting, uncovering—these were the feelings inside him. She really meant it: he didn't have to answer. He didn't have to do anything. He felt both empty and full, stripped of script to recite, full of an easy excitement. He looked straight at her, eye to eye, and neither one blinked or looked away. His voice sounded an octave lower and warm as he heard it, unplanned, unmonitored, spontaneous, uncalculated, "You give me thrills. It's crazy, but it feels like I'm watching a ballet dancer, and I love it. You seem so balanced, centered, graceful." This was not the way he talked with women. Marilyn seemed different from "women," certainly different from mother, wife, Mrs. Wilson. He did not have to talk *to* her, just talk, his words—he—more important than the audience. She had leveled with him, had freed him by taking him off the menacing pedestal.

"The leaping feels good, after a while," she said, "better than the twisting and spinning."

Roger felt something give way inside. Something once frozen melted; something once solid crumbled. At first he thought he was falling in love with Marilyn; it was as though he were seeing her for the first time, even seeing her naked. But maybe it wasn't Marilyn, but himself.

8. Joseph: Father Nevertheless

He was, apparently, a man who loved to be at home. But all we know of him is his life as a pilgrim, an exile, a refugee. He intended and deserved wife, children, and settled homestead. But his wife had prior claims on her, his son was not his son, and he lived his life on the run—trekking to Bethlehem at the behest of an emperor, fleeing to an alien land to escape one vengeful king, and taking up permanent exile to evade another. His dreams of marriage and family and homestead, just because he took them seriously, embroiled him in an eerie drama of virgin birth and god-come-to-earth, and in a bloody rivalry with a ruling king.

We *want* for Joseph—as we want for ourselves—to be settled householder. So we invent for him—as we invent for ourselves—scenes of Joseph surrounded by children, Joseph contented and industrious in his carpentry shop, Joseph manfully and tenderly training his son in his craft, Joseph esteemed among the village elders, Joseph the solid citizen, Joseph the model "man." But all we *know* of is Joseph on the run, Joseph on the verge of the settled life, Joseph in the wilderness. Not the dramatic, unmistakable Moses-wilderness of manna and tablets and assurance of a promised land. Not the dramatic, unmistakable John the Baptist-wilderness of furious call to repentance and heaven-splitting baptism. Not the dramatic, unmistakable Jesus-wilderness of confrontation with demonic temptation. Just a man's lifelong, unheroic, unheralded wilderness; just a man drab and displaced, sidelined, sand trapped, sand bagged. Not the wilderness that is encountered en route to a promised land, but a wilderness that is off-course, off the route, and a traveler who is uprooted, an exile from the land promised and yearned for, not pilgrim marching toward it.

That's the Joseph story. That's the male story, the male predicament: promises hijacked, life diverted, trapped in dreams too big or chores too mean. That's what this book is about: Dreams too big and chores too mean and the excruciating way that dreams become chores.

Trapped by our desperate hunger for the promises to be true, we fiercely latch onto the pieces of the promises that we can reach, and the imitations, and take the part for the whole, the role for the reality, the idol for the god, the empty yes for the hearty yes, the masked yes for the almost yes, compulsive up-ness for genuine loftiness, the other's script as our own destiny, their errands as our life.

Trapped by the urgency of our own dreaming, we try so hard to force the dreams to come true, to patch broken dreams, to make things happen our way, that we lock ourselves into the self-imposed chores of freezing, crippling, staying up, making others, rolling the stone uphill. Our very yearning for the promised land poisons itself, hijacks us into exile. The birthright of life that surges within us gets thwarted by the scripts fashioned to make us "men."

The preceding chapter discussed how to emerge from the predicament; this chapter discusses how to find new life within the predicament, to reclaim the predicament and to make it serve us, not vice versa. What newness can our diverted dreams and diverting chores yield to us?

Joseph did it, Joseph of Nazareth and Joseph of Canaan. Men who would be doers, they got distracted by dreams—their principal encounters were with beings of the night—then in them found vigorous mission. Men who cherished abode, both were driven into exile in Egypt, then in the very exile found themselves newly grounded and located. In their displacement, they found enduring place. If Joseph had known life as he—and we—most wanted it, we would never have known Joseph.

It is the difference between surrendering to the exiling drudgery, letting it own you, and claiming it, living it so vigorously and deliberately, that you own it.

In exile, in any of its forms, what are the choices? One: to escape, to defy, to repudiate the claims on you; they do not provide the structures of your life. Two: to surrender, to accept the claims on you, as though they are, after all, your destiny. Or, there is a third way: You may think I am going to suggest something halfway between escape and surrender. But I don't think such timid temporizing is possible; there is no halfway. These are the only genuine responses, to fight or to join. The third way, I think, is to do both, simultaneously: renounce *and* surrender. Play our role heartily, as though it were the real thing, and disdain it with a hearty horse laugh, knowing it isn't. You may be in a role now, thoroughly playing it out, but you are not the role. You may own it, but it doesn't own you. Accept the script, but know you are more than any script. Live out the looseness and freedom of hearty overcommitment. That's what this chapter will try to say, in several ways.

The preceding chapter celebrated the power of regard as the mode of liberation: just as demeaning regard by others (and by self) cripples and binds, so positive regard by others (and by self) can liberate. Here I propose a different mode of liberation: wrestling the crippledness for a blessing, engaging the role of the moment so intensely, as both intimate and alien, that it becomes transformed. It may turn out that the power of regard, a more passive form of power, is a characteristically female mode of liberation—it *is* the mode that women's groups have best identified—and that the power of wrestling, penetrating as far as you can into the role to achieve release, is more male. That is to deal with stereotypes, perhaps, or real differences, perhaps.

The dreams of the night. The drudgery of chores. Two huge distractions in which Joseph—every Joseph—finds himself; no, loses himself; no, finds himself. First, a man claims his life through taking control, managing deliberately and self-consciously, planning his daily schedule, planning his long career. Then a man loses his life by losing control of himself

in submission to dreams, in submission to tedious chores—
Joseph's two forms of exile—and perhaps also, for other Josephs, in emotional outburst and violence, or in relentless
ennui. Dreams and chores (or violence or ennui) happen *to*
him; they take over; they distract him from his destiny. Dreams
and chores sideline Joseph, put him out of the action. He loses
control—and thereby loses himself. He loses control over his
goals, his daily goals and his life goals, and over the means
of achieving them. When dreams and chores take over, the
man disappears, swallowed up. Men grieve, and for good
reason, at the end of an hour surrendered, in spite of themselves and their best planning, to distracting daydreaming or
to distracting busywork; at the end of a day or the end of a
week that is "shot"; at the end of a life, or midway through
it, when they suddenly, sometimes violently, sometimes in the
"burn-out' of ennui, look up to discover themselves in exile
far from their promised land, hijacked by dreaming and
drudgery never owned, barely acknowledged, just passively
done.

But not Joseph, either Joseph. A doer, deflected into obedience to dreams and to the chores they assigned him, he didn't
fight, he switched. He didn't just tolerate his distractions, he
lived vigorously and thoroughly into them. Like the other
"wise men" who, steadfastly and far from home, followed
their distraction, a wayward star, Joseph gave his all—a surrender of sorts, but an assertive, claiming surrender—to these
unexpected, unwelcome intrusions into his plans, just as though
distractions conveyed meaning and destiny. And they did.
They intruded. They undid him. They turned his life around.
They put him in touch with a new destiny, undreamed of. And
he claimed it.

The dreamer and the chore boy are such different figures,
the one with his mind wafted away, eyes closed, oblivious to
the present, the other with mind numbed, eyes glazed, and
preoccupied with the immediate; the one relaxed and loose,

the other fixed and bent; one in flights of fancy, racing into the unfamiliar, attention leaping up and out and away, the other plodding among the all-too-familiar, facing down and inward and backward. The dreamer and the chore boy are both "spaced out," on opposite sides of normal daily life. But Joseph is both, Joseph of Canaan, Joseph of Nazareth, Joseph of today. Joseph moves readily from one to the other, from dreaming into chores, from drudgery into dreams. For Joseph has discovered that, despite their differences, dreaming and drudgery are one. They are two forms of alienation from life, two forms of discovery and reflection about life, two forms of catapulting into life. Each gives the mind a massage but also a message.

Daydreams, night dreams, superstitious habits, intuitive hunches, idealistic commitments, alcoholic binges, bizarre movies, science fiction; tedious, monotonous chores, such as mowing the grass or sitting through committee meetings or working on an assembly line or yielding to the numbing rituals of office politics—all the fixed and fixing scripts this book has identified—these things, dreams and chores, make you feel out of it, dazed, estranged and alienated, somehow captured or drugged. Giving in to dreams or giving in to chores, you lose control, lose autonomy; you feel somehow under control of another, and you are. Something alien is carrying you along and away. These are mindless moments, usual vigilance and control relaxed. They are automatic, that is, *self*acting; they enact themselves; they enact us. We do not enact the moments. The dream dreams us; the task tasks us.

Yet exactly because they are mindless moments, dreams and chores are moments of message. Yielding control, our usual conscious control, we are ready to receive, to hear from those lively parts of the self that are ordinarily neglected under the frozen dominion of daily self-control. The auto-matic moments are indeed self-making moments, moments when our fuller self, the unfrozen parts of the self, comes forth to be heard and seen. When it feels automatic, it is the self acting, the self taking charge, showing itself, in the absence of that constant

vigilance and monitoring and shaping, which is really an obedience to others. When we go on automatic we are able to set
aside, for the time being—truly a time for being—that preoccupation with the expectations of others. In our daily occupation at best, we occupy ourselves. We inhabit, fully, our
own lives. We possess ourselves.

Self-consciousness is eased off, and the self surges up, those
parts of the self hidden and neglected most of the time when
life is under the rule of those timid, earnest monitors—the
adolescent self-consciousness—peering back over the shoulder
and squinting about, watchfully shaping life to the images of
others. In routines, as in dreams, the self's own images stand
forth, to be discerned and joined by those who will. The
earnest, timid self-containing coach of self-consciousness wants
to dismiss dreams and drudgery as trivial and their disclo-
sures as meaningless. But the daily chores are the fundamental
rituals of life by which the wisdom of the race and the char-
acter of the self are discovered and contoured and transmitted
and celebrated. It has been in the mindless doings of plowing
and spinning, caravaning across the desert and sailing the
seas, marching in formation and splitting wood—rituals of
work as mindless and powerful as rituals of worship or of
sex—that people have always discovered and confirmed the
most significant things about themselves. It was to Mary at
her chores and the shepherds at their chores that the news
came, and to Joseph as attentive, fussing husband, and to the
other Joseph as errand boy for his father and as dutiful steward to Potiphar and as conscientious trusty in jail and as
bureaucratic governor. The most discerning of our friends and
the most discerning part of ourself listens patiently to our
well-chosen, well-controlled words and then says, "What you
are doing speaks more loudly about who you are then what
you are saying."

Though our routines may seem dreary and peripheral to
what our fantasies would like our life to be, our routines are
nevertheless the rootings, the routings by which we are

en-rolled, en-tranced into life. Our lives are grounded and lived out in daily routines just as mean and just as glorious, just as meaningless and just as revealing as—and because of—God's outrageous, squandering dive into the squalid, mean, humdrum routines of daily human life. If God is best disclosed by looking squarely at the dramatically undramatic life of Jesus, by looking squarely at, not away from, the grindings of history and the mean clashes and clatter of daily news, inside pages as much as front page, then each of us may best discover ourselves by attending to the daily drudgery, the mindless drudgery of our own rooting routine, with as much awe as to our soaring dreams.

To be Joseph is to risk taking dreams seriously, to choose to live into dreams, to choose to live by dreams, to choose to be lived by them, not shrinking from their disastrous consequences, right up to the dreary chores or pit or exile; then to choose to persist living into, living by, being lived by, these assignments, until they reap their new harvest of startling, unwelcome, life-displacing, life-giving dreams.

To be Joseph is to dream of a scientific theorem so fanciful it accounts for all the atoms and all the stars, to announce that theory as boldly and as naively as Joseph disclosed his dreams to his brothers, to set one's life by the dream totally—knowing all the while that the more intensely you commit yourself to it and advertise it, the more readily and the more surely you will find yourself exiled and mocked for a dream disproved. You welcome the exile as the necessary condition for the dreaming of new dreams. Only in exile in Egypt is there dream and assurance of new homeland for Joseph and Mary; only in exile in Egypt is there the reassembling of family for Joseph and his brothers.

To be Joseph is to be a carpenter obeying the dream to create with your own hands lovely furniture and gracious interiors; to live that dream so obediently that your business grows and grows until you are exiled from carpentry and spend all your time managing finance, marketing, personnel, and large administrative machinery; then to discover that in this exile there is a new dream, a new destiny—discovered only when the exile is lived as intensely as the first dream—now the vision of creating community, work teams, a coalition of wood-workers; you become skilled at and fulfilled from the art of fitting people with each other and fitting people with their work, and you find as much beauty in the psychic work space you create as in the dens you once panelled and furnished, now designing your own interiors and not others'.

To be Joseph is to dream of becoming a professor and to live that dream intently until appointment and tenure are in hand, only to discover that the professional role is so straitened as to be an exile of drudgery: students and public expect you to pronounce and to profess, not just search and query; the university expects you to chair committees; the politics of academia requires you to connive; publishers require you to shape your ideas to market needs. The dream has led you into exile from itself. But in that exile there is ferment and newness—so long as the exiled role is lived in as fully to the breaking point as was the dream—and discovery of hitherto undreamed ways of shaping ideas and moving students, new ways of being the professor by a forced breaking out of the role of professor.

To be Joseph is to invest, at high risk, everything—money, time, passion—into your business because your dream so compels you, to be tiptoeing constantly on the thin edge, the narrow ridge, daily risking the loss of all in exile, in bankruptcy, as the only way to gain.

To be Joseph is to be drawn, dreamed, by the personal pain surrounding you to become a counselor, to revision and re-shape peoples' lives—only to discover that you don't counsel, but you listen; you don't reshape, but you mirror the mis-shapes; you can't change people, only stand by. But in this exile of decidedly not intervening and rearranging and reshaping peoples' lives, of decidedly not healing their pain, of decidedly not redirecting their priorities, you find yourself providing the necessary conditions—and so you are doing it after all—that enable them to do just such revisioning and reshaping.

To be Joseph is to be called by dreams to minister to a community of the faithful only to be called as the minister of a particular church of people of decidedly ambiguous faith and commitment, people who leave you stranded time after time after time in the role of lonely champion of justice and mercy and faithfulness to God; only to discover that when you leave that lonely championship role, when you yield your call to be representative for God, when you leave that all behind and join the people where they are, in exile from God and from ministry and from faithfulness of community, when you join that community of exile intensely and fully and honestly, there is a new, undreamed-of transaction between God and people, flowing through your very exile of faithlessness.

To be Joseph is to be a physician committed to a heroic lead role in the life-and-death drama at the frontier of illness and health, only to encounter constant interruptions that keep you in the wings or at the stage door while the drama goes on elsewhere, interruptions in the forms of anxieties and half-imagined ailments, routine symptom management, and a dreary recycling of the same common complaints. Living passionately as Joseph the dreamer brought you to this impasse. Living passionately as Joseph the drudge lets you live fully into this exile, and you discover it teeming with life and new dreams. It is just in these chronic, low-key, nuisance ways of dealing with themselves and you that people are thrashing out their crucial struggles with wholeness, making the daily decisions that mean the difference between life and death. Your day-to-day practice resembles Joseph's lean years of famine with day-to-day lonely and difficult administrative decisions required of him. You may call it holistic medicine or general practice, or anything else. It is certainly far from the long dreamed-for spotlight of emergency room or trauma center or laboratory (with its coat of no colors). But a throbbing excitement fills your practice that seems more rooted than the high drama you once dreamed of.

To be Joseph is to come, bursting with high anticipation, to a sexual rendezvous—perhaps your first, perhaps only the newest—tumescent and throbbing with expectation for the intensity and intimacy of the union. And it is disastrous, not just disappointing, not just falling short, but disastrous. The lofting thrill you intended to deliver and receive never happens; instead, self-conscious numbness for both of you. No total merging; instead, an unwanted small secret war and mutual second-guessing and strategizing; the missed communications, as between strangers, rather than the unspoken, intuitive total blending of lovers. So you lie there in this pit and this exile, brought low by your high dreams. But you are Joseph, so you live into the dismay, together. You say to your lover, comfortably, "We messed that up." Not just the stiff, subtly protective "I messed that up," which invites reassurance and more game playing. "*We* messed that up," and there is hugging and mock slapping and tears and laughing and an honest intimacy and union never dreamed of in the first dream.

To be Joseph is to dream of the loving, intimate companionship marriage will be, the bliss of dating made intense and guaranteed. But these dreams lead into the drudgery of housekeeping, nothing like dating. Conversations seem more and more to be limited to budget and carpooling and house maintenance and children—where is all the tender loving talk once dreamed, or even the lovers' quarrels, which once so excited you two? Then, Joseph, you discover it is there, after all, in the gentle, tender, flowing sharing—and the battling—of the drudgery.

To be Joseph is to get appointed, to last, to the committee of your dreams, in your workplace, your church, your club, or wherever, the committee of power and decision—the executive committee, the membership committee, the finance committee, whatever. Now: power and influence and a real use of your vision and wisdom. Out of the muddy road where you have been spinning your wheels, and onto the superhighway. Inside the Holy of Holies. You read background papers, you anticipate the issues and prepare your positions. You compose speeches in your head. You build personal rapport with the other committee members. Your wisdom and commitment to the committee and its mission is so evident that you know that soon this wisdom and commitment will be fully engaged and widely appreciated. You live fully into the dreams and the glorious future to which it points.

Then, Joseph, your very forwardness and intensity—the dream itself and your commitment to it—sabotages the dream. It—you—turn people off and push them away. Your earnestness runs afoul of the sluggishness of the committee, and the sluggishness fouls your earnestness. It turns out that the committee, any committee, has an earnest, relentless, deadly life of its own; to be a member of the committee, to be committed to the committee, is to join this deadly routine. The more you are committed to the committee, the more you get ground into this inertia and your dreams get ground down by it. It's a whole new world, Joseph. The new committee—or new job, new school, any new setting for your dreams—has its own culture, its own history, its own language, its own earnest rituals, this Egypt into which your dreams have led you, this pit, this stable. Your ideals and your speeches don't fit here. This world doesn't move by ideals and speeches, but by subtle political processes and signals. The decisions somehow are all made out of sight. You are Alice dropped down into the rabbit hole, through the looking glass, into a world with exotic logic. Some things are circuitous and delayed and meandering, and other things happen even before you know it in ways you do not recognize. It just doesn't fit. It must be like God walking among the new creation, full of dismay and wonder and intrigue.

But then, as with God, the very fact that this new culture is unfamiliar and therefore frustrating, leading dreams into exile, makes it inviting and challenging. New raw materials to create with, once you get the hang of them, frustrating tedium until you do, then gradually more entrancing. You submit to the stubborn, intransigent, frustrating stuff of this new alien, inviting world; you learn from it, and it gradually submits to you. You adapt to this once-alien ecological niche. And so,

Joseph, you find yourself, after a wandering exile, speaking the new language of the committee, caucusing and patiently waiting out routines and signaling political compromise in the private code language of the committee. It is all very different from your dreams of power, but not so different after all, a natural evolution. It still turns out that you are making things happen—as Joseph dreamed from the beginning. You are doing your thing their way.

To be Joseph is to be a man who dreams of the abundant life and finds that this dream compels him into the junior executive, country club whirlwind, an Egyptian exile of sorts. He lives so hard into this dream-become-pit that he squeezes out a new dream: his daughter, too, will achieve and excel, and this dream compels him into assiduous monitoring and managing of her adolescence. He lives so hard into this drudgery that once when she rebels he strikes her on the cheek: a new low of captivity. But he is able to accept his residence in this pit, to be shocked but not defensive about what he has done, and to learn from it. The blow on the cheek yields a still newer dream of being honest with his daughter, and this precarious new gift of honesty flourishes between them.

To be Joseph is to be God struggling to transform dream into creation, creation into dream, an act that is possible only at the risk of trusting that creation, an act that is stymied and betrayed by the risk of trusting that creation; for the creation betrays the dream and lurches into self-exile, out the gates of Eden, over and over and over again. God struggles from the mountaintop, the place of the gods, to make things right, but the betrayal goes on until finally God gives up, God gives up all, God surrenders Godship, becomes self-exiled from heaven, and eventually even from life, in manger and cross and all the homelessness and humiliation in between, a grand Exile, which welds creation and dream.

To be Joseph is to be any lover, like God, yearning so urgently to make real, to make visible, tangible, reliable, permanent, embodied, vivid, that bond of zesty, warming intimacy that has been promised by dreams immemorial and by some special glimmer in this woman's eyes and lilt in this woman's voice, and toss of this woman's hair. But the efforts to lodge that dream land one inevitably and quickly in the exile of struggle and frustration and disappointment and maneuvering, lost in the cold, dark woods, maybe together, but far from the promised nest. The efforts to make love happen, to make it real, the efforts themselves are the exile: he who would save love, he would make love, loses it. But then, to lose is to find: in despair, the lover abandons efforts to make it happen, lets go and gives up, and there is relief and release—and often in that mood a deep bond of zesty, warming intimacy undreamed of, long dreamed of. The lovers fall into each other's arms, whispering in the bond of despair, giggling, and clinging tightly all night.

To be Joseph is to be any author, like God, yearning urgently to form into words, words of flesh and blood, the aspirations and wisdom that loom so insistently but mistily in the corners of the mind: how to bring into being—how to make the word become flesh—how to interpret the dreams—how to imagine life. And the author is constantly caught in a web of drudgery, an exile that defies the dreams far more than it gives them lodging, but a drudgery and exile that is somehow a necessary and fruitful sojourn and that finally yields up, when the struggle is abandoned—sometimes in the dreams of the night—the words and the metaphors that give life after all to the dreams, give image to life, at least for the moment.

THE FATHER WHO IS NOT THE FATHER, WHO IS THE FATHER NEVERTHELESS

To be Joseph is to be a father, dreamed and destined for a bonded oneness with your own blood and flesh, an intimacy promised by myth and by deep intuition—there is gaping requirement in a man's soul for a child to be companion and completion—an intimacy grasped at exuberantly and awkwardly, and missed, on the arrival of the infant, an intimacy gradually surrendered, untasted, to others, to the child's mother and grandparents, siblings and friends, neighbors and uncles, lovers and spouse, and, perhaps finally, to the child itself, adult and gone. Yet that surrender of dream, that sundering of intimacy, that lifetime of ambiguous love, that is to be father.

Fatherhood, like Godhood, is, after all, a giving of life, a giving in, a giving up, a donation, a surrender. You give your child a life to lead . . . and you follow. You give life to your child and your child to life, and that act of giving creates the most intimate bond imaginable—you do image it intensely— and it also creates an absolute otherness, for the gift is not a gift if it is not an irrevocable donation, a surrender, a sundering. You give with abandon, but do not abandon; the child is forever linked. The gift is by one possessed, but does not possess; the child, once lifed, is forever separate. The child is your very flesh and blood, incarnation, living apart and without you.

No birthing for fathers, no weaning, no gradual transition from having to letting go. It's abrupt and never complete. Weaning never begun is never completed for fathers. The having of the closeness is always there, always total, in the wanting, to the end, and the fissure, the chasm of separation, is always total, from the beginning.

For man there is no sentimental, decisive *pietà*: Mary tenderly holding dead son. The separation is more tenuous, more chronic, more ambiguous, because so is the connection, and therefore more anguished. It is fraught with the ambiguities of blaming self and feeling victimized, of never being sure until it is too late whether the relationship at any moment is becoming closer or more distant, of feeling the potential for closeness has never been realized but it's already time for separation. If a woman can yield up a moment to memory, theman has neither time of yielding nor memory, only the exile of "almost" or "not quite" or "might have been" or "I still want."

Fatherhood is the act of losing one's life and finding it, all at once. Surrender, naked, to a woman, to a moment of passion, surrender control, surrender your seed, surrender to limpness. Everything goes, all you can call your own—except for total well-being and, maybe, a child who becomes all in all. Awkward bystander for the birth of the baby you have made, for the birth of the baby that makes you a father, fatherhood is not much different after the birth. It is an excruciating blend of intense investment, all-out surrender and commitment, and helpless sidelining, watching from the curb while the parade passes by. It is also an excruciating wizardry of finding on the sidelines, in the margins, in the fringes, just that impact that makes you a father. Uncles and neighbors and friends' fathers and teachers and the legendary figures parading across the TV screen—these are the child's heroes, the visible, valued heroes. As for Father—for this is how it is with fathers—you are sloughed off, tolerated, apologized for, kept behind the scenes, in the necessary and inevitable margins of your child's life. For it is from behind the scenes, in the margins, that you make the crucial, unnoticed (until years later) fathering gesture. To be a father is to be crucial and therefore to be unnoticed. To be a father is to be unnoticed and therefore crucial. Fatherhood—perhaps, manhood—*is* like Godhood: standing by, in the margins, straining with eager longing for your creation to be complete but knowing that completion is possible only if you withhold the power to enact it. You want so hard to shape, but know that your shaping will sabotage the creation's capacity to shape itself and therefore subvert its fulfillment.

To be Joseph, to be a father, to be God, to be a man, is to give your all to your creation, all your energy, all your manhood, all your power, put everything to work to make the creation successful—and then, when it's time, to give still more by surrendering all and letting go.

The dilemma of God is the dilemma of paternity: how to create being out of chaos, how to lodge in the stuff of the world a transcendent intention. For the stuff of the world always captures the dream and exiles it. The dilemma of God mirrors the dilemma of the worshipper: how to encounter the God who transcends the world when the means of encounter are—by God's daring decision—the stuff of the world. God is apprehended only with the words and events of the world, which distort as much as they reveal. They give never more than an approximation. The worshipper seems destined either to cling too tightly—in idolatry—to the inadequate words and events and forms, ignoring how much they distort, or else to shrug them off—in apostasy—forgetting how much they convey. God's dilemma, the dilemma of paternity, the dilemma of manhood, seems just like that. Aaron "fathered" a golden bull and idealized it and clung to it, as fathers sometimes do (and as God wanted to do in the Garden?), and thought it the perfect offspring, a solution to all problems. Hot bondage, idolatry. Onan "fathered" by spilling his seed on the ground, retreating from the risk. Cool bondage, letting the risk be sovereign. Refusing to give new life, because it will not be perfect.

The story of Onan, Joseph's nephew, is tucked into the story of Joseph in Genesis 38. With Joseph sold into Egypt, into bleak exile from the only life he knew, an exile in which he was to find a new life, we come upon the short story of Onan, who chose a kind of exile or retreat in which no life was to be found. It was, quite literally, a withdrawal that denied life.

Onan's married older brother had died without children. So he was obliged by the custom of a time and people for whom paternity and progeny were crucial to take his brother's place and to impregnate the widow. As Onan's father made very clear, "Go and sleep with your brother's widow. Fulfill your obligation to her as her husband's brother, so that your brother may have descendants." (Genesis 38:8) But, precisely because paternity was so crucial to him and declining the invitation to be interchangeable stud (one form of frozen power) Onan refused paternity and life: "But Onan knew that the children would not belong to him, so when he had intercourse with his brother's widow, he let the semen spill on the ground, so that there would be no children for his brother." (Genesis 38:9) That Onan's name is used to describe an "offense" of which he was not guilty—the word *Onanism* now means "masturbation"—may seem a confusion and a misreading; masturbation seems to us very different from coitus interruptus, because for us the difference is so crucial between solitude and intimacy with another. But for a people obsessed with fatherhood, with the making of life—and perhaps we are obsessed with it, too—the spilling of life on the ground, however it happens, is the offense.

The struggle to lodge life and to lodge it authentically among chaos and confusions and ambiguities, the struggle to create, Onan's struggle, any father's struggle, any man's struggle, is the drama of Genesis, the book of beginnings. It is the struggle of God, wresting life out of recalcitrant nothingness and recalcitrant creatures. It is the struggle of the Hebrew people, told as the struggle of their patriarchs, their fathers, struggling to implant themselves and their descendants in an alien land among alien people.

The drama of Genesis, man's struggle—and God's—to implant life, to lodge dreams—that drama takes primitive and stark form. It's that moment of first awakening in the murky, chaotic twilight between night and day, when our dreams blur into, and give shape to, the morning sights and sounds. It's the time men of all cultures look back to with legend and myth, when the forces of life and death still struggled in stark combat, and their fathers, gaunt giants all, were totally enlisted in the combat, sometimes on one side, sometimes the other. Everyone in Genesis, including God, seems obsessed with begetting children and with death, and the two are always close. The very first struggle in the Bible is over access to the tree of life, and when the creatures come too close, they are banished from the very garden in which they had found life. The story of the first births (Genesis 4, Cain and Abel) is the story of the first murder. Because Father Abraham is willing to kill his son, he is promised "as many descendants as there are stars in the sky or grains of sand along the seashore." (Genesis 22:17) To create or to kill seem the only choices and become blended; the task of creation is so urgent it becomes stark.

Make life! Onan was ordered. He refused and made death—primitive alternatives then. Of course, he met death immediately. ("What he did displeased the Lord, and the Lord killed him also." Genesis 38:10) For God played by the same rules and was limited to the same choices: Life or death. Yes or no. Up or down.

Suck on the nipple or bite the nipple—the little man's primitive choices. I want life my own way, or I'll hold my breath and die. Make love, make life with me, or I'll slam the door on the way out or beat you or shoot you—the bigger man's primitive choices. Live my way, under my dominion, or I will destroy you—the primitive father's stark choices to his adolescents, and the primitive man's choices escalated to tribal choices, even up to the nuclear age. Make my dreams come true, or else. Wrest new life out of the wilderness on the American frontier and punctuate the claim with quick-draw six-shooters. My own dreams, my own children, or no children at all, Onan meant; life was too urgent and too precarious to tolerate ambiguities. Onan preferred death to ambiguous life. So did the God of Genesis, caught in the same primitive dilemmas of wresting out a creation that remained ambiguous. He, too, dealt with the ambiguities by stark destruction.

The sin of Onanism is the sin of denying life as the way of dealing with the ambiguities in which the life is embedded, the sin of refusing life because it's not perfect, of copping out of the struggle for life. The outcome of the fatherhood/manhood to which Onan was called was not going to match his dream. Actual creation never does. So rather than choose life with ambiguity, which means rather than choose life, Onan chose to opt out, to refuse life.

Onanism is the prevalent sin of the book of Genesis, the book of beginnings, when the making of life is so absolutely urgent and difficult. The God of Genesis seems the least able of any of the patriarchs to tolerate the ambiguities, perhaps because his craving for life was the keenest of any of the patriarchs. His Onanistic temper was felt fatally by a long roster of victims, including one whole civilization on which he rained wrathful torrents for 40 days (Genesis 7:11-24) and by two cities on which he rained burning sulphur (Genesis 19:24). My dreams, or else! Enact, embody life as I want it, or no life.

The sin of Aaronism, the prevalent sin of the book of Exodus, is the opposite of Onanism. In infantile tantrum, Onanism discards and perhaps attacks: it spits out and maybe bites. Aaronism is the next stage: it compulsively clutches and controls; it is preoccupied with its own product, relies on its own doing. Onanism throws out the baby with the bathwater. Aaronism treasures bathwater and all debris as though it were all baby. Onanism can't tolerate contamination. Aaronism can't turn away from it. "Let my people go," the liberator Moses demands of Pharaoh. But Pharaoh, that quintessential Aaronite, retentive to the end, hangs on tight, troublesome slaves and all. It's a struggle for control. No killing, no shoot-out between Moses and Pharaoh; that is still the move, the dying gasp, dying grasp, of the Genesis God, as he engineers one more holocaust, this time against every Egyptian firstborn infant—reprise of Cain's murder of the firstborn.

But after that mass infanticide and one more flood, this time destroying the Egyptian armies, the God of Genesis gives way to the God of Exodus, who adopts a new strategy for coping with the ambiguities: contain them, regulate them. Exalt the ambiguities with detailed attention. The lawgiver plays breathless catchup ball, trying to match his strides to the offenses, but never catching up, always at least a step behind—lawgiver remaining servant to the offense. Father clinging to the flaws and delinquencies of his children in managing them. Men celebrating the oppression of their workplace in the rituals of water cooler, carpool, barstool gripes. Men endlessly and fruit-lessly coaching their teams on television and damning their own team's flaws foremost. So God's lawgiving is one form of clinging obsessively, preoccupied with the ambiguities as though life were no more than the ambiguities. God's sin of Aaronism matches that of the people who clung obsessively and preoc-cupied: to their memories of Egypt, to the golden bull Aaron fathered, and to all the laws themselves.

The Onanistic father exiles or shuns his delinquent adoles-cent. The Aaronistic father manages him closely, forbidding his flaws and demanding perfection and performance.

The Onanistic man goes numbly through his work day, his work life; the Aaronistic man, compulsively. The Onanistic husband is sullen and silent at home, the Aaronitic, busybody manager of spouse and household.

Yet Onanism and Aaronism, both attempts to sort out life and death, are not so different after all. If Onanism turns its back on life for its ambiguities and Aaronism embraces the ambiguities for the life that is embedded in them, these two sins also share much in common. In one, the clenched fist is thrusting, in the other grasping, but it is the same clenched fist. It is the same intolerance of the ambiguities, the same macho determination to deal with the ambiguities barehanded and decisively, to put an end to the frustrations, in an up or down, all or nothing finality. Both are faithless to, and mis-trusting of, the processes of growth. Both respond slavishly to the past rather than enable the future. Both blame; both blame the victim. Both adopt the posture of absolute invulnerability by the father and impose maximum vulnerability on the sons.

How embrace life without embracing the contaminations in which life is lodged but which are not life? How purge the contaminations without destroying the life embedded and em-bodied in it? One cannot. One cannot escape either dilemma. As surely as the same organ discharges semen and urine, seed and waste, as surely as the story of creation is also the story of the Fall, and as surely as the story of salvation is also the story of the cross, so are life and its contamination embedded together, dreams and drudgery, call and exile. One can't avoid either.

The solution is to do both. God finally hit upon this solution, and so do men now and then. Both Josephs learned it. Embrace intensely and wholly and let go intensely and wholly. The woman does it naturally: creating life by holding totally for nine months and then expelling vigorously. And these are the rhythms she continues to practice at her best, embracing and sending away, nurturing and pushing out of the nest, even while the man so often tries to avoid both, shunning coolly the embrace even while avidly, though underhandedly, hanging on.

The God of the New Testament tries something brand new. He combines total investment with total abandonment: Aaronism plus Onanism. The sin of Aaron and all idolators is to make an overcommitment, to dedicate self to the stuff of this world, in Aaron's case the golden bull, far beyond its deserts. That's exactly what the God of the New Testament does, makes a radical overcommitment to the stuff of this world beyond its deserts, from manger to crowds to fishing boats to heedless disciples to cross to faithless, struggling young churches to precarious, improbable visions of the end. But the God of the New Testament transforms this idolatrous overcommitment, unlocks the clenched fist into an open hand, by fusing it with the sin of reckless abandonment, even to the refusal of life: Aaronism redeemed by Onanism.

And vice versa. If the sin of Onanism is to abandon life recklessly, the God of the New Testament commits this sin, too, but transforms it by the intensity of his reckless commitment: Onanism redeemed by Aaronism. If Onan entered Tamar expecting to complete the act by denying it, by wasting the seed the very intensity of the act produced; if a woman— as I know to have happened—can welcome to her breast the firstborn she has just brought into the world with this exhilarating meditation, "This is mine to give up," if she can say each half of that sentence with an exclamation point, each exclamation point made possible by the other; then God came into the world, explosively and intensely (as explosively and intensely as ejaculation and childbirth) prepared, expecting to relinquish, to yield, to waste this life.

Absolute power and absolute vulnerability, each absolute making possible the other. Total investment, grotesquely inappropriate overcommitment, graciously inappropriate overcommitment, to the stuff of the world and the human melodrama—coupled with a heedless repudiating of that stuff and that melodrama.

A God who stays on the mountaintop, whether Sinai or Olympus—or any man claiming his upper niche on any hierarchy—bestows, it seems, "honor" on the life spread below by bestowing his own exalted attention and command, honor to the point of idolatry. But a God who descends into the meanness of life not only humbles himself but seems to display disdain for that life by his descent. "What kind of people are we to have a mean and humble God like that?" "I wouldn't want to join a club that would have me!" becomes "How can I worship a God who joins my club?" which then becomes "If my club attracts that kind of God, it must really be worthless." A God on the margins of life; a God in a smelly stable; a God who disdains property, family, productive job, religious and political authority, and all the other structures of human life; a God dying on a mean cross as a simple outlaw—such a God is plunging into life so intensely as to break out the bottom side, disdaining and mocking all the signs of civilization and his ties to them as the way, the only way, of imploding with full force into that life. Implode into it so as to explode it; explode it so as to implode into it. Just as the intensity of the sexual frenzy is climaxed and fulfilled in the release of that tension, and just as the release makes the tension endurable, tension and release fulfilling each other, so God's absolute commitment to human life is fulfilled and climaxed in his disdain and abandonment of that life. The disciples—of every generation—who find the cross at first a rude abortion soon discover—within 50 days the first time around—that it is much more like a sexual explosion.

What the God of the New Testament learned—and teaches— is what every other creative artist and lover learns: self-fulfillment is found in self-abandonment. As the New Testament puts it, in one place, "Whoever would save his life must lose it." (Matthew 16:25)

Or, as it is put another way in the New Testament, at the beginning: and as we read at the beginning of this book, "When Joseph woke up, he married Mary, as the angel of the Lord had told him to. But he had no sexual relations with her before she gave birth to her son. And Joseph named him Jesus."